PRAISE FOR *INTERNAL COMMUNICATION STRATEGY*

'Combining practical advice and methodology with sharp insight and experience, this book is packed with "need to know" detail. Keep it close – it'll be your go-to reference and guide, equipping you and enabling you to deliver your best.'
Suzanne Peck, President, Institute of Internal Communication

'Rachel Miller has combined evidence-based insights with her experience and expertise to produce this must-have guide to strategic internal comms. Quite simply, this is a strategic IC coach in a book!'
Christine Shukis-Brown, Deputy Director of Communications, King's College London

'What I most admire about Rachel Miller is her clarity. No one explains complex issues more clearly, and this makes her book ideal for students and beginners. But since clear writing requires clarity of thinking, experienced communicators and educators will also find there's much wisdom in here.'
Richard Bailey HonFCIPR, Senior Lecturer in Public Relations, Leeds Beckett University, and Editor of PR Academy's PR Place Insights

'A great resource for IC professionals, offering a blend of practical advice and insightful ideas through The MILLER Framework. It equips readers with necessary skills to craft and implement effective internal communication strategies, essential for thriving in organizational environments.'
Rita Men, Professor of Public Relations and Director of Internal Communication Research, College of Journalism and Communications, University of Florida

'Destined to become a vital resource for those seeking to learn about IC as well as communicators looking to up their game. The MILLER Framework she introduces is not just innovative but profoundly practical, offering a structured yet flexible approach to crafting effective IC strategies. This book bridges the gap between theoretical concepts and real-world application,

making it an indispensable guide for communicators who aim to deliver meaningful results to their organizations or clients.'
Shel Holtz SCMP, Senior Director of Communications, Webcor

'For over two decades Rachel Miller has been a leading voice and advocate for the integral role of IC globally. She has put her thinking, research and passion into one book for her global IC audience. I particularly enjoyed her "Myths of internal communication" and her belief that "internal communication is a business function because it enables a business to function". I couldn't agree more. An important resource and a must-read for IC professionals.'
Priya Bates, President, Inner Strength Communication

'Rachel Miller has written a book that exemplifies her thorough, thoughtful and empathic approach to internal communication. It is a perfect blend of theory and practical application for professionals who aspire to play a strategic role inside their organisations, and is both current and inclusive.'
Katie Macaulay, Managing Director, AB, and host of *The Internal Comms* Podcast

'Rachel Miller is the global IC Oracle and this book is the new IC bible for comms professionals. The book distils Rachel's vast wisdom of developing internal comms strategies that transform organizations into one comprehensive, handy guide. Covering the hot topics in the industry today, it blends practical advice, comms theory and real-life case studies. It will have permanent home on my office bookshelf for years to come.'
Mione Collins, Director of Marketing and Corporate Affairs, Tasman Environmental Markets

'Makes an internal comms and people engagement strategy that's steeped in measurement achievable – no matter your resources. Rachel Miller's years of experience are evident in how she turns complicated topics into tangible and actionable advice. I urge professionals to keep this book on their desk and use it when they need to improve internal communications, engagement and ultimately their organizational culture.'
Sara Luker, Head of People Engagement, OVO

Internal Communication Strategy

Design, develop and transform your organizational communication

Rachel Miller

First published in Great Britain and the United States in 2024 by Kogan Page Limited

2nd Floor, 45 Gee Street	8 W 38th Street, Suite 902	4737/23 Ansari Road
London	New York, NY 10018	Daryaganj
EC1V 3RS	USA	New Delhi 110002
United Kingdom		India

www.koganpage.com

Kogan Page books are printed on paper from sustainable forests.

ISBNs
Hardback   978 1 3986 1466 6
Paperback   978 1 3986 1464 2
Ebook   978 1 3986 1465 9

British Library Cataloguing-in-Publication Data

A CIP record for this book is available from the British Library.

Library of Congress Cataloging-in-Publication Data

Names: Miller, Rachel, 1981- author.
Title: Internal communication strategy : design, develop and transform your organizational communication / Rachel Miller.
Description: 1 edition. | New York, NY : Kogan Page Inc., [2024] | Includes bibliographical references and index.
Identifiers: LCCN 2023057546 (print) | LCCN 2023057547 (ebook) | ISBN 9781398614642 (paperback) | ISBN 9781398614666 (hardback) | ISBN 9781398614659 (ebook)
Subjects: LCSH: Communication in organizations. | Employee motivation.| Organizational change.
Classification: LCC HD30.3 .M5525 2024 (print) | LCC HD30.3 (ebook) | DDC 658.4/5–dc23/eng/20231218
LC record available at https://lccn.loc.gov/2023057546
LC ebook record available at https://lccn.loc.gov/2023057547

Typeset by Integra Software Services, Pondicherry
Print production managed by Jellyfish
Printed and bound by CPI Group (UK) Ltd, Croydon, CR0 4YY

CONTENTS

PART TWO
Implementing an internal communication strategy

5 Leading organizational communication 169

6 Evaluation and measuring internal communication 209

ABOUT THE AUTHOR

Rachel Miller is an internationally recognized authority on internal communication, based in London, UK. She's a Chartered PR Practitioner and Fellow of both the Institute of Internal Communication and Chartered Institute of Public Relations. She's a keynote speaker and member of the Company of Communicators.

Rachel began her career as a journalist, then spent a decade in-house, before establishing her consulting business, All Things IC, in 2013. She's listed in Inspiring Workplaces' Top 101 Global Employee Engagement Influencers. In 2020, Rachel was awarded the Chartered Institute of Public Relations' President's Medal for distinguished service to PR.

ACKNOWLEGEMENTS

To my husband Jon and three children, thank you for your constant support and the lucky penny.

Thank you to my fabulous All Things IC colleagues AKA Team Teal – Louise Mackenney, Caroline Cubbon-King and Dan Holden, and to the Kogan Page team. Thank you for encouraging me to put what's in my head and heart down on paper. Thank you to all my expert view and case study contributors, I'm proud to be able to share your excellent stories and advice via this book.

To all the clients and comms friends past and present who will benefit from this book, this is for you. I know how visible and valuable your role is and I hope my thoughts make a tangible difference to your work.

Introduction

Organizations that understand and harness the power of corporate communication can revolutionize from the inside out. Effective internal communication accelerates a business and unlocks its potential.

Connecting employees with each other and your business strategy, creating alignment and contentment with a compelling sense of belonging can keep, motivate and invigorate a workforce. At the heart of most business issues is communication, or a lack of. This book contains practical advice and inspirational ideas, rooted in theory and underpinned by the reality of communicating inside organizations today.

Developing an internal communication (IC) strategy is a key requirement for professional communicators. This book will not only teach you how to write an internal communication strategy, but how to implement it too, using The MILLER Framework.

I've examined what is meant by working strategically and highlighted some of the key topics facing the industry today, including influencing at C-suite level, accessible communication, communicating with neurodivergent employees, measuring impact and proving the value of internal communication, plus hybrid working.

My aim for this book is to equip, empower and enable professional communicators to thrive in their organizations.

Why does internal communication exist?

The purpose of internal communication isn't telling people what to do, it is to create a shared understanding and meaning. Only then can employees align themselves with a company's goals and purpose. We will examine this more in the next chapter.

At the core is a focus on people and priorities. A company does not have a voice, people do. The amplification of what 'the organization' thinks is a combination of leaders' priorities, market positioning, external messaging and a desire to create conditions where employees feel a tangible sense of purpose and belonging.

The responsibilities resting on professional communicators' shoulders are huge. We create and curate stories, share experiences and attach meaning to help employees understand the importance of their roles, why they matter and how they fit in.

Internal communicators shape, craft and hone the strategic narrative inside companies. Strategic narrative is one of the four enablers of employee engagement identified by MacLeod and Clarke in 2009.

They defined employee engagement as 'a workplace approach designed to ensure that employees are committed to their organization's goals and values, motivated to contribute to organizational success and are able at the same time to enhance their own sense of well-being' (MacLeod and Clarke, 2009).

The four enablers of employee engagement are:

- **Strategic narrative:** visible, empowering leadership providing a strong strategic narrative about the organization, where it's come from and where it's going.

- **Engaging managers:** engaging managers who focus their people and give them scope, treat their people as individuals, and coach and stretch their people.

- **Employee voice:** employee voice throughout the organization, for reinforcing and challenging views, between functions and externally. Employees are seen not as the problem, rather as central to the solution, to be involved, listened to, and invited to contribute their experience, expertise and ideas.

- **Organizational integrity:** Organizational integrity – the values on the wall are reflected in the day-to-day behaviours. There is no 'say–do' gap. Promises are made and kept, or an explanation given as to why not.

MacLeod and Clarke say your organization's strategic narrative needs to have depth and breadth, but not necessarily length. Employees need to see the 'big picture', what your organization's purpose is, where it has come from and where it is going. You need to give clear direction, and where your organization is changing or responding to changes in the external environment, you need to show what will be different, how it will impact your people, and how they will know the change will be successful.

However, only 30 per cent of organizations have a written strategic narrative in place (Gallagher, 2023). Given the fact strategic alignment is cited as the second reason why internal communication exists inside organizations, behind culture and belonging (Gallagher, 2023), this feels like a missed opportunity.

A point to note is you need to have a business strategy in place to bring a strategic narrative to life; if you don't have one, it makes that storytelling a lot harder! I am a visual thinker and when I'm advising on strategic narrative, I often share examples of visual timelines. I have a whole Pinterest board of examples I've curated over the years (Miller, nd). Being able to see the journey of your company, with its many twists and turns, changes of direction, leadership, branding and products, creates clarity and helps employees understand what has led to the company they are part of today. It's particularly useful in a merger or acquisition situation where you are combining the strategic narratives of organizations.

The proximity to purpose

An important part of the strategic narrative definition is visible, empowering leadership. Leaders have a critical role to play in bringing the story of an organization to life. We will talk more about leaders later in this book.

I had a conversation with an in-house internal communicator about the role of leaders and he questioned me about their 'proximity to purpose'. He asked if I thought a reason some leaders can communicate well is because they know how organizational purpose relates to their role. I think that answer is yes. If purpose feels tangible and you know how it relates to your day-to-day work, I'd expect you to communicate in a way that demonstrates that proximity.

What about your workers who are serving customers or driving vehicles? Does their proximity to purpose impact how they feel about the company, which in turn impacts employee engagement? You will have data in your organization's listening activities to help you gauge how relevant this is for your company. If you don't, consider how you can include it.

Designing and developing an internal communication strategy

Creating an internal communication strategy often feels like an overwhelming and daunting task for many who are working in this field. I've devised a method to guide you through designing and developing a strategy, to reduce the overwhelm and set you up for success.

Your strategy needs to be a living and breathing document, a reflection of your daily practice and a guide to the future. You need to know how to pull the thinking through into doing, so you can focus on longer-term planning.

Gallagher's State of the Sector 2023 survey was completed by more than 2,000 respondents worldwide, across 53 countries. The survey is now in its 15th year and is a useful gauge for benchmarking and comparison in the internal communication world. Practitioners use it to see how peers are using channels, discover the size of their teams and even how much people are being paid.

Developing or refreshing an IC strategy is in internal communicators' top three priorities, with 35 per cent of respondents citing it as their second priority for their year ahead. Engaging teams around purpose, strategy and values came first at 51 per cent, with enhancing people manager communication at third place, with 32 per cent. This was a jump of nine points, showing a perceived need to 'recalibrate communications' (Gallagher, 2023).

I recommend using your internal communication strategy to recalibrate the way communication happens. Knowing whether the cadence – or rhythm – has changed, being clear on business objectives and making informed decisions about how measurement will be used to demonstrate impact, resonance and relevancy is a strong start.

Why develop a strategy?

According to the UK Government Communication Service (GCS), developing a successful strategy means preparing for challenges ahead, which are difficult to predict. 'Your internal communication strategy must support your people strategy. It must share key performance indicators, around engagement for example, so you are all working in the same direction. Developing a well-thought-out internal communication strategy and a plan to execute it is critical to the success of an organization' (GCS, 2021).

The Institute of Internal Communication (IoIC) describe a strategy as setting a clear course of action for how an organization can use IC to deliver on its objectives. They say working without one 'is like setting off on a long journey with no map' and recognize developing a strategy is not always straightforward. It involves acquiring a strong understanding of an organization's strategy, operations and people, and using this knowledge to make fundamental choices about how communication within the organization will happen. However, done well, it can 'help IC to make a meaningful and valuable contribution to an organization's success' (IoIC, 2023).

A visible position

Professional communicators have incredibly visible positions inside their organizations. When you are working at a strategic level, you're creating connections between employees and the C-suite. Daily tasks include advising the chief executive officer (CEO) and senior leaders, and creating and curating conversations, ideas and content to enhance and advise how communication happens.

However, only 45 per cent of internal communicators 'frequently have a say in what gets communicated – and how – inside their organization' (Gallagher, 2023). This statistic was in response to the question 'what does your organization's culture enable you to do?'

- Only 45 per cent of respondents frequently have a say in what gets communicated, and how.
- 36 per cent frequently trial new tactics and approaches.
- 35 per cent frequently inject more 'personality' into communications.
- 26 per cent frequently use creativity and humour.

The first statistic is woeful. Effective internal communication means giving your IC team the access, autonomy and permission to do their jobs well. Not involving comms professionals or giving them a say in what gets communicated and how is a missed opportunity. It's a source of frustration for professional communicators, who are striving to influence and impact the way communication happens.

You need to be working in partnership and aligning your internal communication strategy with the business's strategy. Having a robust and comprehensive internal communication strategy in place is essential.

So why have an internal communication strategy if research like this shows you're not having a say in what gets communicated and how? The research doesn't reveal whether the people who don't feel involved have an IC strategy or not; I'd be curious to know whether there's a correlation.

However, it does state 29 per cent of its 2,000 respondents have an overarching internal communication strategy in place covering a period of more than one year (Gallagher 2023).

Demonstrating impact

At the heart of an internal communication strategy is the requirement to demonstrate impact. Determining what is going to add the most value for employees, the C-suite, clients, customers and shareholders is where we excel.

When you can't articulate the value or impact of planned and thoughtful internal communication, it makes your job immeasurably harder. Literally, because you're not measuring.

We need to align employees' needs with the purpose of the business. Whether we're curing patients, selling widgets or transporting people, aligning actions, intentions and decisions is critical. As internal communicators, you need to have an acute understanding of the purpose of your organization. It's never about producing more content or 'noise' inside an organization, but ensuring relevant lines of communication exist, which allow people to have the information they need to do their jobs and feel a sense of belonging.

> We need to align employees' needs with the purpose of the business.

The rise of belonging

Discussions about belonging have increased among the global internal communication community since 2020, not least because physical artefacts and overt and obvious elements of culture (Somers, 2023) were removed in many workplaces during the Covid-19 pandemic.

Creating a culture of inclusion and belonging often includes wearing certain items of clothing, or lanyards, commuting or going to a fully branded place of work. From conversations with clients and comms friends, it's clear the removal of these artefacts during the pandemic impacted the way people felt about their companies and reduced the sense of belonging. Conversely, people on the front line in hospitals or driving trains and buses maintained those visual and cultural identifiers, but felt fragmented and distant from their business functions and colleagues who were able to work from home.

The work landscape has changed. This means an internal communication strategy that was written before the pandemic (before 2019/2020) is out of date. Organizations have had to reinvent and reimagine the way they work and communicate. We've been experimenting, replacing face-to-face communication methods and channels with video and virtual sessions, and determining what to keep.

Working remotely

The shift to a remote work environment 'has introduced new barriers to inclusion that calls for reimagining the contexts and cultures that individuals are now working in' (Byrd, 2022). Belonging has a role to play in retaining employees, with organizations needing to evolve their approach to building community and cohesion (De Smet et al, 2022). Keep belonging in mind while writing an internal communication strategy.

Isabel Collins, Belonging and Culture Consultant, wrote for my All Things IC blog about the role of belonging in light of the Covid-19 pandemic. She says 'our sense of belonging was taken for granted, until it was taken away' (Collins, 2021). Collins describes the 'deep, primal need humans have to belong and how we can do more together than on our own and go further'.

While creating a sense of belonging doesn't sit solely with internal communication (far from it!) we have an important role to play, whether that's considering the types of channels that can help to facilitate meaningful connection, to listening to employees and feeding their views back to leadership, to creating communication that provides clarity.

Research shows 60 per cent of internal communicators believe their channels help connect people on a human level. Tactics you can use to help employees feel more connected to the organization and each other include workshops and cultural events, corporate volunteering, social evenings, appreciation/recognition week, competitions and sports days (Gallagher, 2023).

What to expect from this book

I've written this book in two parts, the first of which introduces you to a framework I've developed based on my years of working as a professional internal communicator.

The MILLER Framework is a logical series of steps that provides the structure of an internal communication strategy. It is a clear process to follow and as we work our way through its structure, I will touch on broader aspects of internal communication theory.

The second part of this book focuses on how to implement an internal communication strategy. This is important because creating a strategy is only half of the story. The life cycle of an IC strategy starts from the moment you begin creating it. Even before you've written the first word or dusted off an old version, the mere fact you're thinking about it focuses your mind in the right place. It deserves careful thought and attention.

An internal communication strategy isn't a quick plan on a page, but a thoughtful and comprehensive approach that will set an organization up for success. The final stages of the framework detail how to do this, as they concentrate on evaluation and revision. Creating an IC strategy is not a 'one and done' task. Evaluation and revision is a continual process.

My aim for this book is for it to be an all-in-one guide professional communicators will want to keep on their desk and refer to for years to come. Whenever it's time to update an internal communication strategy, it is here to prompt and guide you through what to do.

This is not designed to be an academic book; however, I'm a keen champion of knowing communication theory and investing in continuing professional development in my own career. Being able to recall models and theory can boost your confidence, particularly when having tricky conversations with stakeholders inside organizations.

Therefore, this book examines various communication theories by overlaying them with the reality of being a professional communicator inside a modern-day organization. Being able to translate theory into reality equips organizational communicators with everything they need to not only survive but thrive in their role.

I've detailed a breadth of topics for professional communicators to consider as part of their strategy. I know how visible your roles are, I want you to consider this book as an extension of your team for you to check your thinking, spark fresh thoughts and know what to do next. You'll find expert views featured in this book, so you can discover what your peers are doing.

Working strategically

Much has been written about the need for a seat at the table over the years. I'm not intending to cover this topic in any depth, but I will say this. If we are doing our roles well, it shouldn't matter if we're not sat around the boardroom table, because every single leader should know their responsibility when it comes to internal communication.

Not inviting a professional communicator to join conversations, cutting 'their slot' from the agenda or deliberately excluding them is inexcusable. When I've felt excluded from rooms, I have created my own conversations and brought stakeholders together to talk about business problems and come up with solutions. Not being invited doesn't mean you don't have a voice. The best internal communicators are those who champion voices inside an organization and find ways to connect people with each other. That starts with speaking up for ourselves and the communities we represent and serve.

Structuring an internal communication strategy

The fundamental principles of how organizational communication happens have remained unchanged for decades. However, in a Covid-19 pandemic-impacted world, companies have had to adapt their internal communication techniques to reflect the reality of today's workforce.

An internal communication strategy captures a professional communicator's thinking, and they use it to inform and influence the way communication happens inside an organization. Practitioners are struggling to adapt their strategies to mirror hybrid working and the asynchronous nature of communication. We'll talk about this in more detail later in the book.

For many IC professionals, creating their strategy is an overwhelming task. I've worked in internal communication since 2003 and written countless internal communication strategies.

The way I used to approach them was like a map. I viewed an IC strategy as an outline of your organization's journey and the big picture of what you want to achieve.

HOW I USED TO STRUCTURE AN IC STRATEGY

I included:

Where you are now

Where you're heading/want to be (objectives)

How you are going to get there

How long it will take and why

What is involved

Who is involved

Why this approach is the best one

How you'll know when you've got there (measurement)

I often used these phrases as part of the structure. Why? Because packing it full of jargon does no one any favours!

For me, it's the what and why that are the most important for strategy, largely because the how, where and when are more tactical, which inform your IC plans.

The MILLER Framework

My thinking has evolved into The MILLER Framework. It mirrors a lot of the points above, but now includes more in-depth analysis, particularly in the insights section.

I developed this original and trademarked framework to provide professional communicators with a rigorous and robust method. I've used it successfully with clients around the globe to help them write and implement their internal communication strategies. This book details what it is, how it works and how you can apply it today.

The MILLER Framework is:

- **Mindset:** Business priorities, vision and why internal communication is important.
- **Insights:** What we know about the organization and its people.
- **Logistics:** How internal communication happens and what we're prioritizing.
- **Leadership:** How we will deliver this strategy and the role leaders and managers play.
- **Evaluation:** How we measure and evaluate internal communication.
- **Revision:** What happens next in the life cycle of this IC strategy. Next steps and when it will be updated.

FIGURE 0.1 The MILLER Framework for IC strategies

Mindset Business priorities, vision and why internal communication is important.

Insights What we know about the organization and its people.

Logistics How internal communication happens and what we're prioritizing.

Leadership How we will deliver this strategy and the role leaders and managers play.

Evaluation How we measure and evaluate internal communication.

Revision What happens next in the life cycle of this IC strategy. Next steps and when it will be updated.

Every stage of this model earns its place. Creating an internal communication strategy without insights means you put employee alignment at risk. Similarly, writing a strategy without detailing the responsibilities for internal communication in the leadership section leaves it open to interpretation.

In my experience, a lack of clarity leads to assumptions inside organizations, with a sense of 'someone is responsible' for communication, which aids confusion and causes breakdowns in the flow of information.

This book also includes content on the following key topics, which are issues professional communicators are facing: communicating with neurodiverse colleagues, which is an emerging requirement and consideration for organizations; how to operate as a strategic internal communicator and influence at C-suite level; how to measure with impact and prove the value of internal communication; and the impact of hybrid working on internal communication.

If you are grappling with these considerations, you are not alone. I hope you find this book reassuring and helpful as you navigate your way through and unlock the power of corporate communication.

My intention for this book is for you to create your own strategy and use it to reflect on your own professional practice. It's written to align with The MILLER Framework – this is your all-in-one guide that is here whenever you need to dive into the relevant topics it covers.

References and further reading

Byrd, Marilyn Y (2022) Creating a culture of inclusion and belongingness in remote work environments that sustains meaningful work, *Human Resource Development International*, 25 (2), 145–62, doi.org/10.1080/13678868.2022.2047252 (archived at https://perma.cc/BZ8B-6GBJ)

Collins, I (2021) How to create a sense of belonging for hybrid workers, All Things IC Blog, 13 May, www.allthingsic.com/how-to-create-a-sense-of-belonging-for-hybrid-workers/ (archived at https://perma.cc/54M9-X634)

De Smet, A, Dowling, B, Mugayar-Baldocchi, M and Spratt, J (2022) It's not about the office, it's about belonging, McKinsey & Company, 13 January, www.mckinsey.com/capabilities/people-and-organizational-performance/our-insights/the-organization-blog/its-not-about-the-office-its-about-belonging (archived at https://perma.cc/X97U-F46H)

Gallagher (2023) State of the Sector 2022/3, www.ajg.com/employeeexperience/state-of-the-sector-2023/ (archived at https://perma.cc/C9JB-CA75)

GCS (2021) Developing an internal communication strategy, Government Communication Service, 18 May, gcs.civilservice.gov.uk/guidance/internal-communication/developing-an-internal-communication-strategy/ (archived at https://perma.cc/GA32-ZEMP)

IoIC (2023) *IoIC Guide to Internal Communication Strategy*, 2nd edn, Institute of Internal Communication, www.ioic.org.uk/resource/ioic-strat-guide-v2.html (archived at https://perma.cc/9R54-P9DU)

MacLeod, D and Clarke, N (2009) Engaging for Success: Enhancing performance through employee engagement, Department of Business, Innovation and Skills, www.engageforsuccess.org/wp-content/uploads/2020/12/engaging-for-success.pdf (archived at https://perma.cc/9846-XV9B)

Miller, R (nd) Visual timelines in offices, Pinterest, www.pinterest.co.uk/allthingsic/visual-timelines-in-offices/ (archived at https://perma.cc/599Y-SM4T)

Pass, S, Court-Smith, J, Liu-Smith, Y-L, Popescu, S, Ridgway, M and Kougiannou, N (2023) Engage for Success: UK employee engagement levels 2022: Exploring the impact of COVID-19 on employee engagement in the UK, Engage for Success, London, doi.org/10.17631/rd-2023-0001-drep (archived at https://perma.cc/KLT4-7CLR)

Schein, E H (1985) *Organizational Culture and Leadership*, Jossey-Bass, San Francisco, CA

Somers, M (2023) Five enduring management ideas from MIT Sloan's Edgar Schein, MIT Sloan School of Management, 9 February, https://mitsloan.mit.edu/ideas-made-to-matter/5-enduring-management-ideas-mit-sloans-edgar-schein (archived at https://perma.cc/LR4E-RZU2)

PART ONE

Writing a strategy

1

An introduction to strategic internal communication

WHAT THIS CHAPTER WILL COVER

In the introduction we examined what you can expect from this book, and I presented The MILLER Framework for the first time. This chapter is an introduction to strategic internal communication, and it will establish strong foundations ahead of your strategy creation. It examines what internal communication is, why it is important, the role IC professionals play inside organizations, and looks at the need for a strategy. You'll find a checklist at the end of this chapter to help you keep track.

What is internal communication?

This book refers to internal communication, but the term is used interchangeably with employee communication, organizational communication, corporate communication and even iComms. It broadly means the same thing – communication inside a company, where employees are the primary audience and stakeholders/interested parties could be a secondary audience.

There may be some external interested parties involved too, such as shareholders or members. Or even some outsourced colleagues, such as joint ventures, supply chain partnerships or offshore call centres (Quirke, 2008). The core focus of internal communication is what is happening inside the business, and communication between employees and leaders.

Sometimes the term 'corporate communication' includes wider disciplines in a comms function, such as public affairs, external communication or investor relations.

'Employee communication' is popular in the United States and professional bodies such as the Public Relations Society of America's (PRSA) Employee Communication section use the term for its members who are focused on communication inside organizations.

The lack of consistency in the naming convention also extends to job titles, which vary between sectors and organizations. For example, an internal communication executive could be the most senior internal communicator in a business, or someone just starting out in their career.

It's imperative to make sure the title of the vacancy clearly describes the remit of the position and reflects the accountability the chosen candidate will hold (IoIC and VMA Group, 2021).

Defining internal communication

The Institute of Internal Communication (IoIC) is the only professional body solely dedicated to internal communication in the UK. It started life as the British Association of Industrial Editors in 1949. The IoIC says successful internal communication:

> creates an environment of mutual understanding and forges connections between people, allowing them to perform at their best, both individually and collectively. At the most basic level, you have to communicate well at the right time, so employees know what is expected of them and what is happening in the organization. At a deeper level, for employees to feel engaged with their workplace and give their best, they have to see that the organization cares about their views and understand how their role contributes to overall business objectives (Miller, 2020, quoting IoIC).

Performance is also highlighted in the UK Government Communication Service's definition, which describes the purpose of internal communication as being 'to inform and engage employees in a way that motivates staff to maximise their performance and deliver the business strategy most effectively' (GCS, 2020).

Making the connections

Connections and interactions are key themes in internal communication definitions. The Chartered Institute of Public Relations' (CIPR) Inside group, which specializes in supporting internal communicators, defines internal communication as 'the way we connect people within organizations – connect them with our strategy, with news and information and with each other. It's not only broadcast communication, but also driving employee voice' (CIPR Inside, 2017).

In Bill Quirke's book *Making the Connections* (2008) he says companies know employees' energies and enthusiasm need to point in the same direction. However, Quirke cautions against the enthusiastic rush to plug together different components of communication best practice, warning organizations can 'short-circuit' their own efforts. He says people need a better understanding of the connections and urges 'moving from the message and media business to that of creating meaning and understanding'.

Dewhurst and FitzPatrick (2022) state an employee or internal communicator is concerned with the conversation with the organization and not automatically the interpersonal skills of regular colleagues in the office or factory. They describe relationships between co-workers as mostly the realm of organizational communication. They say as communicators we have an important role in creating a sense of shared context and that at a basic level, the value we add is in fostering shared understanding within a workplace. 'If we do nothing else well, getting everyone on the same page immediately makes organizations work better and be more effective.'

Welch and Jackson (2007) describe internal communication as the 'strategic management of interactions and relationships between stakeholders within organisations across a number of interrelated dimensions including, internal line manager communication, internal team peer communication, internal project peer communication and internal corporate communication'.

You may hear the phrase 'internal marketing'. I don't identify as a marketing professional and don't know of any internal communicators who do, either. Internal communication is a stand-alone discipline, it's often closely aligned with, or even reports into, HR/people teams.

Internal marketing is described as the 'planned use of communication actions to systematically influence the knowledge, attitudes and behaviours of current employees' (Stauss and Hoffmann, 2000).

As communication professionals we rarely describe what we do as systematically influencing. However, that definition does resonate with me because we often strive to change behaviours, make a connection or provoke a reaction. I prefer to think about planning intentionally and will talk more about this in the chapter on mindset. Our marketing colleagues use data and insights to know how to drive action and encourage consumer behaviour externally. Internal communicators use data and insights to drive action and encourage employee behaviour that aligns with organizational values. One of the biggest opportunities for internal communicators is knowing how to use data and insights effectively to inform our work. We'll analyse these areas in more detail in the insights and evaluation chapters.

How do you define internal communication?

I conduct an experiment at the start of training sessions with professional communicators, where I urge them to write the words 'internal communication is…' and then complete the sentence.

I encourage you to do the same now. What's your definition? When friends or family ask what you do and you tell them you work in internal communication, and they say 'what's that?', how do you answer them?

QUESTION

What is internal communication?

Internal communication is…

I wonder how easy you found that activity? It appears to be straightforward, but unless you have a definition that is top of mind, it can be a struggle. When creating a definition for internal communication, consider it through two lenses – how you define it and how your organization defines it. Does that definition need to change?

If you have a definition, how well known is it? Does the whole of your comms team give the same answer? If you're a team of one, that's a simple task! But if you are striving to work strategically, consistency is key. Every single member of the team needs to give the same answer when being asked to define what internal communication is. We will come to what it *isn't* later on.

The purpose of internal communication

I disclosed my own purpose definition in the introduction, and we are going to examine it further here. *The purpose of internal communication isn't*

telling people what to do, it is to create a shared understanding and mean-
ing. Only then can employees align themselves with a company's goals and
purpose.

Meaning is at the heart of what professional communicators do. A shared understanding and meaning appears to be a straightforward statement. However, it has many layers and levels.

THE PURPOSE OF INTERNAL COMMUNICATION

The layers and levels include:

- **What is said and done** in the company.
- **What is prioritized** by employees and leaders.
- **How communication happens**, including tone of voice, accessibility and inclusivity.
- **Clear alignment** between employees and the purpose of the organization. They know how their role fits into the wider picture and why the company exists.
- **Clarity of thought** from leaders, with no organizational integrity gap between what is said and done. Values on the wall are reflected in day-to-day behaviours. There is no 'say–do' gap. Promises are made and kept, or an explanation given as to why not (MacLeod and Clarke, 2009).
- **Stories** and peer-to-peer communication employees identify with.
- **Analysing assumptions**, testing recall and jargon busting.
- **Sense-checking** and creating frames of reference for employees.

How these layers manifest inside each organization is different. That's down to a variety of factors, not least the culture, leadership style, type of business, how and where employees work, its history, the maturity of the company and ownership. It's why the world of internal communication is so fascinating and why it differs so much from company to company.

According to the 2023 State of the Sector Survey from Gallagher, 74 per cent of respondents rate culture and belonging as their purpose for internal communication – creating an inclusive workplace where employees feel valued and energized. This is followed closely by strategic alignment at 67 per cent: creating clarity around your strategy and a sense of ownership.

Everything you do as an IC practitioner has to be aligned to the objectives, goals and purpose of the organization. It's why we exist. When I'm analysing an organization's internal communication team, strategy, plans or work, I'm looking for a clear correlation between what the business is striving to achieve and what the comms team's focus is.

What is the purpose of internal communication inside your organization?

Why does your role or the function exist? If you've never considered this before, spend a few moments trying to answer these questions. Then test what you've written against what your team members, leaders or stakeholders say the purpose of internal communication is.

The Institute of Internal Communication states the core role of internal communication is to enable people at work to feel informed, connected and purposeful in order to drive organizational performance (IoIC, 2023a).

Why a lack of clarity impacts internal communication

Let's look at the word 'shared' in my purpose of IC phrase, as it's a critical one.

> *The purpose of internal communication isn't telling people what to do, it is to create a shared understanding and meaning. Only then can employees align themselves with a company's goals and purpose.*

Departments and silos exist inside companies, with sections of organizations determining their own answers to the layers. I've witnessed companies operating with the best of intentions, with departments, countries and regions determining what they *think* strategic priorities are, deciphering how what's on the mind of the CEO translates into their area and making assumptions on the work they need to do.

However, a lack of clarity and communication means everyone is working hard, but not necessarily on the right things. I observed this acutely in a business I was invited to audit. They did not have an internal communication function and the director of human resources wanted to determine the status quo and whether an IC person or team was needed.

I spent time listening to employees, in audit mode. The word audit means to listen, or hear. It comes from the Latin word *audire*, which is a valuable mindset to be in when embarking on something like this. *Audire* is also the root of 'hearing' words in English such as audience, something we are mindful of as communicators.

I try to avoid using audience as it implies a performance, and one-way, broadcasted communication. But it remains a popular way for many to describe employee groups. We'll talk more about employee groups in Chapter 4 when we examine logistics.

From speaking one-to-one with colleagues, spending time with the senior leadership team and talking with people managers, it became clear everyone had their own sense of direction.

However, it wasn't rooted in anything, and at times those different workstreams contradicted each other. Rather than having one destination, colleagues had created their own route in terms of where they thought the company was heading. I realized one of the biggest risks to the business was the lack of clarity. Everyone was striving and felt like they were on course, but ultimately, they were pulling in opposite directions and going around in circles. It's why the company felt taut, people were frazzled and at a loss to understand why their efforts weren't feeling valued. I identified there was no end point or goal that was known, articulated or understood across the company.

Creating a source of truth

My recommendation for that organization was to create a role for an internal communicator, whose first focus would be to create sources of truth and a strategic narrative. I recommended they map colleague groups and established official communication channels. I examined strategic narratives in the introduction and how it's the story of an organization – where it's come from and where it's going (MacLeod and Clarke, 2009).

Done well, the strategic narrative provides a strong hook for employees to identify with, so they can see how they fit in, have clarity on what's ahead and be able to orientate themselves. But to make it work, you need a strategy first.

Without a communicated sense of direction and story, the efforts colleagues were making felt in vain. Something to note from the example I've just shared with you is there was a new CEO in place in that organization. They had been there for six months but hadn't articulated their vision or revealed the business's priorities. Therefore, employees had created their own in lieu of that missing information. It wasn't done maliciously; they were doing what they thought was the right course of action.

It was evident to me the difference an internal communicator would make in that company! Another recommendation was to course-correct by having the CEO increase their visibility and communicate with the whole company. I wanted them to try to make up for lost time, as six months is too long to say nothing. Without knowing it, they had undermined their own credibility and trust among employees, who had interpreted the silence as impending changes and cuts. They were planning nothing of the sort. However, employees had filled the void with their own assumptions.

Myths of internal communication

There are eight myths that prevail in the world of internal communication (Miller, 2017).

They are:

1 Internal communication 'belongs' to one person or team in an organization.
2 External communication should be kept separate from internal communication.
3 Social media has no role to play in internal communication.
4 Internal communication is about telling people what to do.
5 Internal communication is about Sending Out Stuff (SOS).
6 You can't measure internal communication.
7 Employee-generated content threatens IC pros' jobs.
8 Front-line employees aren't concerned with company strategy.

Let's address each of them in turn.

Internal communication 'belongs' to one person or team in an organization

Internal communication is too important to be left to one team, department or person. It is everyone's responsibility in a company. Professional communicators are not responsible for the interactions between a manager and their team. However, we can provide talking points and train them to be effective communicators. We need accountability when it comes to budgets and overseeing the comms strategy. But even though communication is in your job title, I'm confident it's in your stakeholders' job descriptions already. If not, it should be.

External communication should be kept separate from internal communication.

If external and internal communication are viewed independently and there's no correlation between them, you're doing internal communication wrong. Stop thinking about internal and external communication as being separate from each other. Look for ways to work together.

Social media has no role to play in internal communication.

Social media can play an excellent role when it comes to internal communication. A 'medium is only social if it allows for interaction' (FitzPatrick and Valskov, 2014) and this is the mindset you need for internal communication. Social media creates opportunities for employee advocacy and amplifying a brand from the inside out. Empower your people to share their stories externally. Create guidelines to give them flexibility within boundaries.

Internal communication is about telling people what to do

In many organizations it is still about telling people what to do, aka broadcasting or one-way communication. In truth, it's about creating a shared understanding and meaning. Employees expect and deserve more. The roles we need to master now include community management and collaboration.

Internal communication is about sending out stuff (SOS)

Internal communication should be about two-way communication and giving employees a voice. Russell Grossman, Government Communication Service Head of Profession for Internal Communications, said 'Internal communications' function is to help leaders in your department or agency inform and engage employees, in a way which motivates staff to maximise their performance and deliver the business strategy most effectively. It's not about "sending out stuff"' (GCS, 2020).

You can't measure internal communication

Yes you can. It's essential. There are various models and frameworks to not only help you measure but also use the data to transform your communication. We'll talk about this more in Chapter 6.

Employee-generated content threatens IC pros' jobs

Why? It shouldn't. Our role is to equip, empower and enable organizations to communicate. Think curation, not creation, of content, coach your leaders and employees to communicate in a different way. If employee-generated content is happening in your company, embrace it and help colleagues do it brilliantly.

Front-line employees aren't concerned with company strategy

How do you know? Have you asked them? If the role of internal communication is to help an organization achieve its objectives, then every employee has a part to play.

Why internal communication is important

Internal communication helps employees navigate an organization, it signposts them towards people, ideas and work that can motivate and inspire them. One of the main priorities is ensuring people have the information they need to do their jobs safely and compliantly.

The Institute of Internal Communication (2023a) says an organization that communicates well with its people can achieve greater productivity, innovation, reputation, talent attraction and retention.

You need a cohesive set of channels that work independently and collectively, to create consistency, clarity and certainty. Companies that fail to have a robust and structured approach to internal communication find themselves wasting time, money and effort as their people search for information.

I have an unscientific test to find out what a source of truth is in an organization. I call it the 'snow test'. Imagine you are in a company that has offices and people who spend a lot of their time commuting in. If there was snow forecast, where would employees go to know whether to travel or not?

Where or who would they expect to get credible, accurate and reliable information from to know whether their site would be open and if they should travel? It could be their line manager, maybe it's an app or perhaps it's your intranet (internal website). If that channel or person is the source of truth, that's the focus for the IC team, as you would update them first.

You need to test assumptions. The comms team may think the source of truth would be the intranet, but employees may say their line manager. That's what I mean when I say it's our business to *know* our business as professional communicators. Don't wait until you are in a crisis communication situation to figure out the source of truth inside your company. Build this question into any audit plans or comms surveys.

The cost of poor communication

In the US, leaders estimate teams lose the equivalent of an entire workday, 7.47 hours, each week to poor communication – or approximately $12,506 per employee, per year (Grammarly Business and The Harris Poll, 2023).

> Businesses run on communication. Effective communication allows for the exchange of information, ideas and feedback between employees, management, customers and other key stakeholders. When communication is effective it creates value – but when it's not, businesses face avoidable costs in the form of lost productivity, declining morale, customer churn and eroded brand reputation. When the stakes are so high, harnessing effective communication across the organization becomes a critical priority for leaders; however, communication is layered and complex (Grammarly Business and The Harris Poll, 2023).

Internal communication as a business function

Working in internal communication is not about being ego driven. We set aside our own preferences and bylines to truly get under the hood of organizations. I describe internal communication as a business function, because it enables a business to function. Poor communication disrupts organizations as people waste time, money and effort searching for accurate, credible and reliable information to help them do their jobs.

Companies that find themselves in turbulent times and unable to function well need to look at the way they are communicating. The antidote to uncertainty and lack of functionality will have roots in communication. I observe assumptions, egos and silos creating barriers to clear routes of information flow inside organizations. These alone create issues, division and a loss of functionality.

Internal communication should be about adding value to the core mission of the business or project that it supports. Internal communication is not about making noise for the sake of it – as a maturing profession we have the responsibility to make a difference and share responsibility for the strategic goals of our employers (FitzPatrick and Valskov, 2014).

Defining the terms

The phrases 'internal communication' and 'internal communications' are used interchangeably, but there is an important difference between them.

WHAT IS INTERNAL COMMUNICATION?

How I describe the difference:

- Internal communication is the overarching way a company communicates.
- Internal communications are the tools, tactics, channels and methodologies.

The Institute of Internal Communication is so called in recognition of the fact it focuses on the overarching way a company communicates, not just channels. Therefore, it doesn't use the pluralized form. Its mission is to promote the impact of effective internal communication on organizational performance and working lives.

IoIC describes effective internal communication as 'giving employees a powerful and articulate voice' and says internal communication 'is critical in building deeper and longer lasting connections between employees and the organization they work for'. It says 'how we communicate at work has the power to transform lives by helping people feel informed, connected and purposeful – that they matter at work – making for better organizations and a better society overall'. There's a distinct lack of channels being mentioned in that description, and for good reason.

I find when people want to be seen as strategic internal communicators, they're frustrated when stakeholders only talk about tools, tactics and channels, rather than seeking professional expertise and guidance about the way communication happens.

We will look at the difference between internal communication and employee engagement in Chapter 5.

The internal communicator's role

As professional internal communicators, it is our business to *know* our business. This means being tuned in to an organization and its people. Internal communicators need to know what makes a company function well, which means getting close to the inner workings. We have a vital role to play when it comes to translating ideas, objectives and priorities into actionable goals and a path ahead for our people.

The role of internal communication is to help employees at all levels understand what's happening in their organization, so they can do their job as well as they can. Internal communicators plan, create and curate the process of keeping employees informed and engaged. Internal communication can cover 'any and all' communication between employees in an organization (IoIC, 2019).

Having professional communicators at the core of an organization can benefit leaders, employees, customers, shareholders and stakeholders immensely. We are like a central nervous system or the brain, sending signals, decoding information and ensuring all the relevant parts are working in harmony with each other.

The work of professional communicators is akin to holding a mirror up inside an organization and revealing what is reflected. We are often the first to spot issues and detect the low rumblings of discontent in a business. This is not without risk because often companies don't like what they see in that mirror and blame or challenge the communicator. It's easier to question the person making the reflection happen, rather than taking a good look and accepting what is revealed. This can cause internal communicators to be fearful of doing it again.

However, knowing the reality of how employees are feeling and what is top of mind for both the workforce and your leaders is crucial, to ensure sentiment and stresses are known.

Internal communicators need to use these insights to inform our work. If we fail to tune in, then it can feel like leaders are heading in one direction, and employees in another. Internal communication exists to bring a sense of cohesion inside an organization, so we need to know whether that is happening or not.

Holding that metaphorical mirror up means deciphering conversations, gauging sentiment and analysing employee questions. An example of this would be giving feedback to a senior leader after they have spoken at an all-employee meeting. What professional communicators look for in those scenarios is not just *what* the leader said, but *how* they said it. We also look for what they *didn't* say.

Giving tough feedback

You cannot be a great leader without being a great communicator. I recommend developing strong working relationships with your senior leaders where they know you not only for the work you're doing as a communicator, but also as a trusted business adviser. Part of this obligation requires you to give feedback and speak openly and honestly with leaders.

The role of a professional communicator is to help others be better communicators, from empowering front-line workers by providing mechanisms to have their voices heard, to creating effective lines of communication from leaders. If you know a leader's performance wasn't ideal, you need to say so. Hierarchy often inhibits honesty. However, we do not need permission to offer constructive feedback on how people are communicating. Internal communication may be in our job titles, but it's in leaders' job descriptions. Therefore, we have all the permission we need.

> Hierarchy often inhibits honesty.

Getting comfortable being uncomfortable

For professional communicators to start working strategically, they need to get comfortable being uncomfortable. Over time, your comfort levels will increase, but when starting out working as a trusted adviser, it can feel incredibly visible and exposing. You have an important point of view and vantage point inside your organization. Don't be afraid to give professional advice that's in the best interest of the business or employees. Even if your advice is not listened to straight away, it's not a bad thing to be known for giving solid, professional advice every time, keep persevering.

I've shared some example questions for you to consider ahead of sharing difficult feedback with leaders. Use these to start you off. Then develop your own. What are the criteria you look for? What language are you comfortable using with them? The more you practise working like this, the more comfortable you will feel because you will be using phrases that resonate with you and your leaders. They will start to expect you to feed back constructively and challenge them. It takes time, but it is worth it.

WORKING STRATEGICALLY WITH LEADERS

Questions to consider:

Did they remember all the key messages?

Did they look at ease while speaking?

How open were they to questions?

What did they do when they didn't know an answer?

How did they react to employees?

Did they build trust and credibility through their actions?

Did it look like they were hiding something?

What else could you do to equip and support your leaders?

What are the benefits for organizations?

As the needs of employers and employees become more complex, with employers realizing the benefits of an informed and engaged workforce, the demand for internal communicators to provide unique perspectives and skills is growing. Employees are speaking up around topics such as culture expectations and work–life balance (PRSA, 2021).

Working lives can be transformed by good communication, which helps employees feel engaged, purposeful and that they matter at work. Companies that communicate well with their people can expect greater productivity, innovation and reputation, which in turn attracts and retains employees (IoIC, 2019).

'Whether businesses win or lose depends on the effectiveness of their communication. More seamless, empathetic, and high-quality communication among hybrid team leads to cost savings, new deals and a better brand reputation' (Grammarly Business and The Harris Poll, 2023).

Looking back before moving forward

When you're striving to improve the way a company communicates, I recommend looking back before moving forward. Imagine you are plotting the steps ahead of you. Pause and identify the path behind you first. What led you to where you are today? What is in the previous chapters of your story? Only once you know this information can you move forward and create clarity and momentum, to propel the company towards your destination.

Acknowledging a company's history and the values and behaviours that have led to where you are today should be part of your onboarding efforts. When introducing new members to a team or organization, share the history of the company with them. Help them understand what has led to their role being created and at which point they are entering the organization's story.

An internal communicator's role during mergers or acquisitions is pertinent, as you may be collating and curating two or more histories and trying to combine organizations with each other. You need careful attention and consideration, because there can be a clash of cultures, values, leadership styles and behaviours. In these scenarios, holding that mirror up becomes critical, as we may be striving to replace what is reflected with a new image.

What skills do internal communicators need?

The Institute of Internal Communication's Profession Map was designed to help internal communicators identify the key knowledge, skills and behaviours required to achieve what it says is the core purpose of our roles – to enable people at work to feel informed, connected and purposeful, in order to drive organizational performance (IoIC, 2023c).

The Profession Map's aim is to encapsulate the 'vital role internal communicators play in an organization' and describes the underpinning knowledge and skills required to fulfil that role. The IoIC believes that by striving to obtain those knowledge and skills – through continuous professional development (CPD), education and lifelong learning – all internal communication professionals will play a pivotal role in supporting organizations to achieve their objectives.

It was updated in 2020 and 2023. I have used the map in my own professional practice to set the benchmark for internal communication professionals and teams. I encourage you to examine it in detail (Figure 1.1).

The six areas of activity and expertise outlined in the Profession Map are:

- Strategy, planning and business acumen
- Understanding people and cultures
- Creating and curating content and conversation
- Channel and community management
- Conducting research, measuring and demonstrating value
- Influencing and advising

FIGURE 1.1 Profession Map from the Institute of Internal Communication

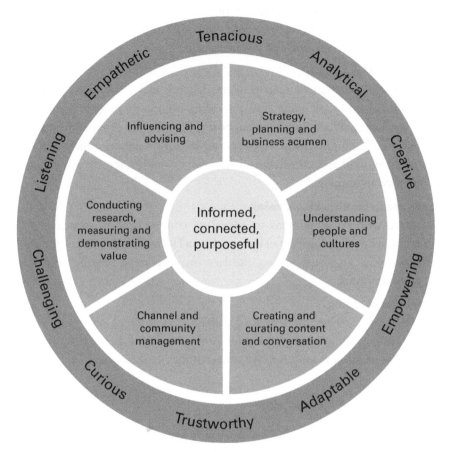

SOURCE The Profession Map, IoIC (2023c). Permission for reuse of this figure has been kindly provided by the Institute of Internal Communication, who also express their appreciation for inclusion

The behaviours around the edge of the map are: listening, empathetic, tenacious, analytical, creative, challenging, curious, trustworthy, adaptable and empowering.

Gauging your professional level

There are four distinct professional levels identified by the Profession Map. They provide an indication of the activities and outputs that professionals at different stages of their internal communication career may be involved in or responsible for (IoIC, 2023c):

Level one: Delivering

Delivering high-quality communication materials, with a focus on content creation, potentially design and the day-to-day administration of communication channels or infrastructure.

Level two: Managing

Responsible for channel management, delivery and evaluation; practical communication planning and providing advice to project teams and other stakeholders. Providing support to leaders and other colleagues in effective communication delivery and creating content which requires advanced skill and knowledge such as more complex, sensitive or change-focused messaging.

Level three: Strategically advising

Working with business areas to advise on communication strategies and approaches; development of overall channel infrastructure and evaluation processes; and supporting leaders in becoming highly effective communicators.

Level four: Leading

Working at a senior level to lead thinking on internal communication; ensuring communication strategies meet business needs and that effective communication is built into the fabric of the organization.

How to use the Profession Map

I use the map to help professionals identify the level they are operating at and spot any skills gaps or areas for improvement. It's also a useful guide if you are helping communicators understand why they haven't been promoted, or what they need to work on to reach that next level. Sometimes I ask practitioners to rank themselves out of 10 across the different areas and explain why they've given themselves the mark they have.

If you are planning an internal communication team's development, recruiting new positions or restructuring a function, the Profession Map could be a useful way of benchmarking. There is a comprehensive Profession Map document available via the Institute of Internal Communication's website that details each level. The language and evidence in there will aid you if you're creating job descriptions for a comms team.

The Institute of Internal Communication developed the Profession Map using insights and advice from internal communication practitioners across a range of organizations and sectors. It says the distribution of knowledge, skills and remit is reflective of combined good practice and encourage using it to help identify additional resource to fill knowledge and skills gaps, and enhance the value that internal communication can add to an organization (IoIC, 2023c).

How internal communicators enter the profession

Many professional communicators do not study internal communication academically. There's an unwritten rule that many 'fell into' the field. In fact, the Institute of Internal Communication has an initiative called #IChoseIC, in an effort to reverse this trend and raise awareness of IC as a career of choice.

This work acknowledges internal communication has come a long way and champions IC as a highly rewarding and exciting profession. They say it is 'integral for organization's performance, the quality of working lives and success of society overall' (IoIC, 2023c).

Regardless of your route into internal communication, I view it as an utter privilege to work in this field. Who else has an access all areas pass inside an organization in the same way?

Related disciplines can be useful to aid your role as an internal communicator. I began my career as a journalist before discovering internal communication and choosing to specialize in this field. Some of the skills I developed over my four years in a newsroom have been immensely helpful. For example, learning how to talk to anyone and draw out their thoughts, actively listening to get to the heart of a story, using persuasion and influencing techniques to dig deeper into a subject matter, discovering how to spot what is newsworthy and how to write in a certain style.

Everyone as communicators?

Whatever the career path that has led you to internal communication, you will have transferable skills. Everyone can communicate in some shape or form; from birth, most humans and animals have ways to attract attention and get their needs met.

However, what sets internal communicators apart is the intentional way we go about our work and the depth in which we hone our mindset and skill set. As a professional communicator, you need to develop your career courageously, and be endlessly curious about people. Yours is the voice that questions why and holds leaders to account. As you create that shared understanding and meaning to align employees with the organization's goals and purpose, you work intentionally.

Comms or PR professionals with 10–20 years' experience may find themselves working in internal communication for the first time, or in charge of a team of internal communicators. What unites us is our sharp focus on communicating the right information, at the right time, to achieve a desired outcome. If you know how to map an audience, plot stakeholders, generate alignment and be transparent in your methods, this will set you in good stead for an internal communication career. All of those elements are required to work in IC, so if you're confident and competent in those areas via external communication or PR, that's a strong start.

In the words of my colleague Caroline Cubbon-King, 'the strongest internal communicators are the ones who consider and understand all stakeholders before they return their lens to what's happening inside the organization'.

Unlocking the power of internal communication

Excellent internal communication doesn't just happen. You may have fallen into your role or the field, but creating outstanding internal communication takes a lot of hard work. There is nothing accidental about planned, robust and rigorous methods of communication inside a company. Behind every successful channel is a communicator who dared to retire an outdated one, or who championed piloting something new.

For every leader who takes to the stage for their first in-person event, there is an internal communicator in the wings (or on mute), who knows their speech by heart and is silently cheering them on.

During change communication campaigns, there is an internal communicator who has tested, refined and debated every single word in the key messages.

A professional communicator's currency is trust. Through our reputations and efforts we earn it, we deserve it and we fight hard to keep it. Being asked for your opinion and advice on business-critical information, knowing you can speak up in any forum to amplify your own and colleagues' voices and calling out what isn't working is in our remit. It takes time and effort, but it is worth it. Advising the business without being trusted casts doubt on your actions. However, creating strong mutually trusting and ethically sound relationships across a business unlocks the power of internal communication.

A professional communicator's currency is trust. Through our reputations and efforts we earn it, we deserve it and we fight hard to keep it.

What is strategic internal communication?

Is there a 'single overarching or unifying conceptual framework to inform the work of the many disciplines relating to the field of strategic communication?' (Hallahan et al, 2007).

In short, no. However, the focus of various communications pursuits has been 'narrowly defined' around specific managerial problems, such as improving organizational performance, selling more products, motivating donors, or building relationships' (Hallahan et al, 2007).

What does it mean to be strategic?

What is the difference between internal communication and strategic internal communication? We use these phrases a lot in the internal communication world. Let's bust some jargon before we move on.

To me, being strategic means being *proactive*. Whereas being tactical is about being *reactive*.

Strategic internal communication is defined as 'the purposeful use of communication by an organization to fulfil its mission' (Hallahan et al, 2007). That phrase resonates with me as the word purposeful implies it's planned, thoughtful and intentional.

Having an internal communication strategy in place helps comms professionals know what they're working towards and what the outcome looks like. An internal communication strategy requires you to set goals. Once you are clear on your goals, you can create a plan, which will detail your outputs. We will talk about this more in the mindset chapter.

The language of strategic communication needs to be focused on outcomes, which I describe as 'so what happens as a result?' If your strategy is a list of outputs, which are channels and tactics, rather than outcomes, you are in the realm of tactical communication, not strategic communication.

Being a strategic internal communicator means:

- Knowing what the organization's priorities mean for employees
- Horizon scanning across the business

- Offering counsel at a senior level
- Setting communication standards and leading internal communication
- Creating strong working relationships at all levels
- Planning ahead to anticipate stakeholder and employee needs
- Prioritizing work based on alignment with strategy and impact
- Using insights and data to inform your approach
- Sharing measurement information to continuously improve
- Helping employees mitigate business risk
- Focusing on outcomes, not just outputs
- Supporting and advising others to be effective communicators
- Keeping updated on industry trends and developments
- Knowing what's important to key stakeholders

What does this mean for an IC strategy?

Being a strategic internal communicator means creating time to think, which then allows you to plan effectively. Another way to look at it is: an internal communication strategy captures the *thinking*, and internal communication planning is the *doing*. You need to think first, to then inform your decision making and what you are focusing on.

Tara McDonagh is President and Chief Communications Strategist at Tara McDonagh Communications in Massachusetts, in the US. I asked her how she defines strategic internal communication, and she told me: 'It's using the lens of communications expertise to advance an organization's business goals.'

Level three of the IoIC's Profession Map is 'Strategically advising' – working with business areas to advise on communication strategies and approaches; development of overall channel infrastructure and evaluation processes; and supporting leaders in becoming highly effective communicators. In a nutshell, that's an excellent description of working strategically.

Level four builds on this and details the requirement for communication strategies to meet business need, with effective communication 'built into the fabric of the organization' (IoIC, 2023c).

The Government Communication Service in the UK says 'a successful communications strategy needs to be integrated into the strategic fabric of your organization' (GCS, 2021).

If you're not sure if you are working strategically, think about the work you are doing with that in mind. Can you honestly say communication is built into the fabric of your company? If not, why not? Is it because of how you work, what the organization's view is or something else?

Creating thinking time

One of the biggest pitfalls I observe from strategic or senior internal communicators is not creating time to think. Setting a weekly recurring meeting with yourself is vital; you are in the position because of the way you think.

As a strategic internal communicator you need to be working *on*, not just *in* your role. No one else can do this for you. Therefore, you need to create time in your schedule to prioritize it, because only then can you plan and measure effectively.

Prioritizing and valuing thinking time is often an indicator that you're operating in a more strategic space. When you step up into a leadership position or a more senior position in an organization or comms team, it's easy to feel guilty that you're not spending time *doing the doing*. However, spending time doing tasks the rest of the team are equipped to do is not a good use of your time.

Consider whether what you're working on is the best use of your skills, knowledge and experience. I champion knowing the reality of all roles in a team; however, you need to create time to pause, analyse, reflect and review. You are in a leadership position, which means unless you are a team of one, your role is not to upload stories to your intranet. On that note, please don't describe yourself as a 'one man band', regardless of gender, if you are a team of one, you are an independent or solo practitioner.

> As a strategic internal communicator, you need to be working *on*, not just *in* your role. No one else can do this for you.

Why companies need an IC strategy

Whether you call it a strategic plan, an IC strategy, a comms master plan or something else, we're using the phrase internal communication strategy in this book. Your internal communication strategy could form part of a wider comms strategy. Do make sure you're aware of what the expectations are inside your organization.

Whenever I am auditing an organization's internal communication I ask to see examples of documentation that supports the IC team. This can range from an IC strategy to a channels matrix or editorial calendar. I will expand on this in Chapter 4, when we look at the logistics of internal communication. How well do you plan in your organization? What's in place to create consistency within your comms function?

The reality for many internal communicators is that they are working inside their organization without having an IC strategy or master plan in place. Data reveals 52 per cent of companies do not have a long-term internal communication strategy (Contact Monkey, 2023).

Does planning help IC pros?

Research conducted by ICPlan and Liam FitzPatrick of Donhead Consultants in 2021 aimed to see if planning was an overlooked tool in the communicators' kit bag and if it was neglected, why that might be the case.

The key takeaway was that many communicators do not have a master-plan for what they are trying to achieve with their operations.

The research revealed:

- Effective communication planners have better relationships with their leaders.
- Teams that plan get better results.
- 38 per cent acknowledge they don't have a clear enough communications plan.
- Those that acknowledge a lack of plan rate themselves as less successful.
- Mid-sized communications teams find it most difficult to plan.

FitzPatrick says: 'We found that the smallest and the largest teams seem to be better at planning and being aligned with each other. For the former it is probably a matter of living in a simpler world and for the latter it's a question of necessity. Yet mid-sized teams seem to struggle to gather intelligence, get involved in projects at an early stage or align communications. Fewer than 40% of communicators in teams of between 21 and 30 practitioners said they had an overarching strategy and/or plan.'

Why have an IC strategy?

The Institute of Internal Communication says 'a strong internal comms strategy can help you attack your goals with clarity and purpose. If you don't understand why you're doing what you're doing or the direction you need to take, you aren't using your skills to your advantage' (Jones, 2022).

An internal communication strategy determines how you oversee internal communication and why your approach is right for your company. It includes evidence that helps you make informed decisions. A strategy helps you be proactive and set standards inside your organization.

Michael E Porter is the C Roland Christensen Professor of Business Administration at the Harvard Business School in Boston, Massachusetts. He says 'if a strategy meets a goal; it's working. If a strategy meets a target: it's a success' (Porter, 1996).

Focusing on the right things

An internal communication strategy written without consideration of the wider business strategy is difficult to quantify, deliver, implement and measure. You may feel like you're working incredibly hard, but are you focused on the right things? If you don't hook your IC strategy into strategic priorities, it's easy to invest a lot of effort and time into workstreams and projects that don't align with what the business needs to focus on and forge ahead with.

Having clarity on what your business is striving for and keeping those deliverables and strategic aims top of mind helps you keep on track. It can also equip you to have difficult conversations with those you are advising inside an organization. We'll look at stakeholders later in the book, including how to work well with them and say no, to keep focused on your core priorities.

EXPERT VIEW

Tara McDonagh

Tara McDonagh is President and Chief Communications Strategist at Tara McDonagh Communications in Massachusetts. We share a passion for strategic internal communication planning and nurturing comms pros to be business advisers.

She champions strategic communications centred around business goals and says they can make a massive impact on an organization and industry. However, she notes internal communications is a skill and area of expertise that doesn't only involve communications expertise or knowledge of engaging employees through communications to support business goals.

McDonagh says it takes business expertise, leadership skills, negotiation and a firm but calm attitude: 'It's changing minds. You can transfer skills from other areas and learn on the job, but it's still an area of expertise that requires some level of knowledge of business, communications, strategy and leadership.'

When considering the difference between an IC strategy and a plan, she says the strategy is the approach to the work and what it is and isn't, and the plan is actionable steps required to marry a company's business goals with the audience (employee) interest. In other words, the strategy is the *why* and the plan is the *how*.

Avoid jumping to the tactics

McDonagh cautions against the tendency for internal communicators to jump to the tactics. 'It's commonplace to hear communicators saying they need an employee app, a refreshed/better intranet or another form of technology. But jumping straight to the technology doesn't solve business problems if you haven't considered how that technology channel fits into your entire communications approach.'

Questions to answer

McDonagh says you need a long-term comms strategy to be successful first, and to answer questions such as:

- How will you support business goals?
- What business goals are they?
- What communications strategies and tactics will you use?
- What processes?
- Who will do what on the team?
- What do you need to accomplish to achieve those objectives (staff, budget, technology – which is where the technology fits)?
- How will you periodically adjust?
- How will you measure results?

SOURCE McDonagh, 2023

The need to create a strong strategy should outweigh investing in new technology. However, McDonagh acknowledges it's 'much easier' to secure budget for the technology! She urges communicators to 'jump the hurdle of strategy and the benefits far outweigh the initial challenges and short-term pains of creating it'.

Busting the industry jargon

I worked in-house as a professional internal communicator in the underground rail network in London back in the mid-2000s. I then went to work in the overground rail network in London in the late 2000s as Head of Communication. The company was 18 months old when I was recruited to set up the comms function, with responsibility for both internal and external communication.

I thought I knew how the railway operated, having experienced it firsthand in the underground. I was confident of the language set, mindset and opportunities an operational workforce presented. However, the difference in the overground shocked me.

The layers I've described above both enhanced and restricted the way communication happened in equal measure.

Disinformation wastes time

Lack of consistency, clarity and certainty was creating disinformation and wasted time, money, effort and resources in the company. The absence of shared understanding and meaning was stark. By the end of my first week, I had written 47 different words and phrases in my notebook that I'd had to bust through the jargon to clarify. It felt like everyone was talking in riddles and when I asked them to explain their terminology, they couldn't, or it varied depending on who I spoke with. Companies need to have sources of truth and mechanisms for employees to check their own understanding and meaning. In the case of the overground, I identified the need for a corporate glossary, as a tactical, but necessary, output.

I worked autonomously inside that organization, particularly because I had been hired due to having a particular set of skills and experience. However, it didn't mean I wasn't left out of conversations, excluded from meetings I should have been at or challenged daily to prove my worth and the value of creating the function.

As a result of the intensity and tenacity with which we make it our business to truly understand what's top of mind for leaders, the impact of culture on the way employees feel and many other aspects, we have the ability to be incredibly knowledgeable business advisers and strategists.

Mixternal communication

The lines between internal communication and other departments have continued to blur. Some organizations combine employee communication with external communication, public affairs and investor relations. Whereas others draw on disciplines such as HR.

Reporting lines are varied, from internal communicators finding themselves in a separate department reporting directly to the CEO, to being part of HR or a mixed team. There has been an increase in the number of teams combining their skills, knowledge and experience to benefit their organizations.

In recognition of this, the term 'mixternal communication' has been growing in popularity. It was the whole theme for the Public Relations Society of America (PRSA) Employee Communications Section's conference, PRSA Connect, in Orlando, in May 2023.

Over the course of two days, 200 employee communicators met to tackle 'Blurred lines: Embracing the new demands of "mixternal" communications'. PRSA described how 'fluid the lines have come between internal communications and everything else. In a world where mashups are expected and lines are constantly blurred, how can communications professionals bring new thinking to their roles?' (PRSA, 2023).

Mixternal comms is 'a relatively new trend that has seen growing interest among internal communicators. This buzzword refers to the internal and external messaging that feeds into driving brand reputation and positioning' (Contact Monkey, 2023).

EXPERT VIEW
Ally Bunin

Ally Bunin is Vice President of Teammate Communications and Recognition for Advocate Health. She was Conference Chair for the Public Relations Society of America's Connect23 event in Florida.

She describes mixternal communications as 'a concept and a way to approach communications, understanding that all employees are consumers and are getting your organization's messaging from both internal and external channels. It's likely externals are even more influential than the internal messages'.

Reflecting on the rise of mixternal communications, Bunin says it's 'more critical than ever to align the brand voice – ensuring you're practicing on the inside whatever you're preaching on the outside. This builds cohesion and trust. It also necessitates communicators to strengthen channel strategy and understand employees' preferences so they can reach employees where they are' and notes it's 'easier said than done!'

Attached to leaders

Bunin says Covid-19 put a spotlight on internal communications 'brighter than ever before' and describes our seat at the table 'becoming more like a backpack: suddenly communicators everywhere were attached to their leaders 24/7, supporting them and influencing their messaging around the clock'.

It was coined THE moment for internal communicators. But she argues it's still our moment and says perhaps what's changed since 2020 is an intense need to cultivate relationships, add value, and influence leaders, employees, shareholders and even customers. Bunin says this is critical as most internal communicators have become mixternal – partnering closely with all aspects of the communications team – internal, external, brand and social media.

She cautions the blurred lines of communications have become blurrier and today's internal communicator is called upon to do far more than write communications and 'just make my PowerPoint deck pretty'. Describing what's in front of us as a 'massive opportunity to help our organizations thrive', she says she wouldn't have it any other way.

Upping your strategy game

I asked Bunin to describe what working strategically means to her. She says 'it's about understanding the business, the bigger picture and the key stakeholders, and being able to put all the pieces together to tell a cohesive story – but also to help solve a problem. It requires a strategic mindset to consider how best to bring all the pieces together – when, to whom and why – well before execution. And not just communicating for communication's sake – to help the business solve a problem is far more valuable than executing a message or a campaign. Solve a business challenge through communications and you'll up your strategy game'.

Working as trusted advisers

Bunin's comments regarding our role during the Covid-19 pandemic are echoed by Lucy Cairncross, Managing Director of recruiter VMA Group. She describes comms leaders and their teams as working non-stop throughout the crisis, which was a 'period unlike any other and CEOs were looking to their most trusted advisers to help make the right decisions'.

Cairncross says communicating with employees was number one priority and the glue that held companies together, the compass that enabled teams to navigate their way out of the dark. She cautions organizations that fail to acknowledge or reflect the pandemic was a difficult time 'will have done long-term damage' to their internal and external employer brand (VMA Group, 2023).

STRATEGY CREATION CHECKLIST

Make notes and decisions on the following points, before moving on to the next chapter. This will help you write your strategy as you read through this book. As a result of working your way through this chapter, you should now:

- Define what internal communication is for you/your team and for your organization.

- Consider publishing that definition internally wherever you talk about IC, such as onboarding or on the IC team section of an intranet.

- Write the purpose of internal communication for your organization.

- Consider how you work with leaders. What questions do you need to ask them?

- Identify your internal communication skills using the IoIC Profession Map.

- Analyse any skills gaps and decide how you're going to work on them. Include the behaviours in your analysis.

- What does working strategically mean to you? What does it mean for your stakeholders? If there's a difference, make a note of what it is.

Review the choices you've made while reading through this chapter. Make sure you've captured what has resonated and what feels appropriate for your organization.

References and further reading

Bunin, A (2023) Communications is about influence: 10 takeaways from our 10th anniversary PRSA Connect Conference, LinkedIn, 4 May, www.linkedin.com/pulse/communications-influence-10-takeaways-from-our-10th-prsa-ally-bunin (archived at https://perma.cc/YZH8-SVMH)

CIPR Inside (2017) Making it Count: The strategic value and effectiveness of internal communication, Chartered Institute of Public Relations, London

Contact Monkey (2023) Report: Global State of Internal Communications 2023, https://www.contactmonkey.com/ebook/global-survey-2023 (archived at https://perma.cc/C49A-HB2J)

Dewhurst, S and FitzPatrick, L (2022) *Successful Employee Communications: A practitioner's guide to tools, models and best practice for internal communication*, 2nd edn, Kogan Page, London

Engage For Success (nd) What is employee engagement, engageforsuccess.org/what-is-employee-engagement/ (archived at https://perma.cc/9WLK-7E59)

Engage for Success (2022) UK Employee Engagement Survey, engageforsuccess.org/wp-content/uploads/2023/02/EFS-Engagement-Survey-Report-2022_FINAL-VERSION-.pdf (archived at https://perma.cc/M8G3-K46P)

FitzPatrick, L and Valskov, K (2014) *Internal Communications: A manual for practitioners*, Kogan Page, London

Gallagher (2023) State of the Sector 2022/3, www.ajg.com/employeeexperience/state-of-the-sector-2023/ (archived at https://perma.cc/J2LW-DQK2)

GCS (2020) Internal communication, Government Communication Service, 12 March (updated 7 September 2023), gcs.civilservice.gov.uk/guidance/internal-communication/ (archived at https://perma.cc/AXP7-FP4T)

GCS (2021) Developing an internal communication strategy, Government Communication Service, 18 May, gcs.civilservice.gov.uk/guidance/internal-communication/developing-an-internal-communication-strategy/ (archived at https://perma.cc/A4F8-GLCG)

GCS (2023) Engaging employees through internal communications, Government Communication Service, 30 January, gcs.civilservice.gov.uk/guidance/internal-communication/engaging-employees-through-internal-communications/ (archived at https://perma.cc/HX3F-AQVN)

Grammarly Business and The Harris Poll (2023) The State of Business Communication 2023: The path to productivity, performance, and profit, go.grammarly.com/business-communication-report (archived at https://perma.cc/GM2U-8EJJ)

Hallahan, K, Holtzhausen, D, van Ruler, B, Verčič, D and Sriramesh, K (2007) Defining strategic communication, *International Journal of Strategic Communication*, 1 (1), 3–35, dx.doi.org/10.1080/15531180701285244 (archived at https://perma.cc/N7YS-DTYA)

ICPlan and Donhead Consultants (2021) Communications Planning Report 2021, icplan.com/if-you-dont-know-where-youre-going-any-road-will-take-you-there/ (archived at https://perma.cc/AXZ4-3RN6); or via Miller, R (2021) How to plan your Comms effectively, All Things IC Blog, 17 March, www.allthingsic. com/how-to-plan-your-comms-effectively/ (archived at https://perma.cc/ PQ4D-EQG2)

IoIC (2019) The IC Career Guide, Institute of Internal Communication, www.ioic. org.uk/learn-develop/careers.html (archived at https://perma.cc/YDY5-93QV)

IoIC (2023a) About us, Institute of Internal Communication, www.ioic.org.uk/ about-us.html (archived at https://perma.cc/P7XE-WWRV)

IoIC (2023b) *IoIC Guide to Internal Communication Strategy*, 2nd edn, Institute of Internal Communication, www.ioic.org.uk/resource/ioic-strat-guide-v2.html (archived at https://perma.cc/G2MA-X7TU)

IoIC (2023c) The Profession Map: The core, Institute of Internal Communication, www.ioic.org.uk/learn-develop/the-profession-map/the-core.html (archived at https://perma.cc/DXX4-GWD6)

IoIC and VMA Group (2021) Internal Communication Hiring Guide, www.ioic. org.uk/learn-develop/careers.html (archived at https://perma.cc/XSH3-SQ7G)

Jones, R (2022) A thorough IC strategy will help you plan your next move, Institute of Internal Communication, *Voice Magazine*, September, www.ioic.org. uk/knowledge-hub/voice/voice-magazine.html (archived at https://perma.cc/ H85D-MYE3) (members only).

MacLeod, D and Clarke, N (2009) Engaging for Success: Enhancing performance through employee engagement, Department of Business, Innovation and Skills, engageforsuccess.org/wp-content/uploads/2020/12/engaging-for-success.pdf (archived at https://perma.cc/P732-PWDB)

McDonagh, T (2023) Interview/correspondence with the author

Miller, R (2012) Employee engagement: How social media are changing internal communication, in *Share This: The social media handbook for PR professionals*, ed S Waddington, pp 195–204, Wiley, Chichester

Miller, R (2013) Engaging for Success in Italy, All Things IC Blog, 3 June, www.allthingsic.com/italye4s/ (archived at https://perma.cc/WT26-EGK5)

Miller, R (2016) Why you need to focus on employee experience, featuring Jacob Morgan's model, All Things IC Blog, 31 March, www.allthingsic.com/ex/ (archived at https://perma.cc/2MM7-2RD8)

Miller, R (2017) Eight internal communication myths, All Things IC Blog, 10 July, www.allthingsic.com/internal-communication-myths/ (archived at https://perma. cc/RWC3-D85P)

Miller, R (2020) What does internal communication mean? All Things IC Blog, 15 February, www.allthingsic.com/what-does-internal-communication-mean/ (archived at https://perma.cc/LW6J-K37V)

Porter, M E (1996) What is strategy? *Harvard Business Review*, November–
    December, hbr.org/1996/11/what-is-strategy (archived at https://perma.cc/
    QWY4-5YN6)
PRSA (2021) Employee Communications Section, Public Relations Society of
    America, www.prsa.org/docs/default-source/about/get-involved/employee-
    communications/section-flyer-employee-comm-12-14-2021.pdf?sfvrsn=
    71d0a299_0 (archived at https://perma.cc/SL6X-ZWDY)
PRSA (2023) Employee Communications Connect23 Conference, Blurred lines:
    Embracing the new demands of 'mixternal' communications, Public Relations
    Society of America, www.prsa.org/home/get-involved/professional-interest-
    sections/employee-communications-section/prsa-connect23-employee-
    communications-conference (archived at https://perma.cc/7BAE-MLLK)
Quirke, B (2008) *Making the Connections: Using internal communication to turn
    strategy into action*, 2nd edn, Gower, Aldershot
Stauss, B and Hoffmann, F (2000) Minimizing internal communication gaps by
    using Business Television, in *Internal Marketing: Directions for management*,
    eds R J Varey and B R Lewis, pp 141–59, Routledge, London
VMA Group (2023) Changing Communications – The CEO experience of commu-
    nications during Covid and beyond, www.vmagroup.com/changing-
    communications-the-ceo-experience-of-communications-during-covid-and-
    beyond (archived at https://perma.cc/HQ82-86B9)
Weick, K E (1995) *Sensemaking in Organizations*, Sage Publications, Thousand
    Oaks, CA
Welch, M and Jackson, P R (2007) Rethinking internal communication: A stake-
    holder approach, *Corporate Communications: An International Journal*, 12 (2),
    177–98, doi.org/10.1108/13563280710744847 (archived at https://perma.cc/
    Q8NX-PWP4)

2

The mindset strategic internal communicators need

WHAT THIS CHAPTER WILL COVER

This chapter focuses on the mindset an internal communicator needs and how it relates to writing an internal communication strategy. We will examine why mindset matters, what start-ups need to know about internal communication, why an IC strategy needs to align with business strategy and how to determine business priorities. As a result of reading this chapter, you will know how to start writing an internal communication strategy. You'll find a checklist at the end of this and every chapter to help you keep on track.

Imagine you have your completed internal communication strategy in front of you. The finished document aligns to your business priorities and determines the path ahead. What difference would that make to your professional practice? My intention through this chapter is to help you start turning that future state into reality.

We're moving away from firefighting to focused work, so you can shift from working tactically to strategically. Mindset forms a huge part of this.

The MILLER Framework: Mindset

You need to know what to include in your internal communication strategy and how to keep it concentrated on what's right for your organization.

I developed The MILLER Framework to guide internal communicators through their decision making.

It starts with mindset, which includes business priorities, vision and why internal communication is important (for your organization). Using that definition, each organization has its own unique mindset.

What is mindset?

Before we look at the mindset from an organizational perspective for strategy creation, let's turn our attention to its importance for internal communicators. To be an effective internal communicator you need to combine your mindset, which is defined by the Oxford dictionary as 'a person's particular way of thinking and set of beliefs' with your skill set 'the combination of skills you can use'.

At the end of this book, you'll discover a chapter called 'What happens inside is reflected outside'. This is the ethos of my business and something I live by. When considering mindset, we need to think about what's inside, which is your *attitude*. Attitude is defined by the Cambridge dictionary as 'a feeling or opinion about something, or someone, or a way of behaving'.

> An internal communicator's attitude (mindset) matters just as much as their competencies and experience (skill set). To be successful as an internal communicator requires working on both.
>
> If you have incredible knowledge about the profession, or your organization, but lack the belief or confidence to have difficult conversations with stakeholders or champion employees' voices, it's difficult to operate at a strategic level.

In Chapter 5 we will look at your personal brand – your reputation and promise – and the role it plays in communicating your internal communication strategy.

Superpowers

I believe kindness, ethics and empathy are superpowers for internal communicators and their organizations (Miller, 2018). Ensure these are at the forefront of your mind, as they are what people relate to, particularly when you are communicating change.

If you can focus on kindness, ethics and empathy and know how employees are feeling, you can unlock the power of internal communication. Having leaders with an attitude of kindness, ethics and empathy can cultivate high levels of trust and motivation in their teams. I recommend reading about servant leadership if you're curious to explore this topic in more detail. We will look at ethical practice later in this chapter.

The point about superpowers is that they are not skills or experiences in a toolbox. Rather they are attitudes or mindsets embedded in our own personal operating systems that we bring with us to our work every day, regardless of where we are in our careers. Whether we are starting out and developing our writing or project management skills, or we have chosen to bring many years' experience to providing strategic advice, what we do is coloured or flavoured by our underlying character and approach. These superpowers may evolve over time as our life experiences ripen and I believe we can cultivate them as well; but they are always in the background. What is inside is reflected outside.

Why superpowers?

I use the term 'superpowers' rather than values, or personality or outlook, because we use them in the service of our work. They are more than traits or features in our psychological make-up or upbringing because, when applied to our daily work, they turbocharge or amplify the craft or professional skills.

Many people can do the things that a communication professional does, but the magic starts to happen when we act with kindness, with an ethical mind, with empathy and with compassion. It is the use of our superpowers that ensure that content and tactics are more than noise; they enable us to move from sharing knowledge to building emotional connection and commitment on the *know–feel–do* journey. We'll talk more about that shortly and I'll share my intentions framework, which has an additional step.

Personal autonomy

Superpowers are also important because a sense of autonomy or agency is central to many theories of personal happiness. Sports psychologist and coach Dr Josephine Perry (who started her own career working in communications) says there are three aspects to personal autonomy: a belief that we are in control of our actions, freedom from being pressurized by others to do things and the flexibility to make our own choices (Perry, 2022: 67). If we are in control and make the choices we want because we are clear about what matters, we stand a better chance of being happy.

Determining your superpowers

I have shared this list in conversation with people who I respect and value as good internal communication practitioners. Building on those discussions, here is a set of typical 'superpowers' that I have noticed. The list is not exhaustive, and the task for internal communicators is to determine the superpowers you want to develop and hone. This is a conversation to have with yourself, or perhaps a mentor or colleague, to focus on your own growth areas and gaps.

SUPERPOWERS FOR INTERNAL COMMUNICATORS TO HARNESS

- Audience insight – curiosity about our audiences and how communication works for them.
- Compassion – caring about the people around us and ensuring that, on balance, communication is a positive force.
- Ethics – having clarity about what is right and not being bent to the needs of a particular situation; being able to guide our colleagues onto the right path.
- Empathy – the ability to understand what our colleagues and stakeholders are (or might be) thinking and needing.
- Kindness – seeking to do no harm and remember the impact we have on the lives of the people around us.
- 'Planfulness' – ensuring that communications and corporate plans have achievable outcomes and a sensible road map to achieve them.
- Equanimity – when there is urgency or turmoil, using our communications brain to be a stabilizing influence, bringing insight to explain what is really happening and reminding ourselves and colleagues of what matters.
- Gratitude – not just for the kindness of others but for our own gifts and the situations in which we find ourselves; seeking out the positive in situations and the people with whom we work.

SOURCE Rachel Miller and Liam FitzPatrick, 2023

In considering what the superpowers are for yourself and your organization, determine what is your kryptonite, or the thing that stops you being successful. What changes your attitude and weakens or disrupts the way you work? Perhaps it's stress, not being brought into conversations early enough, or a lack of time or resource. Maybe it is an overactive inner tyrant telling you that other people know better than you or that your instincts are nonsense.

Working on your internal insight will help you spot the blockers to your superpowers and help you find the support and cheerleaders who can pick you up when you trip or stumble.

Capturing the uniqueness

Let's imagine your completed internal communication strategy is in front of you now and the company logo is covered up. How would you know it was yours? Mindset matters when writing an internal communication strategy, because it should be as unique as the organization it represents.

When I was pregnant with my non-identical twin sons, I absorbed myself in the world of multiple births research. I learnt one of the ways to tell identical twins apart is their fingerprints. I discovered that the whorls, loops and ridges tell the story of your time in the womb. How you interacted with the world around you is reflected via your fingerprints. So even though your sibling/s had the same environment, your personal experience is unique, which is revealed through your fingerprints.

On the day you're born, you are communicating your story through your fingerprints. Therefore, everyone is born a storyteller – don't let people tell you otherwise!

I bear this in mind when looking at organizations and how they communicate. I look for what makes you special and unique. What makes you stand out? It's typically the way you interact with the world, so in the same way each child has their own fingerprints, companies have their stories and employees have individual experiences due to their interactions.

What makes you stand out?

An IC strategy should mirror the company's tone of voice, state what is important and show what makes the organization special. Generic strategies do not help anyone, least of all the internal communicators who try to live and breathe what's in them through their daily work.

This is why mindset is critical for an internal communication strategy, because it needs to demonstrate the particular way of thinking and set of beliefs inside the organization. It needs to show your values, both the organizational values and what you value from an internal communication perspective. If anyone picked up your internal communication strategy, it should be unquestionably yours for all those reasons, even if the logo was covered up.

That's how to make an internal communication strategy appropriate and relevant for each individual organization, and why a one size fits all approach doesn't work. You cannot simply copy someone else's, as their organizational goals, mission, purpose and priorities will differ to yours.

WHAT'S ON THE MINDS OF IC PROFESSIONALS?

I surveyed a group of 40 in-house internal communicators and encouraged them to ask me anything related to strategy writing. I wanted to understand their challenges and barriers, to discover what internal communicators are struggling with.

These were some of their questions:

- How often should I update an IC strategy? How do I adapt it when change happens?
- How can I build an IC strategy for Europe while navigating rogue comms from local offices?
- How to structure an IC strategy – what goes in it?
- How can I use an audit to inform the development of my IC strategy?
- How do I include measurement?
- Should I create one strategy for the group, or individual strategies for each company in the group?
- How much is too much?
- Huge opportunity in my organization – how do I break down what's achievable?
- How do you encourage buy-in or commitment to an IC strategy?

I will address these comms conundrums in this book.

Working in a visible role

Professional communicators have such visible roles inside organizations, as everything we write, say and advise can be seen, heard and critiqued. The behaviours identified by the Institute of Internal Communication's Profession Map in Chapter 1 included many behaviours linked to mindset, including challenging and tenacity.

Their definition of challenging is 'uses evidence and reason, built on a strong foundation of knowledge and skills, to confidently question current thinking, which allows for positive change' (IoIC, 2023b). That strong foundation of knowledge and skills is expressed through your internal communication strategy.

The Cambridge dictionary defines tenacious as to 'hold tight to something' or 'keeping an opinion in a determined way'. The Institute of Internal Communication describe being tenacious as remaining determined and having a 'strong hold in principle, position and course of action, whilst being open to constructive challenge' (IoIC, 2023b). IoIC President Suzanne Peck describes being tenacious as 'championing clarity and transparency' (Peck, 2022).

Questions to ask yourself include: how can you be clear and transparent in your organization's communication efforts? How can you role model the expected behaviours and standards for employees and leaders? Creating deliberately confusing messaging, which has been designed to hide the truth, or overcomplicating details mean communication breaks down.

Core principles

The International Association of Business Communicators' (IABC) Global Standard has a shared career purpose and six core principles as the building blocks of its work.

The six core principles are ethics, consistency, context, analysis, strategy and engagement. The ethics principle requires communication professionals to adopt the highest standards of professional behaviour. It includes being sensitive to cultural values and beliefs, acting lawfully and without deception, representing organizations truthfully, fairly and accurately, adhering to the IABC Code of Ethics for Professional Communicators and enabling mutual understanding and respect (IABC, nd).

The full set can be seen via the IABC website. Use these standards to look at your own professional practice; I think they are an excellent combination of mindset and skill set in action.

Saying what we mean

There is a word within the world of internal communication that grates on me. Every time I hear it, I hope the intended meaning is the right one. I've even banned it from my own internal communication practice.

It's the word land. As in… *How did the comms land? We've landed it to the front-line employees. We're going to land this campaign on Monday.*

Why does it irk me? Because 'landing a message' implies once you've hit send on an email for example, the job has been done. But that's only half the story! I agree with this comment 'we never "land" anything, unless it's an aircraft' (Gregory, 2022).

The difference between information and communication

One of my favourite quotes is from the journalist Sydney J Harris, who said 'the words "information" and "communication" are often used interchangeably, but they signify quite different things. Information is giving out; communication is getting through' (Harris, 1972).

Harris was an American author and syndicated columnist for the *Chicago Sun-Times*. I've been referencing that quote for years as I identify strongly with it, particularly when analysing an organization's internal communication and figuring out what's going on. His book, *For the Time Being* (1972), is worth checking out.

The reason *land* jars with me is because it's often meant in the *information giving out*, or *outputs* territory, whereas the intention should be *communication getting through*, which is *outcomes* territory.

It's easy to focus on the information part, which is implied when internal communicators talk about the word land. However, that puts us squarely into one-way, or fixed, broadcasted, information.

What is priceless for internal communicators is knowing whether something has resonated with colleagues, which requires two-way communication. This means checking for understanding and testing recall.

We'll talk more about measurement in Chapter 6. But I'm going to define the difference between outcomes and outputs now, as this distinction is critical as you prepare to write an internal communication strategy. If you *are* using 'land' and you mean communication getting through, well done. Make sure your stakeholders are also thinking along these lines and don't think the fact you've sent an email means communication has happened.

JARGON BUSTING

Outputs are something quantifiable you can measure, like a click, like, share or number of stories you've published, or number of town halls/all-employee meetings you've held.

An **outcome** is what happens as a result of communication, such as a change in behaviour. I call it the 'so what?' or effect of internal communication. So what's happened as a result of all of those stories or meetings?

Working intentionally

A technique I use to help with strategy creation is my intentions framework. I used to call it my secret sauce for internal communication, but it's really a framework that internal communicators can use to set their intentions and plan their work. It helps you create your aims, which enables you to measure.

There are various schools of thought within internal communication when it comes to planning. Some organizations use know–feel–do, or think–feel–act. My intentions framework encourages internal communicators to know the answers to the following questions. It can also be used with stakeholders when trying to decipher their business needs and determining the editorial strength of their request.

Setting intentions

Before starting to write, ask yourself these questions:

1 What do you want people to do, say, think or feel as a result of your internal communication?
2 How do you want (or need) them to behave?

FIGURE 2.1   Intentions framework

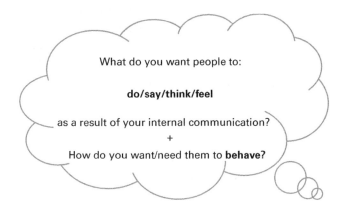

What do you want people to:

do/say/think/feel

as a result of your internal communication?
+
How do you want/need them to **behave?**

The *need* part is pertinent for safety communication or operational communication.

Don't underestimate the power of focusing on feelings. In a world that has experienced the Covid-19 pandemic, how employees *feel* has been brought into sharp focus. If you are communicating change or trying to increase positivity around a certain product or service, gauging and monitoring how people *feel* is essential. You can then see how and if those feelings change over time.

Turning intentions into action

I used my intentions framework with the CEO of a local authority in the UK. They had been through a lot of change, they'd spun off the local authority housing part of the council, which had then developed its own identity, branding and values. Then after only a few years, the local authority reversed that decision and were planning to reunite both parts again.

This meant some employees had worked at the council, then the housing entity, and back to the council again. They had aligned themselves with a new set of values, a fresh vision and way of operating. A lot of hard work had been done to separate the two entities, and they were about to reunite.

I sat down with the CEO and head of communications to discuss the scale of the change and what was ahead for their people. I started by asking the CEO to imagine it was a year's time, I asked him what he wanted employees to be feeling about the changes. What would they be doing, saying, thinking and feeling?

His answers were instrumental in helping the internal communication team and I to plan the way ahead. Knowing the outcome we were aiming for was for employees to feel involved in the changes, confident explaining the rationale, knowledgeable about the process and excited about the future gave us a lot to work with. We were then able to determine what needed to happen over the next 12 months and identify the gaps.

If you are communicating complicated change, look for ways to demonstrate empathy and kindness. Spot opportunities to reinforce feelings through messaging and take employees through the change. You don't want employees to feel like the changes are being done *to* them, but *for them and with them*. This means not leaving the thinking or messaging down to chance.

TIP FROM RACHEL
Questions to ask

When working with stakeholders, ask *them* to articulate the answers to those questions. What do they want people to do, say, think or feel as a result of the internal communication? How do they want (or need) people to behave?

Asking why

If you find yourself setting an aim relating to something people should do, feel or know, ask yourself why these things are needed.

Dewhurst and FitzPatrick (2022) say:

> Keep asking 'Why?' until you reach a business or organizational target or statement. For example, if you want people to better understand the safety processes for their area, presumably that's because you want them to follow the processes more consistently. The reason for this is probably because you want people to be safer at work, that is, you want fewer accidents to happen. There's the core aim: reduce accident rate. (By how many, by when?).

They caution not going too far with the 'why' questions and say many aims can ultimately be related back to reducing costs or increasing sales. They urge communicators to 'keep things focused on the problem your customer wants to solve'.

Dewhurst and FitzPatrick suggest working the other way around from 'know–feel–do' – they urge professional communicators set out the 'do' first. 'Work backwards from the core business/organizational aim. What did you discover in your stakeholder conversation? Be specific about *what* behaviour is needed, by *whom*, and if appropriate, *in what situation*.'

How to write a strategy: Formatting

Formatting an internal communication strategy is something internal communicators struggle with. It's one of the first hurdles when comms professionals are thinking about creating an internal communication strategy and can lead to a delay in starting the work. Therefore, let's address it before looking at mindset and business priorities in further detail.

Which format to choose

The answer to knowing which format to write your internal communication strategy in depends on the culture of your organization. If everything that gets debated, discussed and decided goes to your board as a presentation, that's the format you should use.

If you are a spreadsheet-first organization where everything is mapped out in that way, then you need to write your strategy in a spreadsheet. If you're a document-led organization, then that's the format to use.

Be informed by your organization

There's never a one size fits all approach in the world of internal communication. When considering formatting, be informed by your organization. Once you know what your senior management team or director of comms' preferences are, it's unwise to present a strategy in a different format.

You need to understand how internal communication happens and how decisions are made, which means knowing how they're presented. Look inwardly to the company to help you make the appropriate choice. If there's no standard way topics are debated, discussed and decided, choose your preference. You need to write confidently, so do not let the type of document stop your work from flowing.

Communicating clearly

Whatever format you decide, there are some key parts that you need to work through, which we will do together in this book. They are applicable regardless of the format, and it's where The MILLER Framework comes in. Make sure your internal communication strategy makes sense to whoever reads it. This means using jargon-free language and explaining industry terms.

I'm a visual thinker, so presentations get my vote, especially because they allow me to present the internal communication strategy to relevant parties without having to reimagine or rewrite the content into that format. We'll touch on this topic again in Chapter 5 when we address buy-in for your internal communication strategy.

What's your reason?

Which of the following reasons resonate with you when thinking about writing an internal communication strategy?

- Having a clear plan for what's coming up in internal communication
- Demonstrating to my line manager that I can think strategically
- Sharing my strategy with my stakeholders, so they can understand what we do
- Being able to say no to what's not in our strategy
- Having something to refer to when I'm writing my personal objectives, or setting objectives for my team

These are all considerations internal communicators have and they are good reasons to think about creating an internal communication strategy.

How long should it be?

The question of 'how much is too much?' is a common query among comms professionals. When it comes to the length of an internal communication strategy, the truthful answer is it can vary. Again, this can come down to the culture of your organization – the 'way you do things around here' (Deal and Kennedy, 1982) – which determines what you create. If your senior leaders expect a one-page summary on everything, you need to be able to produce one. Or if everything is a large presentation slide deck, do you have enough to fill it?

The MILLER Framework creates a logical flow, and as a minimum I suggest one to two slides/one page for each letter. This means you are looking at a minimum of six presentation slides or six pages. There's obviously a huge difference in the word count between those two! Which is why the formatting considerations are worth thinking through.

Two versions

I often create two versions of an internal communication strategy. One is the comprehensive version, which contains all the information a leader or team member needs. That detail needs to be documented somewhere. The other is a shortened summary that explains how internal communication happens, this could be a visual summary or one-pager, which can be shared with employees and leaders. Some internal communication teams stick this shorter version on their desks.

In Chapter 1 I shared the difference between internal communication and internal communications. A strategy is focused on internal communication – the overarching way the company communicates; if you use The MILLER Framework, your internal communications – tools, tactics, channels and methodologies – are reflected in the Logistics part. The focus is the thinking, which is why the language needs to align with the way your business communicates.

CREATING A SHORTER VERSION

A summary version of an IC strategy would not talk about channels. It would include sections such as:

- Internal communication vision
- Internal communication mission
- Organizational objectives
- Internal communication objectives
- Outcomes
- Activities
- Impact
- Inputs and enablers

Trying to distil information is tricky as strategy is 'inherently complex, we see this in the thick reports and complex frameworks that companies use to describe their strategic choices and how they connect with each other. Describing a strategy favours complexity, but executing it requires simplicity' (Sull et al, 2017).

What's the timescale?

You may choose to write an internal communication strategy that will see you through for the next 12 months. Or you could choose to write a three- or five-year strategy.

I'm hesitant to suggest creating a longer-term one, for say 10 years' time, because it would require so many updates between now and then. However, if your company regularly communicates in 10-year timescales, then go for it.

The benefits of longer-term strategies come when you are trying to create objectives that change behaviours, as behavioural change, or changing habits, takes time. Picture a scenario where people managers are not communicating well inside the organization. The lack of consistent communication is impacting productivity, adding to confusion and wasting time, money and effort all round.

You could create an internal communication objective to increase opportunities for two-way communication by people managers. However, it is unlikely a one-year strategy would see the desired outcome happen, whereas a three-to-five-year strategy would allow you to change or break communication habits, upskill people managers, introduce a dedicated IC channel or peer network for them, and introduce plans and processes to support robust communication habits.

TIP FROM RACHEL

Ask to see any previously created internal communication strategies inside your organization. It's useful to see the format to give you an indication of what has been written before. It can also be valuable to view any wider comms strategies such as external communication, or your organization's HR/people strategy. What format are they written in?

Who should write an IC strategy?

You don't need to be the most experienced communicator in your company or in a leadership position to write an internal communication strategy. Your strategy is a chance to show what you know and influence communication positively in the organization.

Writing an internal communication strategy is a good development opportunity. Your tactics are *what* you do and *how* you do it, and your strategy is *why* you do it. If you've not written a strategy before, you will probably be more familiar writing *what* you do and *how* you do it – which we'll cover in Chapter 4. The development opportunity comes through the requirement for you to write *why* you communicate in a certain way in your organization. Or why you need to communicate that way in the future, with a longer-term ambition clearly mapped out.

Whenever I am setting out to write an internal communication strategy, I consider the inputs that need to go into it. Another way to think about inputs in this context is as ingredients. I may know the outcome I want, which is my longer-term ambition of what the ingredients will make, but to make it work well, I need to assemble the correct ingredients. This is where mindset comes in as part of The MILLER Framework.

Strategy creation is typically considered the remit of the comms director or head of internal communication. This makes sense because the most senior professional in the function sets the direction of travel and their objectives should be mirrored in their team's objectives. They also have the most access to senior leaders and should be closer to the *why*, or purpose, of the organization.

However, if your company does not have an IC strategy in place and you think it should, you now have all the guidance you need via this book to attempt to write one. If there is someone in a senior role above you, I would inform them of your intention, in case they are working on it. You'll also be able to gauge how they feel about you writing one.

How long it will take to write depends on your ability to collate all the information I've suggested, the format it is in and what state your internal communication is in today.

How easy is it to write?

The Institute of Internal Communication (IoIC) recognizes developing an IC strategy 'isn't straightforward, it involves acquiring a strong understanding of an organization's strategy, operations and people, and using this knowledge to make fundamental choices about how communication within the organisation will happen'.

I agree with their stance of it being 'thoroughly worthwhile'. They state 'done well, it can help IC to make a meaningful and valuable contribution to an organisation's success' (IoIC, 2023a).

EXPERT VIEW
Debbie Chapman

Debbie Chapman is Head of Communications at Battersea Dogs & Cats Home in the UK. Alongside the internal communication team, she used The MILLER Framework to design and develop their internal communication strategy, to support Battersea's organizational strategy.

The organization has employees working across operations, on the front line in clinics and in three sites, including 250 people in animal-facing roles. It also has hundreds of volunteers who contribute over 100,000 hours across the year.

Just over a third of employees are working in a hybrid fashion and they have rotas that include working weekends and public holidays.

Most employees are motivated by a connection to the cause. The charity's vision is 'Battersea is here for every dog and cat, and we believe they should have the chance to live where they are treated with compassion, care and respect.'

Defining the IC team's mission

The internal communication team's mission is to support Battersea's organizational goals by providing the channels and expertise to empower colleagues to effectively carry out their work, communicate, collaborate, and share their own stories and lived experiences. The team say they raise awareness, build understanding, promote inclusivity and help their people play their part in achieving their mission to help more dogs and cats.

This mission sits alongside their internal communication vision of having 'a culture where open, honest, two-way communication is the norm and employees feel informed, listened to, involved and valued. Colleagues are purposeful and engaged with the cause and understand how everyone plays a part in contributing to Battersea's vision, mission and strategy'.

Chapman says The MILLER Framework sets out a clear course of action for how the charity can harness the power of its people to achieve its goals. Their internal communication strategy is a detailed PDF document containing images and evidence, plus a one-page Word document.

The IC team has worked hard to become the go-to people in Battersea when it comes to communications. They say they're good at giving out information in a timely fashion, but recognize the need to focus more on communication (getting through), admitting sometimes there is too much 'noise'.

Roles and responsibilities

Understanding of internal communication in the organization is still in its infancy. The IC team was highly valued during the pandemic for providing updates. However, internal communication is still seen as the responsibility of the small IC team, rather than a shared responsibility. Only a few colleagues share their own stories and update the intranet, with the photo gallery and thank you board being the most popular.

When creating her internal communication strategy, Chapman used a strengths and weaknesses table to identify where the organization is now and where it needs to go to. Her IC strategy is a five-year one, which gives scope for some stretch targets. She also identified the organization's values and matched internal communication goals against them. For example, one of their values is Determination – *We stay focused and solve problems to achieve our goals and our mission to be here for every dog and cat*. The IC goal against it is *Colleagues can help shape decisions and input to business plans and organizational strategy*.

Enablers

The charity's organizational strategy cites some enablers: 'ensuring our people, income, technology and systems support the effective delivery of this strategy, recognizing their vital impact and contribution'.

These are underpinned by Battersea's theory of change, which they say are essential for change to be delivered:

- A motivated, highly skilled and committed staff who are supported by a high-performing working environment of collaboration, empowerments and trust
- A culture of diversity, equity and inclusion as an organization which is open to everyone
- Engaged and motivated volunteers who provide vital support for Battersea through their time, effort and expertise

They also have three key themes, including a determination to increase charitable impact, a commitment to making Battersea an even better place to work and volunteer, and a recognition of the need to invest in systems, data and technology to drive growth and improvement.

Gathering insights

Chapman used the following insights to inform the IC strategy:

- Staff survey results
- Discussions with leadership team
- HR's plan on a page
- IC survey results
- Feedback forms from events
- Webinar polls
- Channel statistics
- Organization chart
- Meeting minutes
- Shadowing of front-line and animal-facing roles
- Benchmarking with peers in the IC community

She created IC objectives and stated the desired outcomes. For example, one of the objectives is 'Maintain high levels of engagement through the delivery of internal communications that focuses on the impact we are having for dogs and cats everywhere.' The outcome is 'Staff and volunteers understand the role they play in contributing to the organisational strategy. Increased sense of belonging and shared purpose.'

All of the internal communication objectives support the organizational objectives and are measured through employee and volunteer pulse surveys, focus groups, engagement with internal communications channels and content, engagement with recognition scheme, social media comments on LinkedIn and Glassdoor, attrition rates, digital engagement (number of campaigning actions), event engagement and fundraising/legacy data. They are also tracking behaviour change for their transformational change programme, working with learning and organizational development colleagues to look at engagement with new systems, training sessions, focus groups and surveys.

Stating intentions

One of the strengths of Battersea Dogs & Cats Homes' IC strategy is the clarity with which they have stated their intentions and identified priorities.

Chapman says: 'The MILLER Framework helped me know what to include and how to get started with my IC strategy. I was stuck knowing which format to use, which made it hard to even start. However, planning it to be a presentation format, plus a one-pager made sense for our business, and it helped me focus on what to write. We now have a clear sense of direction as an IC team and organization and know what we are aiming towards.'

Involving the team

I like the way the whole internal communication team were involved in the creation of Battersea's IC strategy. Chapman held a session with the internal comms officers to show the work in progress and where they were planning to go with the strategy, so they could provide input into it. This is critical because the whole IC team needs to align their efforts to the strategy, so I recommend involving them in its creation. You may find IC officers or executives are particularly good at knowing what employees are currently doing/thinking/feeling/saying inside the organization.

Another strength of their strategy, and something that was a result of involving the whole team, was a sign-off framework. This details how content is approved and decisions are made. Could something like this be useful for your internal communication strategy? It has three columns: activity, consulted and sign-off.

What's in a name?

Two of the comms conundrums I identified earlier in this chapter were whether to have one internal communication strategy, or separate strategies across countries or as part of a group of companies.

In these situations, I create an overarching IC strategy for an organization, then either have a specific and separate one that addresses a certain market, or have a section of the overarching document dedicated to that region.

Whether it's in one whole document or two separate ones, they need to correlate with each other. What you are trying to achieve in each area may be different. That could be for a wide variety of factors such as leadership style, culture or how the business operates in that area. Be guided by how the organization communicates and operates, and how realistic it is to have two separate strategies in place. When I have two in place, I make sure to give each one a name and cross-reference each document. This means if someone in a company reads one, they don't think the comms team has omitted a whole country or part of the organization.

When to write an IC strategy

Companies that say 'we don't have internal communication' should take a closer look. Every organization has internal communication happening inside it. What it may not have is a planned and methodical cadence (rhythm) of internal communication, with defined channels (methods) and owners.

Internal communication happens whether you are ready for it or not. Wherever humans are involved, communication is taking place.

Your internal communication strategy sets boundaries for the way communication happens. The strategy's author determines what good looks like, explains the potential for effective internal communication and guides the organization towards the future state. The best time to write your internal communication strategy was yesterday. The second-best time is today. Don't let a lack of experience hold you back, you can write it, you just need the inclination and a structure.

If you are reading this book because you're aware of the need or desire to create an IC strategy in your company, then the answer about timelines is today. *Now* is the time to start writing your IC strategy.

TIP FROM RACHEL

Do not wait until the end of this book to start writing your IC strategy. If you are reading in chapter order, make notes as you go. There are prompts at the end of each chapter to help you gauge the stage you should be at.

Internal communication inside start-ups

I find new companies, or start-ups, fascinating from an internal communication perspective. Typically, these sorts of companies are in the first stage of operations with a founder or owner. Over time, they hire people around them and start to expand. Teams are recruited, services grow, and processes and systems are created. However, there's a point in the life cycle of an organization where a lack of structured communication is evident.

Owners realize information and communication is not flowing effectively and they don't know who everyone in the company is. You don't all fit around one table, on one office floor or on one screen. As a company scales, you need to scale the culture and communication.

What is your culture, or rules of the game? As you grow in number, do they still stand? What behaviours do you have in place to support the culture you're striving to create? Are those behaviours known by all employees or just the founder/s? At a fundamental level, the lack of clarity here creates shaky foundations for the company to build on. As you recruit new people and expand operations further, the values and ethos need to be the cement that binds the building blocks of the company together.

The desire to hire

Start-ups get to a point where they decide to hire a professional communicator. From my own observations, this is after realizing time, money and effort is being wasted due to employees searching for credible, accurate and reliable information. This is when attention turns to investing in internal communication and creating a first comms hire. I welcome the move for organizations to invest in professional internal communication. I love the fact comms pros are being recruited to set up functions inside fledging companies. I've seen companies with as few as 50 people have a dedicated internal communicator.

Gaps between expectation and reality

The confidential conversations I have with professional communicators have led me to discover a disconnect between expectation and reality. When a company is starting out (or when an organization has been without an internal communicator and has realized they need one), you need to make sure you know what you're getting into. On both sides.

Being part of an organization at the start of the journey can be exhilarating. You help define, refine and shape the way communication happens and the way things are done.

However, I've lost count of the number of conversations I've had with senior-level comms practitioners who have been headhunted into start-ups and then had a difficult and frustrating experience. I experienced it myself in my own in-house career. Scenarios I've encountered include employees communicating via established internal forums and messaging boards, in lieu of having 'official' channels in place. They are not controlled by anyone, and the internal communicator has to break colleagues' habits, or jump in and try to get corporate messages to stand out. It can also be hard to get founders to articulate a coherent vision for the future, with a realistic time-line in place. If they are ideas people and have grand plans, that can be exciting to witness. However, creating certainty for employees is difficult when plans constantly change or they acquire other companies along the way. My colleague Caroline Cubbon-King says: 'Acquisitions can lead to little offshoots all over the world, which impacts the company's sense of togetherness and belonging. You may also find a common sense of purpose is lacking as a result.'

If you are reading this book because you are about to hire your first inter-nal communicator, or you are considering moving to a start-up, I have some advice in the form of questions to think through.

WHAT START-UPS NEED TO KNOW ABOUT HIRING AN INTERNAL COMMUNICATOR

- What is the business problem you are hoping your first internal communication hire will solve?

- Are you recruiting a senior-level professional? If so, how are you going to support them and provide them with resources? What's their budget? What size will their team be?

- If you don't intend to support your senior-level hire via resources, they will be working tactically. This won't be fulfilling for them or you.

- If you are recruiting a strategic internal communicator (e.g. someone who has led a large team), trust their advice. Listen to their questions, they know more than you do about internal communication. It's why you hired them.

- Who will line manage the internal communicator? Do not make them report into HR or marketing without direct access to the founder/s.

- It doesn't matter *where* they report into, as long as you give your internal communicator the access they need to all people across the company.

- As professional communicators, it's our business to know our business. Therefore, you need to be comfortable with the fact the comms professional will be asking questions, questioning why things are done in certain ways and will speak to whoever they need to in the company.

- You need to trust the internal communicator and share with them the information they need to do their job.

- If your internal communicator is asking for something, it's because they've identified a business need for it.

- Internal communication is too important to be left to one person, team or department. It's everyone's responsibility. This person will not single-handedly solve every communication problem your company has. Others need to take accountability for the way they communicate too. Including you.

- Respect boundaries with your internal communicator. When you're a founder, you're thinking about the business 24/7. But your people need to rest. If you expect them to be on call 24/7, you need to make that clear and hire in that way. Being 'on call' is usually required for external comms and resourced in that way. Crisis situations require your internal communicator to be involved. But unless you've specified, they are not on call and cannot be expected to respond in the early hours of the morning.

- What support can your internal communicator access? For example, if you have an agency working with your external comms colleagues, can your internal communicator ask them to assist them too?

- What equipment are you providing for your internal communicator? If you are expecting them to produce channels (ways for people to communicate) in-house, be prepared to equip them with software and hardware so they can do their job effectively.

- How will you be supporting their professional development?

What internal communicators joining start-ups need to know

- Why are you being hired? What's the problem they are hoping you will solve?

- Look at the wording of the job advert – how mature is the company's understanding of internal communication? How do they describe internal communication?

- Ask to see the business plan and anything that lives in the hearts and minds of the original employees or founders. What's their company story? Where have they come from and where are they heading?

- Whose responsibility is internal communication? What do the founder/s think?

- If you're a team of one, will it expand? Who will deputize for you when you are on holiday?

- How open are the founder/s to constructive feedback?

- Who is overseeing internal communication at the moment? Does it sit with one person or a department?

- Who are the internal influencers?

- What channels are in place already?

- What is the tone of voice? Is there a cultural playbook in place? How can you get up to speed quickly about the company?

- If you are on a fixed-term contract, what are the measures of success?

- Comms pros are often hired because you're a strategic operator who coaches leaders and sets standards. Then when you join a start-up, you're expected to do that, but also everything else. Expect to work tactically for a while, until you can expand the team. But make sure you prioritize what you work on.

- If you are the first internal communicator and people don't really know what to expect, you will find yourself repeating things constantly. Document as you go, share your observations and work out loud.

SOURCE Miller, 2021

Ethical practice for internal communication

Working ethically is a core consideration for internal communicators and needs to be not only part of our mindset, but our skill set too. Confidentiality and ethics go together in our professional practice. We need to be sensitive and respectful in our work, being attentive of what we advise and the information we know. Being an internal communicator means being placed in an exceptionally trusted role, with access to leaders and employees in a manner unlike most other functions. In situations such as impending change, we regularly know information in advance of most of the organization. This can make our jobs incredibly difficult at times.

I can recall numerous occasions in my in-house career when I felt the weight of responsibility on my shoulders, knowing certain teams were facing change. I knew they were going to be listening to their leaders saying the words I was writing, when learning about changes to their jobs.

That's a responsibility to take seriously, we need to be mindful of those types of scenarios and making sure we are taking care of our own mental health too. Longer-term change and business transformation not only impacts employees embroiled in the outcomes, but the communication professionals at the heart of the messaging and talking points. When our own teams are impacted, it makes it even harder.

Certain projects, such as mergers and acquisitions, or floating on a stock exchange can be highly confidential. Professional communicators need to work ethically in every situation. Consider non-disclosure agreements (NDAs) to provide clarity around what you can and cannot communicate. Don't forget to keep protected information to yourself in both the personal and professional space.

I've also encountered ethically challenging situations as a consultant, where I've been asked to disclose information that has been shared in confidential environments, such as focus groups as part of an audit. Which I have refused to do, because it would break the trust placed by employees as part of that process. The mindset for me when auditing is always presenting back and analysing *what* was said, not *who* said it, down to an identifiable and individual level.

Operating effectively

It is a privilege to work at the heart of an organization as a professional communicator. You do not need permission to talk with anyone and need unfettered access to all employees. If you are working in an environment that restricts, hides and shields leaders and employees from a professional communicator, it impacts the ability for the communicator to operate effectively.

In its ethical practice guide, the Institute of Internal Communication defines good ethical communication as 'ensuring all communication within the organisation is truthful, fair, and demonstrates respect'. It also describes how ethical values provide the moral compass by which we practise and help our organizations make decisions, acting as a foundation upon which professionalism and ethical practice is promoted (IoIC, 2022).

The only way is ethics

Ethics are at the root of most codes of conduct from professional bodies. All members of the Chartered Institute of Public Relations (CIPR) are bound by their code of conduct. They make the commitment on joining and renew this annually when they renew their membership. It is a critical part of their Chartered PR Practitioner assessment and ethics feature under the principles of the code. Members agree to deal honestly and fairly in business with employers, employees, clients, fellow professionals, other professions and the public. They also pledge to maintain the highest standards of professional endeavour, integrity, confidentiality, financial propriety and personal conduct.

The Public Relations Society of America (PRSA) states ethical practice as the most important obligation for its members and it is committed to ethical practices. It views its member code of ethics as a model for other professions, organizations and professionals.

Core values form the foundation for the Code of Ethics, as a set of fundamental beliefs that guide behaviours and decision making. They are: advocacy, honesty, expertise, independence, loyalty and fairness. The 'level of public trust PRSA members seek, as we serve the public good, means we have taken on a special obligation to operate ethically. Each of us sets an example for each other – as well as other professionals – by our pursuit of excellence with powerful standards of performance, professionalism and ethical conduct' (PRSA, nd).

Aligning with business strategy

An internal communication strategy needs to align with a business strategy. This sounds simple, but it rarely is, and internal communicators struggle to gather the information they need.

We need to have organizational alignment in place, which is 'the process of creating unity between the company's ultimate vision of success and the way leaders and individual contributors drive business results' (CMOE, nd).

Creating strong strategic pillars

The UK's Government Communication Service (GCS) is the professional body for more than 7,000 public service communicators working in government departments, agencies and arm's length bodies. It has three pillars to its 2022–2025 Communication Strategy, Performance with Purpose.

The pillars are:

1 Collaboration
2 Innovation and improvement
3 Great people

The wording of the collaboration pillar is applicable to all, as it concentrates on fostering better collaboration, describing it as the need for a 'clear, shared plan, an ability to overcome institutional barriers to join up campaigns' (GCS, 2022a).

Specifying goals

The Government Communication Service has outlined its strategy's goals, which include building public trust, to retain, attract and develop the best communications talent and to improve the ability of government communications to work together. It also says communication 'makes a real difference' to individuals and society (GCS, 2022b).

Business priorities

Do you know what your business priorities are? They may be stated in a different way, for example, they could be called strategic priorities, pillars or goals.

What happens if your business doesn't have its priorities communicated anywhere? Well, it makes our roles a lot harder! An internal communication strategy is not the business strategy, they should be two distinct and separate documents. However, in lieu of having clearly articulated business goals, mission, vision and strategic priorities, it's not uncommon for the professional communicator to find themselves identifying what the priorities should be, following conversations with stakeholders.

In an ideal scenario, you should be able to easily collate these documents. However, I know that's not always the case. If you can't find them internally, look externally. Documents such as annual reports, recruitment websites and even the press release and media centres on websites can contain this information. I hope you have access to such data if it already exists inside your organization, but sometimes we have to seek it out, and I regularly find external communication contains valuable insights we can use internally.

Strategic priorities

Strategic priorities are defined as 'an explicit set of prioritized actions to execute strategy over the mid-term' (Sull and Turconi, 2017). Think about your organization's strategic priorities or pillars. If you don't have them as part of your business strategy, what could you put in place to underpin your internal communication strategy?

Consider the actions you want to take. Strategy research suggests instead of trying to summarize strategy in a pithy statement, translate it into a handful of actions the company must take to execute that strategy over the medium term.

Your strategic priorities 'should be forward-looking and action-orientated and should focus attention on the handful of choices that matter most to the organization's success over the next few years' (Sull, Sull and Yoder, 2018). You can apply this thinking for an internal communication strategy.

Do your leaders know your strategic priorities? Could they recite them if you asked? If not, you're not alone. Analysis of 124 organizations revealed only 28 per cent of executives and middle managers responsible for executing strategy could list three of their company's strategic priorities (Sull, Sull and Yoder, 2018).

Collating the evidence

Collate the following information about your organization, to inform the start of your internal communication strategy creation:

- Business priorities
- Vision
- Mission
- Values

You may need to write the following from scratch:

- An internal communication vision
- An internal communication mission
- Why internal communication is important for your organization
- The outcomes you are aiming for

You will then use this data to inform the creation of your internal communication strategy. The types of documents and thinking in this list is what makes organizations individual, because you are adapting what you are writing to suit your company.

Writing an internal communication vision

Decide whether you need a vision for the comms team *or* the organization's internal communication, or both. This doesn't replace your company's vision, but outlines what good looks like for internal communication inside your organization.

I sometimes create visions with a team as communication principles. I think of it as the blueprint for the team. It's not just their reputation and promise as practitioners and as a team, but an aspirational positioning statement they can measure themselves against. We'll talk more about these in Chapter 5.

Why would a business need an IC vision?

Organizations typically have a lot of feedback indicating internal communication needs to be improved. This ranges from anecdotal feedback in exit interviews, to formalized comments in employee surveys and questions via line managers.

Creating a vision for the way an organization communicates can be helpful to provide a check and balance against which to measure the efforts of your people. It's also useful if you are part of recognition schemes such as Investors in People or Best Companies.

CREATING AN IC VISION

Questions to ask yourself:

What are we aiming for?

What does good look like for our company?

Tip: If you find them hard to answer, flip them: *What does bad look like for our company? What do we need to avoid?* Then build it up from there.

What makes a good vision? Like any other vision, it needs to be aspirational – *this is how we would like the organization to communicate in the future*. Then the supporting statements around it and detail in your IC strategy help you realize, work towards and measure that ambition.

STRATEGY CREATION CHECKLIST

Make notes and decisions on the following points, before moving on to the next chapter. This will help you write your strategy as you read through this book. As a result of working your way through this chapter, you should now have:

- Thought about what aids you (superpowers) and what gets in your way.
- Decided on the formatting. What will the document be? Slides? A Word document? Start that document.
- Thought about the need for one or more strategy documents and chosen names for them.
- Considered whether you'll create a shorter summary one-pager, and what format it will be in.
- Thought about how the IC strategy aligns with your organizational business plan.
- Reflected the language of your business strategy in your internal communication strategy.
- Looked at the terms you are using, making sure to include outputs and outcomes.
- Written your internal communication vision and mission.
- Articulated where are you now in terms of your internal communication (current state).
- Outlined where you are heading (future state). What do you need internal communication to be like in future, and why?
- Defined what the business needs communication to do. (What are the desired outcomes?)
- Considered internal communication versus internal communications. What's the difference in your organization?

Review the choices you've made while reading through this chapter. Make sure you've captured what has resonated and what feels appropriate for your organization.

References and further reading

CMOE (nd) Glossary: Organizational alignment, Center for Management & Organization Effectiveness, cmoe.com/glossary/organizational-alignment/ (archived at https://perma.cc/J3SL-E5U4)

Deal, T and Kennedy, A (1982) *Corporate Cultures: The rites and rituals of corporate life*, Addison-Wesley, Reading, MA

Dewhurst, S and FitzPatrick, L (2022) *Successful Employee Communications: A practitioner's guide to tools, models and best practice for internal communication*, 2nd edn, Kogan Page, London

GCS (2022a) Performance with Purpose: Government Communication Service Strategy 2022–2025, strategy.gcs.civilservice.gov.uk/wp-content/uploads/2022/05/gcs-strategy-2022-25.pdf (archived at https://perma.cc/PJG2-82XD)

GCS (2022b) Government Communication Service: Our strategy for 2022 to 2025, 10 October, gcs.civilservice.gov.uk/about-us/government-communication-service-our-strategy-for-2022-to-2025/ (archived at https://perma.cc/28WN-VNNG)

Gregory, S (2022) A simple guide on words to avoid in government, UK.GOV, Civil Service blog, 16 August, civilservice.blog.gov.uk/2022/08/16/a-simple-guide-on-words-to-avoid-in-government/ (archived at https://perma.cc/PN9W-DNGC)

Harris, S J (1972) *For the Time Being*, Houghton Mifflin, Boston, MA

IABC (nd) The Global Standard of the Communication Profession, International Association of Business Communicators, www.iabc.com/About/Global-Standard (archived at https://perma.cc/UWR3-AUPM)

IoIC (2022) Guide to Ethical Practice, Institute of Internal Communication, 20 July, https://www.ioic.org.uk/about-us/professionalstandards/ethicalguidance.html (archived at https://perma.cc/D3RH-ZJ5Q)

IoIC (2023a) *IoIC Guide to Internal Communication Strategy*, 2nd edn, Institute of Internal Communication, www.ioic.org.uk/resource/ioic-strat-guide-v2.html (archived at https://perma.cc/UK23-D6RJ)

IoIC (2023b) The Profession Map: The core, Institute of Internal Communication, www.ioic.org.uk/learn-develop/the-profession-map/the-core.html (archived at https://perma.cc/P5AS-QAHR)

Miller, R (2018) How to communicate change, All Things IC Blog, 14 October, www.allthingsic.com/how-to-communicate-change/ (archived at https://perma.cc/D9GA-9WD3)

Miller, R (2021) What start-ups need to know about internal communication, All Things IC Blog, 8 July, www.allthingsic.com/what-startups-need-to-know-about-internal-communication/ (archived at https://perma.cc/62GN-VAJ9)

Miller, R and FitzPatrick, L (2023) Interview/correspondence with the author

Peck, S (2022) An end of year message from our President, Institute of Internal Communication blog, 20 December, www.ioic.org.uk/resource/an-end-of-year-message-from-our-president.html (archived at https://perma.cc/GF8F-T7UE)

Perry, J (2022) *The Ten Pillars of Success: Secret strategies of high achievers*, Allen & Unwin, London

PRSA (nd) PRSA Code of Ethics, Public Relations Society of America, www.prsa.org/about/ethics/prsa-code-of-ethics (archived at https://perma.cc/VLD6-DVEM)

Sull, D, Sull, C and Yoder, J (2018) No one knows your strategy – not even your top leaders, *MIT Sloan Management Review*, 12 February, sloanreview.mit.edu/article/no-one-knows-your-strategy-not-even-your-top-leaders/ (archived at https://perma.cc/K62S-UGUX)

Sull, D and Turconi, S (2017) How to recognize a strategic priority when you see one, *MIT Sloan Management Review*, 28 September, sloanreview.mit.edu/article/how-to-recognize-a-strategic-priority-when-you-see-one/ (archived at https://perma.cc/H5TU-Y3ZG)

Sull, D, Turconi, S, Sull, C and Yoder, J (2017) Turning strategy into results, *MIT Sloan Management Review*, 28 September, sloanreview.mit.edu/article/turning-strategy-into-results/ (archived at https://perma.cc/EN7M-AADN)

3

How to gather organizational insights

WHAT THIS CHAPTER WILL COVER

We're going to focus on insights in this chapter and how to use them to inform an internal communication strategy. We will also analyse some of the key topics facing companies and communicators, including the impact of hybrid working on internal communication, and communicating with neurodivergent employees. You'll find a checklist at the end of this and every chapter to help you keep on track.

The MILLER Framework: Insights

Insights form the second stage of The MILLER Framework – *what we know about the organization and its people.*

Using organizational data

Perhaps you're reading this book because you are an HR professional who wants to learn more about internal communication, or maybe you're an internal communicator who needs to write an IC strategy. Whatever situation you are in, you'll be surrounded by organizational data.

We need to look at the bigger picture of your organization. The strategy creator needs to use insights to determine how to develop the internal communication strategy, so it supports the organizational priorities. Let's bust the jargon before we move on. Insight is 'a form of analysis that turns interesting data into actionable data... At its core, insight is about understanding audiences to support communication planning' (GCS, 2021). Actionable data is an excellent description to keep in mind for an internal communication strategy.

We addressed mindset in the previous chapter, which examined organizational goals and priorities. Insights delve deeper into the composition of an organization and build on the nuances and need for uniqueness.

JARGON BUSTING

Insight is a form of analysis that turns interesting data into actionable data.

SOURCE GCS, 2021

Why research matters

An internal communication strategy requires research and data gathering. It must be personalized to the organization, which means collating insights.

A strategy is 'not a long planning document; it is a set of interrelated and powerful choices that positions the organization to win' (Lafley and Martin, 2013). Internal communicators need to make the right choices for their organization. Once data has been collated and analysed, you can make informed decisions and choices that influence and shape the strategy.

JARGON BUSTING

Research makes public relations activities strategic by ensuring that communication is specifically targeted to publics who want, need, or care about the information. Strategy 'deals with the bigger picture' and longer-term, whereas tactics focus on short-term effects.

SOURCE Davis, 2007

How to gather insights about an organization

When you apply for a job, you conduct as much research as you can to gather insights, and learn about a company and the people who work there.

This could include looking at its careers site, reading annual reports, seeing how employees rank their experience via websites like Glassdoor, and even talking with past and present employees. If you are called for interview, you'll be assessing whether what is reflected outside matches up with your experiences as a prospective employee or candidate.

Go and see for yourself

In Chapter 1 I revealed as professional communicators, it's *our business to know our business*. This is brought into sharp focus when you are gathering insights about an organization and the people who work within it. You cannot devise strategies, create content or reflect the reality of your work-force via internal communication until you invest time getting to know who they are and how work happens.

Toyota operates *Genchi Genbutsu* as part of its Toyota Production System (2013). In English this literally means *go and see for yourself*. It uses this practice to make sure a production line is working at maximum efficiency.

Going to see the location or process where a problem exists allows them to solve it quickly and efficiently to 'grasp problems, confirm the facts and analyse root causes' (Toyota, 2013). It also requires a high level of management presence on the factory floor, so a problem can be correctly understood before being solved. The nature of the phrase is more to do with understanding the full implications of any action within an environment, rather than the physical act of visiting a site. However, as professional communicators, we need to do both.

Why internal communicators need to be visible

When I worked in-house in the railway, the employees who were reading what I was writing and listening to their team briefing worked in a completely different way to me. I was based at the headquarters in London and worked as an internal communicator during daylight hours. I would walk past numerous designer shops and restaurants in the Canary Wharf area of London, with their dazzling goods on display and sunlight bouncing off the skyscrapers.

The colleagues I was communicating with and for were working underneath escalators to repair them in the middle of the night. They were maintaining stations, wearing hard hats and high-visibility vests while walking through the train tunnels that run underneath the city. They ate food they'd brought from home and didn't see daylight until the sun rose at the end of their shift.

Our working worlds could not have been more different. If I had stayed sat at my desk and never spent time on the train network or doing night shifts, I would never have truly understood our people. It would have impacted the effectiveness of my work and created a disconnect between my view of the company presented via our internal communication, and theirs.

Internal communicators need to *get their boots dirty*. In my case I remember putting steel toecap boots on and stomping all over my high-vis vest before my first night visit out on the network. I knew turning up to site with packet-fresh personal protective equipment would not go down well!

Being visible within the workforce meant I could build relationships and establish an internal network. I worked in-house for a decade and being visible was how I learnt about each business, whether it was financial services at Visa, pharmaceutical at Novartis, automotive at Visteon or the underground or overground railway networks. What unites every organization I worked for is dedicated experts who were passionate about the purpose of the business and how they could play their part. Internal communicators need to understand deeply what employees care about and what concerns them. IC pros need active relationships with the people behind the job titles. You won't be able to address every single perspective, but you need to be listening to them.

TIP FROM RACHEL

Factor-in time to create strong relationships inside your organization and get your boots dirty. This means spending time on the shop floor, hospital ward, factories or wherever work happens inside your organization. Internal communicators need to be constantly gathering insights and developing effective relationships.

What data exists in your organization?

Companies are rich with interesting data; the task of the internal communicator is to determine what is meaningful, and what to act on.

When trying to unlock the potential of data inside organizations, *meaningful* is an excellent word to bear in mind. It appears in the *conducting research, measuring and demonstrating value* professional area of the Institute of Internal Communication's (IoIC) Profession Map. It states communicators need to use effective research, measurement and evaluation techniques to 'deliver meaningful insights and evidence and robustly demonstrate the value and impact of high standard internal communication' (IoIC, 2023b).

Meaningful or interesting data should provide actionable insights, which help internal communicators gauge the culture, experience and views of employees. Insights lay the groundwork and ensure a strategy has a firm foundation, as it is rooted in the reality of how the organization operates. You can then build on them to support what you are trying to achieve, as you'll understand the intended recipients and make considered choices.

Research by the Institute of Internal Communication reveals 57 per cent of UK workers are clear on their employer's strategy. The proportion of UK employees who 'don't hear enough' about their organization's strategy is 33 per cent and those who receive 'too much' is 11 per cent, which is a 22 point gap (IoIC, 2023a). I wonder what your employees would say?

EXAMPLES OF INTERESTING DATA INSIDE ORGANIZATIONS

- **Employee survey data.** This not only gives you the results, you can also see which groups of employees actively participate in answering the survey, or where you have clusters of certain types of feedback.

- **Organization charts**, 'organigrams' and other ways of representing the structure of a company can tell you a lot about how complex they are, what pressures may exist for line managers and how many layers of hierarchy there are to consider.

- **People data** such as recruitment and retention figures.

- **Pulse surveys** can give you some great real-time data about your people.

- What your external and public affairs and HR colleagues have in their **strategies** can help inform an IC strategy. You need to at least make sure they are complementary and aligned.

- Any previous **internal communication audit** outcomes would be helpful insight, even if they date back a few years.

- **Exit survey** information can be very helpful, if your HR team capture those. They can tell you why people are leaving the organization, which can indicate cultural tensions and issues.

- **Employee personas** or any form of employee groups insight. This isn't just *who* you have in the company, but what is top of mind in the form of employee group discussions.

- **Great Place to Work** or **Investors in People** applications or awards submissions and outcomes can show you key points of achievement and highlights, with some independent analysis and feedback.

The impact of the pandemic on companies

The impact of the Covid-19 pandemic on the way organizations communicate has been unprecedented. Some organizations emerged stronger, with modern methods of communication in place and high levels of trust. Comms pros were invited into high-level discussions, operated as trusted advisers and provided invaluable advice. Investment was made in people and channels, and doors that had felt closed were opened, with IC pros beckoned inside.

However, this was not the experience for all. Other comms pros' working lives have been damaged by mismanaged efforts, hastily introduced channels and frenetic communication.

Some comms teams found themselves working reactively to guide their organizations through a constantly changing situation. Strategic planning and creating certainty were tough to maintain due to the prolonged period of uncertainty.

The challenge today for many comms teams is trying to get back to a strategic way of working, as their reputation was set in the minds of stakeholders because of a sustained reactive response. Comms pros did what they had to do to get through an incredibly difficult period. Internal communicators will be unravelling or building on their new reputation for many years to come.

According to the Institute of Internal Communication we are 'living in a state of "permacrisis", reeling between the immediate consequences of the pandemic, an ongoing climate crisis, and pressing cost of living concerns'. It says the way we work is undergoing the 'most profound transformation in a century, emphasising the essential role of effective communication to give employees a powerful and articulate voice' (IoIC, 2023a).

Hybrid working

The rise of hybrid (or flexible location) working has demanded a new approach for how internal communication happens. This has provided challenges for communicators as we've reimagined channels, helped leaders learn how to communicate in different ways, introduced new methods of communicating with colleagues and managed expectations from employees and leaders alike.

I've worked flexibly since 2013 and agree 'work is a thing you do, not a place you go' (Murgatroyd, 2015). However, for many employees, work is a place you go – it's your bus, train, shop floor, hospital ward or factory.

Organizations that failed to maintain a sense of belonging during the pandemic will continue to pay the reputational price. Memories and scars run deep for employees, particularly those on the front line or in customer-facing roles.

FIGURE 3.1 Working considerations model

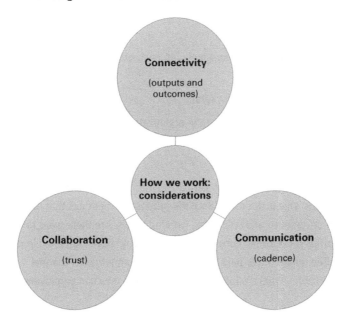

Working considerations

What does this mean for an IC strategy? There are three areas of consideration to determine how work happens: connectivity, communication and collaboration.

You need all three in place inside an organization as their effectiveness is reduced if one is underperforming or non-existent. I've used this model to help clients plan internal communication for hybrid working. However, it is applicable in all organizations. An internal communication strategy requires an internal communicator to know how connectivity, collaboration and communication happen in the organization (Figure 3.1).

WORKING CONSIDERATIONS
(using hybrid working as the example)

Connectivity

This is the outputs and outcomes of work, rather than location. This relates to how connected employees feel to an organization's purpose and to each other (sense of belonging). It also includes technology considerations. Employees are judged on the *impact* and *outcomes* of their work, and a close eye is kept on the volume (outputs), to ensure it is achievable.

Questions to ask

- How connected do employees feel with each other and with the organization?
- What are the barriers or blockers?
- What enhances connectivity in the organization?

Communication

This is the rhythm or cadence of formal and informal channels and conversations. This includes defining the purpose of meetings that require an in-person attendance and respecting working hours. Are there ways to create opportunities for informal conversations that would have happened in person in the coffee queue or car park? Consider multichannel/cross-channel communication – where is information shared and how can employees provide their views?

Questions to ask

- What or who do employees rely on as a single source of truth?
- How does the *communication flow* align with the *workflow*?
- How do channels need to change or adapt (to account for hybrid working)?

Collaboration

This is all about trust. *'Trusting employees to do the right thing, rather than assuming they'll do the wrong thing.'* My husband Jon shared that trust quote with me years ago from an IT perspective. I use it a lot in my work, and when focusing on hybrid or flexible working; you need to create a culture of trust that enables people to work together and make their own choices. Some of the best and most innovative ideas happen when you create a culture of openness.

Questions to ask

- How can employees work together towards a common goal?
- How autonomous are employees in the decision making around where and when to work?
- What is in place to help employees *work out loud* (Williams, 2010) and feel able to share their thoughts with each other?

SOURCE Miller, 2021

Ways to turn these three areas into action include inviting employees to choose the working patterns that will enable them to meet their objectives, leaders *checking in* – not *checking up* – on their teams and creating environments where employees can work well together, even if they are not physically in the same room or even the same continent.

For true collaboration to work, you need to have a high degree of trust, mutual respect and dialogue. Organizations that are trying to entice employees to work in an office need to clearly communicate the benefits.

When I am trying to encourage action, which is a frequent occurrence as an internal communicator, I view it from different perspectives and challenge myself to answer the following questions: *What will I/we gain* and *What will I/we lose?*

Merely addressing every situation from a positive stance – *what we gain*, or *what's in it for me?* – misses the mark if employees have negative views. They need to see those reflected in the communication too.

WHAT DO WE GAIN OR LOSE?

Answer the following questions several times using different perspectives.
  Try employees, leaders and 'the company'. Use this insight to inform your internal communication messaging.

1 What do we gain?

2 What do we lose?

This technique will help you if the purpose of your internal communication strategy is to change behaviour. Changing behaviours and breaking habits takes a long time, which is why it is vital employees see their views reflected. Writing gain/lose perspectives allows internal communicators not only to put themselves into the mindset of the varying colleague groups, but also to know how to use that insight.

Trying to persuade employees to work in offices without clearly communicating what the benefits are will fail. Until 2020/21, this wasn't something I'd had to communicate a lot in my internal communication career. However, today's workforce looks different in a lot of organizations, and this is more commonplace in recruitment and retention conversations.

Why planning feels tougher

From conversations with clients and cohorts of the All Things IC Inner Circle, which are groups of in-house professionals, I know internal communication planning has felt tougher since the Covid-19 pandemic. This is for a variety of reasons, not least trying to create certainty during a changeable and volatile time, and the impact of hybrid working.

Whenever internal communicators have been stuck, I've encouraged us to look at employees in a different way. Rather than examining segmentation data such as the categories you'll find later in this chapter, I've proposed an alternative lens to look through – *when they joined the company*. I have realized through my work that length of service has a significant role to play. Let's examine it in more detail.

FIGURE 3.2 Impact of the Covid-19 pandemic

	PRE-PANDEMIC EMPLOYEE	PANDEMIC EMPLOYEE	POST-PANDEMIC / NEW HIRE
JOINING DATE	Pre-March 2020	Post-March 2020	January 2022
CULTURE COMMENTS	Company feels different. New hires have no idea who we *really* are.	I like the culture and how well we've been looked after.	I was attracted by the flexibility and openness.
HOW THEY VIEW LEADERS	Leaders have adapted their styles.	I like how open and informal leaders are.	I can tell who has recently joined the leadership group.
EXPERIENCE OF INTERNAL COMMS	Our reliable channels have changed. Too many video calls.	I'm kept updated constantly and can share my views.	There's little in-person internal communication.

ANALYSING EMPLOYEE DATA

There are three types of employees inside organizations:

- **Pre-pandemic employees** – people who were in role pre-March 2020.

- **Pandemic employees** – people who joined organizations from March 2020 until January 2022.

- **Post-pandemic employees** – people who joined organizations from January 2022 to date.

Does your demographic data allow you to view employees in this way? It's unlikely you're able to categorize employees by length of service into neat distribution lists and it's not typical to plan content according to how long people have been with a company.

However, the impact of these three distinct employee groups is tangible. Length of service impacts their expectations of how the organization and leaders communicate. What these employees have experienced culturally varies incredibly. If you divided your organization up today, what would the percentage split be between these three groups?

You could create your own categories against the groups. In Figure 3.2 I've used joining date, culture comments, how they view leaders and experience of internal comms.

Additional categories could be: where they work, who or what is their trusted source of communication, how much they trust leaders – the list is endless! Knowing the answers to these queries provides rich insight and it can help inform decisions you make in your internal communication strategy.

What we know about employees

Segmenting employees

Internal communicators need a deep understanding of the people who make up an organization. This isn't surface-level analysis, you need to invest time getting to know and understand your employees, both *who they are* and *how they think and feel*.

We segment, or categorize, employees into groups to know *who they are*. Some IC pros use hierarchical segmentation such as CEO and board, senior leaders, managers and employees. Others use location-based segmentation such as continents, countries or cities. Additional segmentation could include length of service, age, type of role, psychographic data, language, accessibility, diversity or access to technology. We will examine neurodivergent segmentation later in this chapter, which I expect to see increase in the years to come.

Be wary of segmenting for segmentation's sake. For example, if you have demographic data such as age, how would it impact the way you communicate? It's unlikely you would create channels or target messaging per age group, and if you wanted to, would your systems support it and serve up the necessary data? Insights into length of service can be useful – start-ups face their own challenges as most employees are new. In more established organizations, being cognitive of the fact you have long-serving employees allows you to plan change. This group may be resistant to ideas or have long-held assumptions and opinions about the organization.

TIP FROM RACHEL

Consider creating a stakeholder map and including it in your IC strategy. The axes need to suit your organization and could include *levels of influence* and *urgency*. Determine whether the stakeholder map is for the IC team and who you work with, or for the organization as a whole.

Inclusive internal communication

How inclusive is your workplace and how accessible are your internal communications? We will examine accessibility in Chapter 4.

Inclusive internal communication 'enables powerful connections, demonstrates curiosity, and cultivates belonging through two-way engagement. This results in trusted, clear and effective communication, allowing people to thrive in their work and impact organizational performance' (Bates and Patel, 2023).

Diversity, equity and inclusion are critical considerations for an organization. You cannot contemplate creating an internal communication strategy without examining these areas, and I encourage you to know the make-up of your business.

Bates and Patel (2023) say organizations are 'actively starting to explore a variety of traits including: age, disability, gender, race, religion and sexual orientation (listed in alphabetical order)', and encourage internal communicators to 'consider if your workplace has a DEI (diversity, equity and inclusion) strategy or a communications strategy for DEI'.

Assess the language you are using in an internal communication strategy. Language 'has the power to reinforce or deconstruct systems of power that maintain poverty, inequality, and suffering. Writing can subvert or inadvertently reinforce intersecting forms of inequality' (Oxfam, 2023).

Inclusive internal communication includes being mindful of the language you are using, not just jargon-free, non-corporate speak, but being culturally appropriate too.

TIP FROM RACHEL

Consider creating a principle around inclusive language use, which you can include in your internal communication strategy.

Gathering the data

Consider what you have access to inside your organization and how useful it could be. In the Battersea Dogs & Cats Home Expert View in Chapter 2, Debbie Chapman, Head of Communications, revealed the insights she used to inform her IC strategy.

They included: job shadowing front-line and animal-facing roles, staff survey results, discussions with the leadership team, HR's plan on a page, IC survey results, feedback forms from events, webinar polls, channel statistics, organization chart, meeting minutes and benchmarking with peers in the IC community.

Did you notice the job shadowing of animal-facing roles? This relates to being visible, which we've already addressed in this chapter. If you're trying to create a shared understanding and meaning about how the business priorities translate and relate for all employees, you need to know *how* your people are working and *how they feel*. You are tapping into the subconscious, so not just clarifying who your people are, where they work and how they work, but *how they feel* about the work they're doing. Job shadowing is an excellent way of doing this and it also helps internal communicators build their internal networks.

Listening to employees

To know *how employees think and feel* you need to be actively listening to them. Why? Because you're dealing with multiple numbers of people, who each have their own views and experience. There won't be one collective answer. Listening allows communicators to complement the segmentation work, to know what's concerning or motivating people inside the organization. Around half of UK workers 'don't feel listened to' by their employer and 'there's no strong sense organizations welcome open and honest feedback' (IoIC, 2023a).

Internal communication academic Dr Kevin Ruck (2015) defines internal communication as 'corporate information provided to employees that is also tailored to specific internal stakeholder groups (middle managers, line managers, function and project teams, and peer groups), combined with the concurrent facilitation of employee voice that is treated seriously by all managers'.

The 'Who's listening?' research conducted by Howard Krais, Mike Pounsford and Dr Kevin Ruck is valuable for the comms community to learn from. The research suggests 'a prevailing mindset that sees communication as *primarily a process for getting messages across, rather than a process for building trust and collaboration*'. The research is full of actionable insights to overcome this mindset and access the benefits of effective listening inside organizations.

FIVE PRINCIPLES FOR GOOD LISTENING

1 Openness: good listening requires an open mind

2 Planning: thorough planning across the organization

3 Distributed leadership: listening needs to be led at multiple levels in the organization

4 Empathic and creative: creating impactful and emotive feedback approaches

5 Human: understanding how people think and feel

SOURCE Ruck, 2019

Sensegiving and sensemaking

When planning your internal communication strategy, consider sensegiving and sensemaking.

- Sensegiving is 'the role of directing and influencing meaning-making by others' (Gioia et al, 1994).
- Sensemaking is about 'people negotiating meaning and seeking plausibility to understand ambiguous and confusing events' (Weick et al, 2005, cited in Yeomans and Bowman, 2021).

When I am creating an internal communication strategy or analysing the way a company communicates, I want to know who the internal 'meaning makers' are inside an organization. It can vary from leaders to people managers, peers to external commentators.

Influential voices and internal influencers make and shape an organization. Knowing the spheres of influence and who helps information make sense for employees is critical. We'll talk about comms champions in Chapter 4 as they can be a useful way for a comms team to listen, check for understanding and refine messages.

Dewhurst and FitzPatrick (2022) advise understanding the 'main characteristics of the workforce so far as they might affect how things are explained, the detail and context provided and the methods by which they are communicated... to decide how to earn and keep their attention'.

Personas

Do you use personas inside your organization? They are 'models that represent different groups of employees'. Personas 'synthesize data and insights from multiple data sources and incorporate multiple variables to create rich profiles of segments of people that describe their needs, values, behaviors, etc' (Yohn, 2021).

The IC Index from the Institute of Internal Communication (2023) says people in the workforce tend to fall into one of four broad groups: unconvinced cynics, confused followers, miserable moaners or informed cheerleaders. I wonder if any of these descriptions resonate with you?

I often create personas when auditing an organization's internal communication. I may group them into senior leaders, people managers, customer-facing colleagues, call centre employees, new starters. The list is endless! But be clear why you are creating personas, what's the problem you're trying to solve or evidence you're trying to collate?

Categories I apply against them include: needs, challenges and barriers, what they expect and opportunities. If at the end of an audit, I can articulate who the employee groups are, and have enough insights and evidence to complete those categories, I know it gives the IC team a lot to work with. I recommend finding real people who represent each persona group. To avoid being generic, test your findings and assumptions with them.

Using personas

I've used personas at various times during my 20-plus years in communication. I was first introduced to the idea in 1999 when I began my career as a journalist. I was encouraged to think about who read the newspaper, what mattered to them and what they expected to read. I found it hard to do that because the audience was so broad, as it was a whole community.

During my journalism diploma training, I remember one of my tutors giving a mock press briefing for us trainee reporters in the room. It was a fictional scenario of a fatal road traffic incident. We asked a lot of questions and managed to gather all the relevant information. Or so I thought.

Once we'd written up our stories and read them back to each other, we were shown the error of our ways. Yes, the majority of us had accurately reported who, what, when, where, how and why. We'd been mindful of sensitivities and even managed to get some of the trickier details that had been carefully planted.

However, what we all missed was the *impact* of the incident on the local area. I remember the tutor telling us 'I'm a local resident who was stuck in a huge traffic jam on that day, I had to be rerouted and I'm trying to work out why. I picked up the paper to tell me the answer. But it's not clear to me whether the story about the incident and the jam I was in are one and the same, as it doesn't mention the traffic or rerouting.'

That stayed with me because it taught me the importance of zooming out – to consider the wider perspective. So not just what happened and the details, but how situations and what you are communicating have a broader impact. In this scenario, I should have asked what happened in the area because of the incident.

In future press briefings, their words rang in my ears and I tried to think beyond what I was being presented with. Nowadays of course, you would simply look online via social media to uncover what was going on, but at that time that wasn't possible. But the point remains; their intention of buying the paper was with the expectation there would be information to find the answer. But it wasn't there because we'd not asked about the impact.

It was at that time I started to use the question that I have heard myself use every single week since: '*Is there anything else you think I should know, or you want to tell me?*'

I can't count the number of times that question has elicited a response that has become a whole story. It's led me to hear about an employee with 40 years' service, to discover local office moves inside the company I'd not known about and much more. I also use it in meetings with my own team today, as it invites additional information that hasn't naturally occurred in the preceding discussions.

TIP FROM RACHEL

The best question to ask:

'Is there anything else you think I should know, or you want to tell me?'

The question is a reminder for me to not just focus on what is in front of me, but to widen my perspective and be open to something I've not thought of. It creates space for additional ideas to flow.

There may be other insights specific to your organization's culture or industry sector that could help you understand your audience. I shared my personal preference in Chapter 1, which is to avoid the term *audience* where possible as it implies a performance, or one-way communication. However, for the purposes of data gathering and insight analysis, it's an appropriate term. I've seen organizations replace the word audience with employee groups or recipient. I use 'who it's for' when analysing channels.

Impact of neurodiversity on internal communication

I live in a neurodivergent household. I'm acutely aware of the criticality of communication and the impact of not being able to process information or emotions. Uncovering the specific communication needs of my family has led to a journey of self-discovery and appreciation of my own neurodivergence.

The word neurodiversity was coined by Judy Singer in 1998. It's 'used as an umbrella term for neurological differences' (The Law Society, 2021).

Neurotypes can include attention deficit hyperactivity disorder (ADHD), autism spectrum disorder, dyscalculia, dysgraphia, dyslexia, dyspraxia and tic conditions.

Let's examine the language, as it's important to get it right. I've referred to 'working definitions' from the Chartered Institute of Personnel and Development (CIPD).

JARGON BUSTING

Neurodiversity: Neurodiversity is, ultimately, a biological fact of the infinite variety of human neurocognition. It is also being used to describe the subcategory of workplace diversity and inclusion that focuses on people who are neurodivergent.

The neurodiversity paradigm: A perspective on neurodiversity that suggests it is the result of natural human variation and that there is no one 'normal' brain type.

Neurodivergent: Having cognitive functioning different from what is seen as 'normal'.

Neurodivergence: The state of being neurodivergent.

Neurotypical: Given the biological fact that there is no such thing as a 'normal' brain, neurotypical is best thought of as 'not neurodivergent'.

Neurominority: A group such as autistic people, or dyslexic people, defined by sharing a similar form of innate neurodivergence.

It's important not to draw simple lines in the sand between 'neurotypicals' and neurodivergent people – human neurodiversity is a highly complex spectrum, in which everyone sits (CIPD, 2018).

You may also see 'ND'. This can refer to neurodevelopmental disorders (NDs) or be used as an abbreviation for neurodiversity.

Neurodiversity is 'gaining in prominence in organisational practice with specific programmes springing up; yet we witness varied levels of organisational practice and support. Employee experience at work drives performance and productivity, as well as job sustainability, inclusion and mental wellbeing. Work makes a huge contribution to our overall wellbeing, our social and financial health and even our life expectancy' (McDowall, Doyle and Kiseleva, 2023, citing Weinberg and Doyle, 2017).

Reasonable adjustments

As the neurodivergent parent of a neurodivergent child, I've adapted the way we communicate at home. For example, when planning a day out, I must give my family advance warning, detailed plans, visual and verbal cues, show videos or photos of where we are going, outline what they can expect to happen and what I think will happen.

Once we are out, I keep checking in to manage the environment, scan the horizon, answer questions and defuse situations. Once we're back home we have a debrief and I know a detail of something that happened during that trip can be referred to for months to come, particularly if it was negative. Something I couldn't have predicted, such as a pre-planned menu choice not being available, or an inability to decide something, causes a meltdown as their nervous system is dysregulated.

This isn't dissimilar to the way I manage change communication! The parallels between my personal and professional life have converged. I've had to relearn how I communicate and make reasonable adjustments in every area of my life as I've discovered more about myself and my family.

Consider your organization, do you know how many employees are neurodivergent? How are you making internal communication work for them? Are there reasonable adjustments you could make to your internal communication to aid neuro-inclusivity?

For example:

- The option to turn off cameras during online meetings
- Replacing verbal instructions with written
- Allowing extra time to read
- Variety of activities in training scenarios
- Noise-cancelling headphones
- Captions on videos
- Circulating meeting/employee event agendas
- Clear visuals, such as maps
- Making fidget toys available to aid concentration (I provide postcards to doodle on and LEGO in my training courses)
- Transcripts from audio such as podcasts
- Software to record and transcribe meetings and town halls
- Coloured paper to support people with dyslexia
- Using different colours to help organize and process information

The best way to know insights about your workforce is by listening to them. Don't make decisions about your neurodivergent colleagues in your internal communication strategy without involving them. Speak with your HR or people colleagues too, to hear their perspectives about your workforce.

Key priorities for neurodiversity

The Neurodiversity at Work 2023 report was commissioned by the Neurodiversity in Business Report Commission in partnership with Birkbeck, University of London and sponsored by Rolls-Royce, McDonald's and Sage. It was undertaken by Professor Almuth McDowall, Professor Nancy Doyle and Dr Meg Kiseleva (2023). The report's authors identified key priorities for the neurodiversity in business movement:

- Make well-being and inclusion for everyone, including ND workers, a pillar of corporate strategy to harness diverse talent.

- Objectively evaluate and promote the effectiveness of adjustments to find out what works for whom, and how quality of provision can be bench-marked and shared.
- Focus on relationships, in particular psychological safety and line manager confidence, to foster joint responsibility.
- Consider how policies and practices can develop careers and ambitions, beyond surviving, to thriving.

TIP FROM RACHEL

Committing to communicate well with neurodivergent employees could form a principle in your internal communication strategy.

EXPERT VIEW
Adele McIntosh

Arm is a leading semiconductor IP company, whose technologies reach 70 per cent of the global population. It has more than 6,000 employees from 85+ nationalities and has shipped more than 250 billion Arm-based chips to date.

Adele McIntosh is Arm's Vice President, Internal Communications. She says the organization gives its people the capabilities, processes and infrastructure to enable them to develop and thrive as the business scales and strengthens.

At the same time, Arm seeks to nurture a work culture that remains true to its founders' original vision; 'empowering engineers to be innovative and drive Arm-based technology into all areas where computing happens, maximizing their creative potential and enabling all of our people to be their brilliant selves.'

Celebrating neurodiversity

Part of that work to enable people to bring their authentic selves to work every day and reach their full potential, is the company's focus on celebrating and supporting neurodiversity.

'We're focused on bringing awareness to our neurodivergent community by sharing a range of support specifically designed for those with neurodivergent traits or a diagnosed neurodivergence, as well as guidance for their managers. We're supporting our neurodiverse employees while building a workplace that works for everyone' says McIntosh.

Some of the methods in place at Arm include:

Dedicated quiet rooms – for those that struggle to engage due to ADHD, photophobia or sound sensitivity, there are focused work areas in dedicated quiet areas in Arm offices, including the company headquarters in Cambridge, UK.

Neurodiversity Employee Resource Group – set up to enable all neurodivergent colleagues to reach their full potential, while building understanding for those who are neurotypical.

Partnership with Genius Within – to help support neurodiverse employees, Arm has partnered with Genius Within to offer a screening assessment tool, workplace needs assessment and coaching.

Neurodiversity Parent and Carer Group – an open community of people offering support, experiences, guidance and resources for parents and carers of neurodivergent children.

Partnership with Neurodiversity in Business – to enable Arm to operate as a neuro-inclusive workplace, with good practice on neurodiverse recruitment, retention and empowerment.

Neurodivergent, equity and inclusion training – for managers to support neurodiverse employees within the workplace.

McIntosh adds: 'One of the pillars of my team's work is community and belonging, where we focus on helping our people to feel included and part of the wider Arm community through our communications. We use our internal communications principles to guide us, including that we are curious; we understand and amplify the voices of our people; and that we are evidence-based in our decision making. As part of this, we are mindful of how we communicate with our neurodivergent employees.'

The organization has worked alongside employees to make decisions that impact them. McIntosh says: 'We have consulted with them on how they can have a great experience at our internal events, for example, ensuring that music is not loo loud, and we have quiet spaces at our big events. Expectations for meetings are set in advance with pre-reading to ensure time for reflection, if possible. We also amplify their voices by supporting our neurodiversity ERG (Employee Resource Group) awareness campaigns internally, helping everyone at Arm to understand how you experience the world if you are part of our neurodivergent community. Key to this are our efforts to minimize bias by modelling vulnerability at all levels, including senior leadership. During our awareness campaigns, employees across the company – including leaders – have spoken openly about their experience and coping methods.'

Analysing integrity gaps

Organizational integrity means the 'values on the wall are reflected in the day-to-day behaviours. There is no "say–do" gap. Promises made and promises kept, or an explanation given as to why not' (MacLeod and Clarke, 2009).

Internal communicators are well versed in spotting integrity gaps and dealing with ambiguity because companies are rife with haphazard communication methods, speculation, and assumptions. Our role includes creating clarity and certainty inside organizations, and we rely on accurate information to inform our work. We strive to create sources of truth and are tenacious in our approach.

Internal communicators root out speculation, rumours and myths and replace ambiguity with certainty. We spot the integrity gaps and recommend ways to close them. Sometimes this is through IC channels, leaders, internal networks, comms champions or ambassadors.

As communicators create clear lines of sight and plot the path ahead, our position as strategic counsel and trusted advisers embeds itself. We need to zoom in and out constantly; focusing on the broader organizational perspectives, but also pinpointing accurately to inform a cohesive narrative. I think of this like a camera lens; you need to concentrate on sharpening the focus and understand what makes it blurry. Promises being made, but not kept, are one sure way of creating integrity gaps, as employees have long memories.

Mapping the knowns and unknowns

There is a method I use when planning communication or when facing an uncertain situation, such as organizational change. I turn to a fresh page in a notebook or create a new document on my computer. I put a vertical line down the centre and write 'known knowns' on one side and 'known unknowns' on the other side.

Transformational communication is deluged with unknowns. I keep the chrysalis-to-butterfly image in mind when talking about transformation. It's wholescale; you're changing form from one state to another, such as a restructure or merger/acquisition. It could also be a change in mindset, which could be an updated purpose, new leadership or values. Something that fundamentally changes the fabric of an organization is a transformation. Everything else is iterative and evolutionary.

TABLE 3.1 Known knowns and known unknowns

Known knowns	Known unknowns
No formal IC strategy in place	Whether there's ever been an IC strategy
CEO is asking to see an IC strategy	When the CEO expects to see it
Departmental strategies are in PowerPoint	Haven't seen external/PR/HR ones yet
We have company purpose, mission and vision	Unsure if employees know what they are
There are five strategic pillars in place	Don't know if there's a prioritized order for pillars
Organizational strategy runs for five years	Whether to create a one-year or five-year IC strategy
We will be merging with another company	Timeline is unclear. Don't fully know the impact
Attrition is high	Why people are leaving
Organizational pride is low	What stops employees feeling proud to work here
People managers unclear how to communicate	Investment in people managers' skills to date
We have a full suite of IC channels	Individual channel purpose is unknown. No analytics

Former US Secretary of Defense Donald Rumsfeld spoke about known knowns, known unknowns and unknown unknowns (CNN, 2016). It's now referred to as the Rumsfeld matrix, a four-box model that includes *known knowns, known unknowns, unknown knowns* and *unknown unknowns* (Krogerus, Tschäppeler and Piening, 2012).

I use a simplified version of this technique, which works when gathering insights about an organization for an internal communication strategy. Table 3.1 reveals how it works in practice.

You could complete it twice; the first time to help you think about why the strategy is being created, and the second time to help you analyse your organization. Sometimes I use this method to help me create the hypothesis for an audit.

If you are trying to create strategic objectives, it can help you get to the heart of why the strategy is needed, and therefore what you need to focus on through setting objectives or goals.

How to create strategic objectives

Dewhurst and FitzPatrick (2022) caution against 'vague' communication objectives, which don't stand up to questioning:

> Wanting people to feel 'engaged' is a common *feel* objective; but how many questions does your organization have in its engagement survey? What does it mean to feel engaged? How would you measure it? What about a *do* objective of 'embrace change'? What does it mean? Ask yourself whether you'd be prepared to stake your annual bonus on attaining the targets you set. It's a good way of focusing your mind on what's achievable.

Being smart

Chapter 2 highlighted the need for strategic objectives. When you are gathering insights for an internal communication strategy and considering creating objectives, remember to make them SMART.

This stands for:

- Specific
- Measurable
- Achievable
- Relevant
- Timely/time-bound

In Chapter 6 you'll find an example of a SMART communication objective, which relates to a business objective.

Here are some examples of SMART objectives:

- The IC team will work with line managers to increase in-person attendance at the monthly town halls by 20 per cent by the end of the next financial year.
- We will oversee an internal campaign aimed at US-based employees, to encourage 50 per cent higher completion rate in the annual employee survey over the next three months.
- Over the next six months, the IC team will provide leaders with targeted training to increase their confidence answering questions about the upcoming office moves.
- All content created by the IC team will reflect our refreshed company values, which employees will be able to accurately recall within three months.

TIP FROM RACHEL

You need to know why your internal communication strategy exists. Is it an overarching one that will run for 12 months or longer? Is it targeted to a specific goal such as improving safety or to guide your organization through an upcoming merger?

EXPERT VIEW
Alexandra Bîrlădianu

Alexandra Bîrlădianu is Head of Corporate Communication at Guardian Industries. The privately held company is one of the world's largest manufacturers of high-performance float glass; coated and fabricated glass products for architectural, residential, interior, transportation and technical glass applications; and high-quality chrome-plated and painted plastic components for the automotive and commercial truck industries. Her team includes internal communicators in Luxembourg and America. Guardian Industries has employees in manufacturing sites and factories around the globe and operates facilities throughout North and South America, Europe, Africa, the Middle East and Asia.

Communication in action at Guardian Industries

The Corporate Communication vision is focused on innovatively using the company internal communication channels to create, maintain and nurture a meaningful and mutually beneficial relationship with employees. Through these channels, we are providing content that is helping colleagues in their roles and is easily accessible. Our aim is to enable a dialogue where employees feel they can share information and knowledge, ask questions and engage with our team. We want to be a preferred partner to both business leadership and our colleagues, and create value for the organization. As we work and learn what our audiences value, we can enhance our offerings.

Internal comms objectives at Guardian Industries
Our internal communications should help employees do better in their roles by:

- **Transforming how senior leadership communicates** with the organization, making it inclusive (so employees can relate to it), accessible (in content and presentation) and measurable (to understand engagement and respond).

- **Partnering organizational change** to ensure employee commitment: that they are aware of it, understand it, believe in it and commit to it.

- **Supporting the role of the supervisor** by providing a helicopter view of the business through a digital internal communication platform (The Hub). Together with supervisors, The Hub is a source of truth on business priorities, performance and achievements.

- **Acknowledging and recognizing employees' contribution** to improving people's lives (both inside and outside of work), increasing pride in their work, raising employee retention and strengthening our employer brand.

SOURCE Alexandra Bîrlădianu, 2023

When considering the importance of having an internal communication strategy, Bîrlădianu says 'if you want buy-in from your company leadership and from colleagues across the business, you must have a solid internal communication strategy in place. It needs to help others understand where you want to go and hold you accountable for achieving your vision and objectives. These need to be aligned with the business vision and objectives because as a function, we exist to support the business and our employees'.

It's not enough to design and develop an internal communication strategy, we need to know how to implement it too. Bîrlădianu recognizes this and says 'applying a communication strategy is crucial because when we are brought to the table early, we have trust and buy-in'. She says having a robust internal communication strategy they can talk through helps the team to be effective and efficient as they can focus on:

1 Strategic planning

2 Channel mix, based on how well they know the audience

3 Measuring the effectiveness of their efforts

At Guardian Industries, its internal communication strategy is seen as a mechanism to have a joined-up view across the organization. Bîrlădianu says 'in times of change or business transformation, while we might work on initiatives separately, our employees experience everything at the same time. Therefore, it is crucial we have a joined-up view of everything happening in the organization, and this needs to be communicated. Our strategy helps us to formulate our thinking and demonstrate what we are focusing on and why'.

Questions to answer

Bîrlădianu and her team view preparing their IC strategy as an opportunity for experimentation. They've challenged themselves to know the answers to the following questions:

- When is the best time to publish a message on our internal platforms?

- What's the best day to send an email to inform the organization? When can we have the best open rate or click rate?
- There are many tactics in place, such as videos, podcasts and infographics. What is the best tactic for what we are trying to achieve?

She acknowledges the benefit of industry data and case studies. However, Bîrlădianu urges internal communicators to gather insights and conduct their *own* internal experimentation. 'Internal evidence and insights mean you can advise your stakeholders best when it comes to your internal audience. Your research helps you know what they need in terms of information to succeed in their roles.'

Measurement is vital for internal communication. You cannot assess success, design new experiments, learn and pivot (when needed) without measurement. Guardian Industries has a quarterly report they discuss as a team every month.

It includes:

- Monthly priorities and experiments, informed by the business vision and business priorities. This section of the report gives an overview of various actions taken during the previous quarter, and the results.
- Lessons learnt and overall stop/start/continue actions.
- Upcoming priorities and experiments – giving an overview of what they will try to achieve in the coming quarter.

The report then goes in-depth, including quantitative numbers and key performance indicators (KPIs) for key corporate communication and content, such as their intranet, The Hub, traffic (return visits, visits, views, content count, traffic flow), live events, resource centres, top content and internal emails, and leadership communication. They draw conclusions from the numbers, with overall takeaways and stop/start/continue suggestions for each stakeholder.

Every three years they conduct an in-depth audit with surveys in multiple languages and focus groups, targeting 20 per cent of employees.

Measurement strategy

Bîrlădianu attended the All Things IC Live 10th anniversary event I hosted in London in 2023 and says it inspired her to review and simplify her measurement strategy. She says it takes into consideration the following areas:

1 **Inputs:** our audiences and the information and materials we need.
2 **Outputs:** quantifiable information, such as number of articles published, clicks on stories, likes, comments and shares.

3 **Outtakes:** response and reactions of our target audiences to internal communication activities.

4 **Outcomes:** what happens as a result of the communications we are developing – such as change in behaviour in the context of transformation initiatives, for example. How we will identify these:

    a. **Colleague sentiment:** pulse surveys, employee surveys, networks of knowledge, coffee corner discussions.

    b. **Behaviour change:** examples may include more safety incidents reporting, the quality of questions during town halls, peer-to-peer recognition.

    c. **Focus groups:** bringing colleagues together to discuss their views on specific topics.

    d. **myHR data:** recruitment and retention rates, internal moves, etc.

Establishing a knowledge network

If you have a small IC team, Bîrlădianu advises establishing a *knowledge network* for internal communication. 'It can be hard to fully connect to the local reality at each facility, and having a local internal communication ambassador can help with making communication inclusive, accessible and measurable.'

Guardian Industries' IC team wanted to tap into the dispersed knowledge in the business, so they launched a network of ambassadors for their intranet, The Hub. This has helped them to identify local and regional communication opportunities, and take the Hub to shop floor colleagues. The IC team benefits from feedback on how they're doing and has helped them constantly improve. The ambassadors are a cross-regional, cross-business network of people, dedicated to developing interesting, relevant content to engage employees with the company's vision and priorities and advance their culture.

Bîrlădianu says that working together, they have two-way conversations, share global and regional news locally (and vice versa), and develop better methods for doing so.

Knowledge network

The knowledge network and local ambassadors have a number of goals:

- Share better stories using appropriate methods at a local level.
- Promote effective two-way engagement and communication.
- Ensure communication happens at the right place and right time.

They also have Hub Regional Coordinators, as well as Hub Ambassadors in most of their locations globally. The IC team meet with them every four to eight weeks.

Cultural considerations

Bîrlădianu says while the company has one organizational culture, it has 'different ways in which people interact. This means as communicators we need to experiment with different approaches and try to create tactics, because not all the content we share will work in all markets. What we're trying to do is help them stay informed and do better in their roles'.

EXPERT VIEW
Dr Leandro Herrero

Dr Leandro Herrero is the CEO and Chief Organization Architect of The Chalfont Project, an international firm of organizational architects. He is the pioneer of Viral Change™, a people mobilizing platform, a methodology that delivers large-scale behavioural and cultural change in organizations, which creates lasting capacity for changeability. Dr Herrero is also an Executive Fellow at the Centre for the Future of Organization, Drucker School of Management.

He has written several books on change, leadership and management innovation, including *Viral Change: The alternative to slow, painful and unsuccessful management of change in organizations* (2006, 2008) and its follow-up, *Homo Imitans: The art of social infection;* Viral Change *in action* (2011).

Telling the story

His advice when considering strategy is that if you care about the journey and the place, you need a story. 'If you have a good, compelling one, there will be lots of good people travelling with you.'

Herrero champions success and failure scenarios in his work, encouraging organizations to imagine it's a year from now and employees are in front of the CEO saying 'we screwed up!' – he encourages writing the script for that year, what happened to take you there? Herrero runs these exercises with parallel sub-teams of boards, top leadership teams or management teams. They are asked to write those scripts, or at least find all the pieces and assemble them as a script would have been constructed – novel, film, short story.

He says people are incredibly good at writing these scripts and the failure scenario is invariably faster, and they can relate to them much better than an account of goals and targets as written in the strategic plan. Why? Herrero says 'the storytellers inside all of us seem to enjoy the questions and the production of answers.'

Use of language

Putting this into action inside organizations means being conscious of language use. For example, Herrero says he's switched from 'mission and visions' to 'space in the world' and 'compelling narrative' instead. However, it's not a simple change of terms. The questions are different. The emphasis is 'what do you want to be remembered for?' and 'what's the story?'

This is built upon by writing down the headlines you'd like to see in a year's time, or whatever the time frame. A couple of lines. Herrero says he 'has seen more Executives surprise each other in this exercise than in many other times of interaction. These visual narratives are very powerful and bring the authentic part of us to the surface.'

When thinking about the way companies communicate, Herrero says 'it's scripts, narratives and stories, not targets, numbers and earnings per share. There is nothing intrinsically wrong with such figures, but the signposts are not the places themselves.' This is where storytelling comes in.

What about culture?

Herrero urges professionals to consider how everything works together. 'If the business is the mission, culture is the strategy', and describes culture as 'probably your most important asset. Entire companies thrive commercially on the back of a culture, or fail miserably because of it.'

However, Herrero warns culture is never 'done', like a project finished and milestones achieved. He says culture is not the simple sum of components, processes, systems and behaviours; written and unwritten rules; leadership and fellowship. Instead, he says culture is 'in construction' every day.

What is culture?

Herrero says that even the type of furniture and the size of the windows is a component of the culture. The size of your inbox, the number of meetings per week and per capita is also culture. Leaders eating in the cafeteria, or not, is culture. The voice at the other end of the telephone in the call centre is culture. It is the smile of the receptionist, the way a nurse introduces themselves in a hospital, the hotel room service, the speed of a reaction to a complaint.

He says 'all working practices are culture. All ways of doing, all airtime, the concept of a priority, and the differences, or matches, between the values on the wall and behaviours on the ground. The alpha and omega of culture is behaviours.

'*Behaviours create cultures*. I don't have to study reams of corporate documentation; tell me what behaviours you have and I will tell you what culture you are in. Tell me what you do, not what you think, not what you proclaim.'

Herrero frequently uses the model of the 'Petri dish' as a proxy for culture. Culture is the Petri dish of the company, that is 'where things grow'. Good or bad but they grow, he says. Behaviours are the input, 'what to put in it'. What grows may be something we might call 'a culture of accountability, or trust, or any other outcome'. Herrero says that many problems in the organizational world come from confusing input and output. Trust, for example, is an output. You can't inject trust. You can however inject behaviours that, when at scale, an external observer could say 'This is a culture high on trust'.

In conclusion, Herrero says culture is 'simply strategy in action. Magnificent or sloppy, ambitious or middle of the road, thriving or broken. Culture is strategy.'

SOURCE Dr Leandro Herrero, 2023

How to turn insights into action in an IC strategy

One way to illustrate turning insights into action is through an IC audit.

Using an audit to inform an IC strategy

There are various reasons why organizations decide to audit their internal communication. Audits can be conducted by an in-house team or outsourced to a consultancy.

When I was working in-house in the railway, we conducted our own audit and I found the whole process enjoyable. It's crucial to remain impartial, which is tough to do when it feels like employees are critiquing your work! It is possible to conduct your own. If remaining impartial feels like it would be a challenge, I recommend asking a trusted colleague in another department, such as HR, to facilitate focus groups on your behalf.

Listening to employees

You may choose to use an audit to collate insights to inform the development of an internal communication strategy. In Chapter 1, I highlighted the origin of the word audit, which is to listen, or hear. Professional communicators need to be in listening mode constantly inside organizations. Audits are just one method of listening and the whole process is something I love doing, it taps into my inquisitive nature as I love uncovering what's happening inside an organization and experiencing it from the inside out.

Audit advice

Consistency is key with IC audits, I've developed my own techniques to ensure I'm able to gather the required quantitative and qualitative data. I always advise having a hypothesis – or conclusion – in mind and being clear on the purpose of the audit; this helps you keep focused and on track. It also means you can gauge whether you have collated relevant evidence as you go. Refer to the hypothesis throughout the process to guarantee you're not deviating from the audit's goal.

Not having a hypothesis means the fascinating insights you uncover can veer you down a different path. Therefore, you can end up with a lot of data, but it will be vast. You need to have a clear goal in mind and seek out quality information to evidence your hypothesis.

Your hypothesis can be one line. It is the purpose of your audit – why you want to conduct it. Ask yourself what conclusion you want to be able to make at the end. Here are some examples – you would then seek to prove or disprove the statement:

- Shop floor employees don't receive operational information from leaders in a timely-enough manner.
- Our current internal communication methods are suitable for the organization.
- Leaders are not viewed as trustworthy inside the organization.
- People managers know how they need to communicate.
- It is not clear how internal communication happens here.
- Our crisis communication plans are robust.

Being clear on the purpose of the audit helps you to keep on track. Once you know your hypothesis, you will then go into 'listening mode' and find evidence, or proof points that help you create a full picture of how internal communication happens.

Once you know the current state, you can then design the future state and decide how you reflect it in your internal communication strategy to turn it into reality. Don't do an audit for audit's sake. They take a lot of time, effort and investment to do well. Do not listen if you're not intending to take action. This is not the best use of time and doesn't honour the investment you and your colleagues have made. If you are committing to audit, you need to see it through and commit to do something with what you learn.

QUESTIONS TO ASK YOURSELF BEFORE
AUDITING AN ORGANIZATION

Why do I want this audit to take place?

What outcome/s am I aiming for?

Who will own the process?

What do I hope to do as a result of conducting this audit?

How will the audit help me in my work?

What do I want to prove or disprove?

Who are the best people to conduct it?

Can I do it all myself internally?

Should I invite peers or an external party to help?

What are my available resources in terms of time and budget?

What will I do with the results?

Aligning interesting data across a comms function

In Chapter 2, I encouraged you to read and consider your organization's external communication strategy. The organizational goals, vision and mission are the same for the respective disciplines, so the foundations of each strategy should align. The main differences are the objectives, intended outcomes and employee groups. However, the lines between internal and external blur constantly, not least due to the rise of employee advocacy.

In internal communication we look at the business's strategic aims, goals and objectives from an employee (internal) perspective and what they mean inside the organization, whereas external communication considers those aims from an outside (external) perspective and what they mean for customers, clients and stakeholders. Areas such as advocacy create a grey area, as they blur that hard line between internal and external when employees' voices are heard externally, advocating for the company. The same is true for our careers sites, where internal stories are shared to help potential colleagues get a glimpse of our culture, through the views and voices of existing employees.

The way to use the information you gather through your insights research or audit, is to analyse the business problems it helps you solve. Or how it informs your approach. For example, if the insights you gather reveal colleagues feel like change is done *to them*, not *for and with* them, this will impact how you create messaging in future. Or if there is an issue with line manager communication, it's likely you'll want to address this to aid the flow of communication inside the organization.

STRATEGY CREATION CHECKLIST

Make notes and decisions on the following points, before moving on to the next chapter. This will help you write your strategy as you read through this book. As a result of working your way through this chapter, you should now have:

- Researched what insights exist in your organization.
- Looked at employee data and spotted any gaps.
- Spoken with the HR or people team to understand more about neurodiversity in your organization.
- Written personas or captured relevant demographic data to inform your IC strategy.
- Thought about known knowns and known unknowns that are relevant for your strategy.
- Determined strategic objectives and outlined what you want to achieve.
- Considered whether you want to conduct an audit.
  - o Decided to audit? Think through your hypothesis.
- Read relevant strategies from other departments.

Review the choices you've made while reading through this chapter. Make sure you've captured what has resonated and what feels appropriate for your organization.

References and further reading

Bates, P and Patel, A (2023) *Building a Culture of Inclusivity: Effective internal communication for diversity, equity and inclusion*, Kogan Page, London.
Bîrlădianu, A (2023) Interview/correspondence with the author

CIPD (2018) Neurodiversity at work, 15 February, www.cipd.org/uk/knowledge/
    guides/neurodiversity-work/ (archived at https://perma.cc/9WLF-M25J)

CNN (2016) Donald Rumsfeld Knowns, online video, 31 March, www.youtube.
    com/watch?v=REWeBzGuzCc (archived at https://perma.cc/R3CU-JJ8R)

Davis, A (2007) *Mastering Public Relations*, 2nd edn, Palgrave Macmillan,
    Basingstoke

Dewhurst, S and FitzPatrick, L (2022) *Successful Employee Communications: A
    practitioner's guide to tools, models and best practice for internal communica-
    tion*, 2nd edn, Kogan Page, London

GCS (2021) RESIST 2 Counter Disinformation Toolkit, Government
    Communication Service, gcs.civilservice.gov.uk/publications/resist-2-counter-
    disinformation-toolkit/ (archived at https://perma.cc/EAB2-X29J)

Gioia, D A, Thomas, J B, Clark, S M and Chittipeddi, K (1994) Symbolism and
    strategic change in academia: The dynamics of sensemaking and influence,
    Organization Science, 5 (3), 363–83, doi.org/10.1287/orsc.5.3.363 (archived at
    https://perma.cc/A3ES-ZDMV)

Herrero, L (2023) Interview/correspondence with the author

IoIC (2023a) IC Index 2023, Institute of Internal Communication, www.ioic.org.
    uk/resource/ic-index-report-2023.html (archived at https://perma.cc/QHD5-
    CBHA)

IoIC (2023b) The Profession Map: The core, Institute of Internal Communication,
    www.ioic.org.uk/learn-develop/the-profession-map/the-core.html (archived at
    https://perma.cc/GWF2-L7HV)

Krogerus, M, Tschäppeler, R and Piening, J (2012) *The Decision Book: Fifty
    models for strategic thinking*, W W Norton & Co, New York

Lafley, A G and Martin, R L (2013) *Playing to Win: How strategy really works*,
    Harvard Business Review Press, Boston, MA

MacLeod, D and Clarke, N (2009) Engaging for Success: Enhancing performance
    through employee engagement, Department of Business, Innovation and Skills,
    engageforsuccess.org/wp-content/uploads/2020/12/engaging-for-success.pdf
    (archived at https://perma.cc/R59Q-7SFQ)

McDowall A, Doyle, N and Kiseleva M (2023) Neurodiversity at Work 2023:
    Demand, supply and a gap analysis, Birkbeck University of London,
    eprints.bbk.ac.uk/id/eprint/50834/ (archived at https://perma.cc/4SYP-ZB4Z)

Miller, R (2021) The internal communicator's guide to hybrid working, All Things
    IC Blog, 17 April, www.allthingsic.com/the-internal-communicators-guide-to-
    hybrid-working/ (archived at https://perma.cc/VK2S-U7F2)

Murgatroyd, S (2015) Work is a thing you do, not a place you go, All Things IC
    Blog, 6 August, www.allthingsic.com/office/ (archived at https://perma.cc/548U-
    CSSN)

Oxfam (2023) Inclusive Language Guide, 13 March, policy-practice.oxfam.org/resources/inclusive-language-guide-621487/ (archived at https://perma.cc/YPJ2-C5EF)

Ruck, K (2015) *Exploring Internal Communication: Towards informed employee voice*, 3rd edn, Gower Publishing, Farnham

Ruck, K (2019) Who's listening? PR Academy, 18 November, pracademy.co.uk/insights/whos-listening/ (archived at https://perma.cc/JJH8-3GXV)

The Law Society (2021) Reasonable adjustments in organisations – guidance for best practice, www.lawsociety.org.uk/topics/lawyers-with-disabilities/reasonable-adjustments-in-organisations-best-practice-for-disability-inclusion (archived at https://perma.cc/WWE5-TQ2P)

Toyota (2013) Genchi Genbutsu – Toyota Production System Guide, Toyota UK Magazine, 31 May, mag.toyota.co.uk/genchi-genbutsu/ (archived at https://perma.cc/QK3W-9667)

Weinberg, A and Doyle, N (2017) Psychology at work: Improving wellbeing and productivity in the workplace, British Psychological Society, www.bps.org.uk/guideline/psychology-work-improving-wellbeing-and-productivity-workplace (archived at https://perma.cc/GV2M-XB4J)

Williams, B (2010) When will we work out loud? Soon! TheBrycesWrite, 29 November, thebryceswrite.com/2010/11/29/when-will-we-work-out-loud-soon/ (archived at https://perma.cc/9HP3-5C7W)

Yeomans, L and Bowman, S (2021) Internal crisis communication and the social construction of emotion: University leaders' sensegiving discourse during the COVID-19 pandemic, *Journal of Communication Management*, 25 (3), 196–213, doi.org/10.1108/JCOM-11-2020-0130 (archived at https://perma.cc/N2C7-D6PP)

Yohn, D L (2021) Use employee personas to design employee experience for a hybrid workforce, *Forbes*, 4 May, www.forbes.com/sites/deniselyohn/2021/05/04/use-employee-personas-to-design-employee-experience-for-a-hybrid-workforce/?sh=7b13709d5f47 (archived at https://perma.cc/F7XS-GA38)

4

How internal communication happens

WHAT THIS CHAPTER WILL COVER

This chapter analyses the logistics of internal communication. We'll examine how to create strong foundations and why you need to set internal communication standards. As a result of reading this chapter, you will know how to include logistics in your internal communication strategy. You will find a checklist at the end of this and every chapter to help you keep on track.

The MILLER Framework: Logistics

Organizations need to ensure their internal communications tools, tactics, channels and methodologies are robust, planned and measurable. The logistics stage of The MILLER Framework for strategy creation focuses on *how internal communication happens* and *what is prioritized*. It's crucial to address both these areas to create a shared understanding and meaning for all employees and help them align their efforts to an organization's strategy.

We enable employees to deliver the organization's strategy and purpose; this doesn't mean 'selling it in' to them, but empowering and equipping them to live it daily through their work. They are critical stakeholders and need to feel that way. When internal communication is an afterthought, your people are the first to realize.

Employees feel second best when press releases are published internally, without highlighting the people behind the story, or any additional context.

Internal communication deserves careful thought and attention because your employees deserve thought and attention. They need to be treated as valuable stakeholders or interested parties; you need to attract their interest and attention. Therefore, you need to know how internal communication happens.

In Chapters 2 and 3 we examined the mindset and insights required for an internal communication strategy. You cannot determine the logistics required to transform an organization's communication before knowing *business priorities, vision and why internal communication is important* (mindset), plus *what we know about the organization and its people* (insights). Mindset and insights create the destination and why you're heading down a certain path. Logistics are the route you will take.

Bringing vision to life

We examined creating a vision for internal communication in Chapter 2. The logistics part of an IC strategy includes *how* you are bringing that vision to life. If you aspire to *connect all employees so they know what's happening in the organization and why their role is important* for example, what needs to be in place to turn that into reality?

You need to highlight priorities, otherwise you run the risk of trying to do everything, which can create a sense of overwhelm for employees and yourself. You may decide a traditional IC strategy can be replaced with something shorter, such as a mission statement (why the team exists) and what communication needs to focus on.

QUESTIONS TO ASK

- What is the internal communication strategy aiming to achieve?

- What is important to the organization? (See Chapter 1.)

- In succinct form, why does the strategy exist? For example, to inform, engage and inspire employees. Or perhaps to increase employee voice or increase leadership visibility.

If you know what your internal communication strategy is aiming to achieve, that's the language and priorities to mirror in the strategy document. Clearly show the business priorities and how they have informed the IC priorities.

Designing internal communication

Communication should not be left to chance. You need to know how communication flows, or what stops it from rippling through a company.

Professional communicators frequently talk about *cascading* inside organizations. I dislike the term because it invokes an image of a waterfall – a one-way deluge of water flowing from the top to the bottom. We invest a huge amount of effort as internal communicators championing two-way flows of communication.

We encourage conversations to flow from the bottom to the top of a company and vice versa. Therefore, I prefer to think of organizational communication as a water wheel. The inputs are converted to output energy in the form of conversations, which power an organization. The cyclical nature requires a shift from monologue to dialogue, where employees feel involved, listened to and encouraged to contribute.

As internal communicator Katie Macaulay noted in her 2014 book of the same name, we need to be moving *from cascade to conversation* inside organizations.

In this chapter I will share techniques with you that I use to determine the logistics of an organization's internal communication, and how to include this in an internal communication strategy.

Being intentional with internal communication

My Internal Communication Relevancy model depicts how internal communication is designed inside organizations (Figure 4.1).

FIGURE 4.1 Internal Communication Relevancy model

MAKING INTERNAL COMMUNICATION RELEVANT

Let's look at communicating change. In this scenario, I typically observe internal communicators using a *global–local–me* approach when designing messaging and developing the internal communication.

The linear path goes something like this:

- **Global** messaging from CEO: 'We need to save $20 million over the next year and will be restructuring the business to achieve those savings. Your people manager will give you more information and tell you if your area is impacted.'

- **Local** messaging from people leaders: 'We need to save $20 million over the next year and will be restructuring the business to achieve those savings Unfortunately our team is impacted. Let me tell you what I know about what's happening.'

- **Me** concerns from employees: 'What's happening to my role? Do I need to worry? When will I know what these changes mean?'

NOTE You could put arrows from *me* to *global* and vice versa.

Deciphering and translating

Internal communicators often design and plan internal communication in that way, creating messaging and content with a global mindset first. It's important to note *global* doesn't only mean international, it can also mean *across the organization* or even *from one department.*

We strive to communicate with a diverse group of employees; therefore, each stage causes the information to become more relevant and targeted. How? The arrows in the model.

The arrows depict the translation and increase in relevancy, from *global* to *local*, and *local* to *me*. Translating or increasing relevancy can mean language, but it also means deciphering, reframing and explaining. When this is not in place, the flow of information stops, which means communication doesn't happen.

The role of people managers

We rely on leaders and people managers to make sense of the data for their people. They are required to adapt and personalize it for their team members, to increase the chance of communication happening successfully.

Organizations need to be championing 'meaningful interactions which promote dignity, self-appreciation, and a sense of worthwhileness' (Kahn, 1990). From an internal communication perspective, meaningful interactions include personalization and having clarity of the value – or worth – that you have as an employee. Our people need to feel what they are hearing and experiencing has been carefully created and made relevant for them.

We expect employees at the *local* level to feed questions, concerns and feedback back up to the *global* level, as depicted by the arrows.

For this to work, leaders and people managers need to understand their role is the translation. This is where communication can break down. Our role as professional communicators is to ensure leaders at all levels understand their role is to facilitate conversations and drive dialogue. Leaders need to be able to determine what the information or change means to their teams/individuals and to listen and collate questions. We will address people managers further in Chapter 5.

People managers are often described as 'middle' managers. Field, Hancock and Schaninger (2023) say the word *middle* implies the person in that spot is on the way to somewhere else – ideally the top. However, they say, 'that thinking is misguided. Middle managers are at the centre of the action. Without the ability of middle managers to connect and integrate people and tasks, an organization can cease to function effectively. Middle managers act as key players in an organization's competition for talent.'

This model implies a hierarchical – top-down vertical flow – structure in place in an organization. However, you can also use it across a horizontal network or matrixed organization, where employees report to multiple leaders. In that case, the local level could also mean internal influencers, comms champions or advocates.

Developing internal communication

I've designed intranets using my *global–local–me* approach – content that is applicable across the organization goes at the top, then country-specific or departmental content is in the middle of the page or screen, then personalized *me* content is at the bottom. Guess what employees do? They scroll straight to the bottom of the page or screen, to get to what's important and relevant for them.

FIGURE 4.2   Internal Communication Relevancy model (inverted)

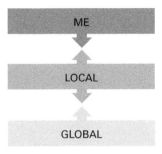

In the change scenario I've outlined, do you think employees can listen to the messaging their people leader is saying, particularly if they are repeating what's been shared at a *global* level first? No.

So, what's the answer? I recommend inverting the model to become *me–local–global* (Figure 4.2).

Therefore, the messaging becomes *me* focused from the outset. A people leader's conversation with their team wouldn't merely repeat *global* messaging, they would start with *me*.

- **Me** messaging from people leaders: 'Unfortunately our team is impacted by the proposed restructure you heard the CEO announce at the all-employee meeting. Let me tell you what I know about what's happening and the potential changes we are facing. You can ask me any questions and I will share what I can and pass your questions on.' (They would then have individual discussions with team members.)

- **Local** messaging from people leaders: 'We are not the only department being impacted in our region. Your colleagues in XYZ department are also having conversations with their people leaders now.'

- **Global** messaging from people leaders: 'These proposed changes are because we need to save $20 million over the next year. It is hoped the restructure will achieve those savings.'

You need to reverse it because the team want to hear how they are impacted first. They won't listen to the *global* or *local* bits because they are relying on people managers to share 'this is what it means for you/us' – the *me* element.

My experience of internal communication reveals this to be true and every single time I've shared this model with clients or masterclass attendees, they confirm it. The arrows are critical because we need to be listening actively at every stage *and* ensuring we have effective two-way channels in place.

FIGURE 4.3 Circular relevancy model

Circular communication

I've used the linear version of my relevancy model since 2013 and developed a circular version in 2023 (Figure 4.3). This aligns with my thinking of the water wheel and *conversations* rather than *cascades*.

It also allows you to have communication flowing from *me* to *global* and vice versa.

Using this model in your internal communication strategy

TIP FROM RACHEL

You could use either the linear or circular version of my relevancy model in your internal communication strategy, to outline how internal communication happens in your organization. If you are striving to transform organizational communication, determine *who* or *what* is referred to at each stage.

Considerations

- What does *global* mean in your organization? Who or what does it relate to?

Ask the same question for all three stages.

- Map your channels to show where they fit in and how they flow to and from each other. Or how they inform each other (signposting).
- How does relevancy increase or decrease in your organization? What impacts it?
- Who are the key internal groups or influencers?
- How can this model support your strategic aims?

One of the core benefits of using the relevancy model is increasing personalization in an organization. Research reveals 'the highest levels of understanding and engagement happen when direct managers and senior leaders both play a role in communicating strategy – and do it effectively' (IoIC, 2023a). Jen Sproul, Chief Executive of the Institute of Internal Communication says: 'In an increasingly complex world, clarity and alignment of communication are crucial. It's vital that all stakeholders share a common understanding of their context, situation, purpose and vision. Creating alignment delivers strategic value and is the new work of an internal communicator.'

EXPERT VIEW

An institutional history of internal communication

Internal communication has a longer history than many realize and is coupled with the emergence of large-scale organizations in the late 19th century.

Dr Michael Heller (Brunel University), Professor Michael Rowlinson (University of Exeter), and Dr Joe Chick (Brunel University) are a research team working on the Economic and Social Research Council (ESRC) funded project 'An Institutional History of Internal Communication in the UK'. Dr Heller and Dr Chick began as social historians, with Dr Heller studying London clerical workers at the turn of the 20th century and Dr Chick interested in long-term trends in social history from the medieval era to the present day. Prof Rowlinson previously studied sociology and moved into researching management at Cadbury.

Charting the history of internal communication

Their project is integrating historical research with organizational theory and involves 20 organizations, 6 that have been fundamental for the practice of IC in the UK, and 14 with historically practised internal communication.

According to the project, there are 45,000 people employed in IC in the UK and its aim is to document occupational history for practitioners to help enhance professional identity.

Dr Heller and Prof Rowlinson say today's organizations frequently wrestle with the risk of appearing 'impersonal' to employees. They say internal communication between employers and employees has become 'a vital element' of personalizing the organization and of creating and augmenting organizational voice and engagement among employees. They note how IC is used for other strategic organizational goals such as change management, stakeholder relations, innovation, equality, diversity and inclusivity, and organizational sensemaking.

Defining internal communication

> Internal communication (IC) is the strategic and operational use of
> communication by management within organizations which treat employees as
> stakeholders.

An Institutional History of Internal Communication in the UK, 2023

Employee voice

In Chapter 5 we will examine employee voice and the work of Engage for Success. Dr
Joe Chick says the term 'employee voice' gained prominence in the 1990s, but its
roots and the underlying concept can be traced back to 1913.

The Chartered Institute of Personnel and Development (CIPD) turned 110 years
old in 2023. The following quote, from one of the CIPD's founders, appeared in
Welfare Work, the magazine of the Welfare Workers' Association, which then became
the CIPD.

Listening to employees' voices

> By giving voice to the hundred and one thoughts it made it possible for each
> individual who played a part in the particular business to broaden his outlook and
> connect up his own activity with that of his fellow-workmen and to create an
> interest in him beyond the confines of his own particular task which he
> performed day by day, year by year (*Welfare Work*, May 1923).

Dr Chick says 'That quote was written over a hundred years ago, yet it expresses a
vision that resonates with present-day campaigns.'

I was interested to note it talks about a sense of community, something we
looked at in this book's introduction, when focusing on belonging. Dr Heller and Prof
Rowlinson coined the term 'imagined corporate community', in which organizations
describe their activities as though they were a family. These imagined communities
have been around for as long as internal communication itself. They say that early
company magazines aimed to instil a sense of *esprit de corps*, meaning a feeling of
togetherness.

Until the later 20th century, company magazines were the key tool in creating
this sense of belonging among employees. While the idea of a community is
important, it hasn't always meant that everyone has an equal say. Early company
magazines were often employee-written publications but, when their production
began to be professionalized in the mid-20th century, some outsourced their articles
to journalists and the tone sometimes became more of a mouthpiece of

management. They say the rise of 'employee voice' as a concept in the 1990s has seen a shift back towards some of the early traditions (Heller and Rowlinson, 2020).

The role of company magazines

Welfare Work examined healthy workplace atmospheres and the role company magazines played. In an article by a founder member, A S Cole, they argue there were three types of articles in company magazines: 1) to 'impart an uplift' to the employees, 2) written by outside journalists, 3) by employees for employees and within the four walls of the business. The article concluded this final type was the only kind to be regarded as justifying the existence of the works magazine (Cole, 1923).

Dr Chick observes the *Welfare Work* article highlights employees expressing themselves via a magazine and a healthy workplace atmosphere going hand-in-hand. He notes that CIPD's original name, Welfare Workers' Association, reflects the importance of welfare as its central purpose. Internal communication was seen as a part of the welfare of the employee.

He says creating a magazine 'isn't a panacea for a negative workplace atmosphere as it states a magazine would not create the correct atmosphere; the correct *spirit* created and maintained the magazine'. This is as true today as it was then, as introducing modern communication channels 'is not a guarantee to begin a two-way conversation or dialogue between employers and employees'.

Including priorities in your IC strategy

What will you include in an IC strategy as priority areas? Table 4.1 provides some examples – logistics and channels, employee voice, the way leaders communicate, creating a sense of belonging and safety communications.

Use the intentions framework I shared in Chapter 2, when looking at the way a company communicates. What do you want employees to be doing, saying, thinking and feeling as a result of the way the organization – or more accurately – the people, communicate?

What is right for your organization to prioritize? Once you know, create your own *do*, *say*, *think*, *feel* answers. A table like this can be included in your IC strategy if you want to demonstrate what you are prioritizing. You could also create them as IC principles to define priorities – you'll find more information about these in Chapter 5.

TABLE 4.1 Intentions table

	As a result of the way we communicate, employees...			
	Do	Say	Think	Feel
Strong suite of IC channels	Proactively seek out information and read/respond to calls to action in internal communication channels	I know where to go to get credible, accurate and reliable information to help me do my job	There are communication methods in place suited to the way I work, and my accessibility needs	The company values creating ways for us to communicate well
Encouraging employee voice	Actively participate in employee discussions, stories and forums	I can ask questions and expect answers	The company genuinely wants to hear from me and makes it possible for me to be included	I feel empowered to contribute to organizational discussions and decisions
Enhance leadership visibility	Hold leaders to account and expect to hear from them	I know who our leaders are and how to talk with them	Our leaders are visible and transparent in the ways they communicate	I trust our leaders and feel like they value communicating with employees
Amplify our sense of belonging	Collaborate across the organization and have mechanisms to communicate with each other	There are meaningful connections and conversations happening at work	Communication is personalized to my role and how I work. I can see how everything fits together	I feel connected to the organization and understand the work we do
Improve safety comms	Know their responsibilities, which are outlined in safety guidance and policies	I am aware what is expected of me and how to work safely	The company cares about my safety and helps me know how to stay safe	I feel supported and able to raise any safety issues or concerns

TIP FROM RACHEL

Consider how you would measure against each priority. How would you gather evidence and proof points? Setting the intentions is only half of the story, you need to track against each priority. You need to know the current state across these priorities, to then be able to measure any change.

The outputs could be quantitative, such as numbers of questions asked in town halls, and the outcomes could be qualitative – *tell me what's happened as a result* – this measurement is how you would *really* know whether what you've prioritized has had an impact. In this scenario, the number of questions asked (outputs) plus type/tone of questions asked (outcomes) could indicate that priority's impact.

Actions to take: create priorities, collate the as-is or current state, determine what and how you will measure the actions you are recommending in an IC strategy.

Remember: this is the strategy – the thinking.

How to be more strategic with channels

A channel is a medium for communication, and internal communicators are spoilt for choice. If you analyse the internal communication methods inside an organization, there will be a set of 'official' channels in use. They're typically owned, controlled and managed by the internal communication team. They could include an internal website (intranet), forums, employee app, noticeboards, podcast, digital signage, emails, all-employee meeting or town hall, magazine or email newsletters.

There are more than 280 million monthly active users of Microsoft Corp's Teams, Zoom's business customers have nearly tripled to more than 210,000 and Salesforce Inc's Slack is also growing (Chaker, 2023).

Shadow comms

There will also be other methods in place inside an organization, which I call *shadow comms*. In the same way employees have filled the technology gaps in organizations by creating their own ways of transferring large files, having video calls or exchanging information via messaging platforms (also known as *shadow IT*), we are experiencing the same for internal communication.

Wherever there is a gap that is not filled by 'official' channels, employees find their own techniques to get the right information, at the right time to help them do their jobs. They may produce localized newsletters, create closed groups on messaging platforms or use technology to produce information and stories for their part of the business.

Internal communicators need to know how communication happens inside an organization. If you have a set of 'official' channels in use, but employees rely on their own localized methods, there's a chance they could miss the 'corporate' content entirely.

From my own professional practice, I've uncovered various reasons why this happens.

WHY EMPLOYEES CREATE THEIR OWN CHANNELS
AND COMMUNICATION METHODS

- Content from the company doesn't feel relevant.

- News isn't new or noteworthy.

- Company news doesn't load instantly.

- Lack of trust in corporately produced stories.

- Organizational communication is not timely enough.

- They have trusted sources who are closer to their roles, team or location.

- Employees want to consume content in the ways they are familiar with in their personal lives.

The 'company news doesn't load instantly' point relates to not having the intranet as the default browser landing page. What message does it send to employees if the company does not prioritize that site? There is an assumption employees will actively seek out the site, which may not be realistic.

Being strategic with channels includes analysing your organization and determining why employees may be missing 'official' internal communication. Think about what this means for your internal communication strategy.

Is it clear how internal communication happens inside your organization? What stops communication from being successful? Could it be because employees rely on other methods in place of the corporate ones? Or is it because you're not segmenting employee groups or tailoring content to feel relevant for them?

Maximizing channels

Research among workers reveals six out of ten employees 'rely on and prefer' email as a channel to hear news about and from their employer. Email is also the most preferred channel for communication from senior leaders and CEOs. CEOs can 'get away' with communicating via email. However, there is a much higher demand to see departmental leaders in a face-to-face and interactive setting (IoIC, 2023a).

EXPERT VIEW
Marks and Spencer

Leading retailer Marks and Spencer (M&S) was established in 1884. It employs around 65,000 colleagues across stores, support centres, logistics operations and international teams.

In 2022 the organization introduced a CEO suggestion scheme called 'Straight to Stuart'. Victoria McKenzie-Gould, the organization's Corporate Affairs Director, describes it as 'truly one of the best things me and my team get to do.'

Every colleague at M&S can talk to the CEO, Stuart Machin, to share an idea and potentially see it put into action. McKenzie-Gould says: 'What makes it so special – and effective – is how much our leaders get involved and listen and take action. The two-way programme means colleagues are empowered to make M&S the best place to work for colleagues and the best place to shop for our customers. No idea is too big or too small.'

In the first year of the scheme, almost 10,000 ideas were submitted, which McKenzie-Gould says demonstrates how passionately they feel about driving positive change. Suggestions range from life-saving guidance on spotting the symptoms of cancer, to introducing identifier symbols on name badges to make colleagues feel more comfortable.

Visual communication

Visual communication 'has become a strategic imperative' according to research conducted with 1,600 business leaders in the US, UK and Australia by Canva. Its Visual Economy report defines the term as the process of using visual elements to convey ideas, information and data.

FIGURE 4.4 The Visual Economy Report

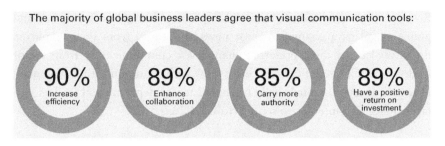

The majority of global business leaders agree that visual communication tools:

SOURCE Canva (2023)

The majority of business leaders agree visual communication methods increase efficiency (90 per cent), enhance collaboration (89 per cent) and carry more authority than other methods (85 per cent). Plus, 89 per cent of business leaders agreed that visual communication methods have helped remote and hybrid team members connect with each other (Figure 4.4).

Findings reveal leaders prefer using visual methods, over text and audio, in any work situation. This includes communicating with their teams about status updates, receiving input on their work and conveying business updates. 'From presentations to whiteboard sessions, proposals to recruiting videos, visual content is becoming the fuel that's driving the modern-day workplace with every passing day. Data storytelling is becoming an increasingly critical part of visual communication for many organizations across many industries' (Canva, 2023).

However, Canva's findings also revealed 53 per cent of global business leaders said content is not aesthetically pleasing, 56 per cent said it's not consistent and 64 per cent said employees lack access to the right tools to make meaningful business impact.

THE VISUAL ECONOMY REPORT 2023

Nine different methods or platforms are used by business leaders to communicate and collaborate at least once per day:

- Presentation programmes
- Video comms software
- Shared documents

- Digital whiteboards
- Email
- Phone
- Graphic design platforms
- Instant messaging
- Shared documents (hosted)

With more than one billion presentations created on Canva, its platform data reveals there is a method to creating presentations in a standout way.

Less is more: Ten pages is the sweet spot for presentation length. Engagement (views and shares) increases with page count from 1–10, with engagement dropping between 11 and 30 pages.

Add motion to boost engagement: Animations, videos and GIFs all tend to increase design engagement (views and shares). In fact, the number of views and shares per design is 70–80 per cent higher for presentations containing one animation.

Canva, 2023

How are you using visual communication inside your organization? How can you use visual methods to maximize your channels?

Investing time in internal communication

At the start of this chapter, I highlighted the need to attract and keep employees' attention. How much time do employees invest daily in internal communications – not the day-to-day interactions with their teams, but updates from their employer? According to the IC Index (IoIC, 2023a), nearly 7 in 10 employees spend only 15 minutes or less a day reading and reviewing updates from their employer. The research found 23 per cent of employees spend 15–30 minutes per day, 7 per cent spend 30–60 minutes per day and 2 per cent spend over an hour per day. Regardless of the time employees invest, we need to ensure it's time well spent and the quality of the content they interact with is high.

If you knew you only had 15 minutes or less a day from employees, what decisions would you make? Knowing you have such a short time frame forces you to prioritize and concentrate on what is critical for employees to access and contribute to. It certainly gives internal communicators permission to push back on unwieldy and lengthy videos!

What is the reality for your organization? Perhaps this is a question to add to an employee survey. I wonder how long employees spend reading news and updates from peers? Are they spending part of their 15 minutes navigating channels and content to find what they are looking for?

Consider the impact it would have on an internal communication strategy if you knew how long people spend reading and reviewing updates.

If you work in an organization where employees must have time set aside for communication, for example an operational environment, this figure won't be a surprise to you. You'll be used to making content work hard for you and being mindful of restricted timings.

Communication preferences

Do you know the communication preferences inside your organization? There are many ways to determine what they are, including a DISC analysis. The DISC model is based on psychologist William Moulton Marston's 1928 work on human behaviour, which led to the theory behind the DISC (Dominance, Inducement, Submission and Compliance) personality dimensions. Today it stands for Dominance, Influence, Steadiness and Conscientiousness and is a way to determine behavioural and motivational styles. I did this with my own team when I recruited new members. It helps me as a leader know how to tailor the way I communicate. For example, I know who to give a heads up to that I'm about to announce something and I know not to use Teams chat with my Executive Assistant as she prefers phone calls or email.

On a larger scale, these preferences become more important when you're trying to communicate with thousands of colleagues across multiple time zones and geographies.

How well do you know employees? How many options do you give line managers to help them determine the best way to communicate with their team?

Repurposing content

Organizations invest a lot of time, money and effort trying to communicate well. One opportunity that is often missed is repurposing content.

This doesn't mean repeating the same messaging everywhere, as the quality goes down. Repurposing means reimagining and future-proofing internal communication. If you are creating video content for an all-employee meeting, how can you repurpose that footage for an end-of-year video? Or if you are recording an all-employee meeting, how can you strip out the audio and turn it into audio clips or a podcast? Channels are thought of in isolation from each other, but working strategically means thinking ahead and being proactive. Your future self will thank you!

Addressing noise

The mother of all comms models is the Shannon–Weaver model, which describes how communication happens from a sender to a receiver. It was published in an article by Claude Shannon called 'A Mathematical Theory of Communication' in the *Bell System Technical Journal* in 1948 and was expanded upon in the book he co-wrote with Warren Weaver in 1949. The model's main components feature a lot of the terminology we use today, including message, receiver and noise.

The model was later updated by mathematician and philosopher Norbert Wiener, to highlight the two-way nature of communication and turn it from linear to cyclical, by including a feedback loop.

What stands out to me is the *noise* part of that model. It originally referred to communications systems, such as telephones, therefore noise could be a crossed wire or a crackle on the line.

Internal communicators need to know what or who is stopping information from flowing and communication from happening. It may be the sheer number of channels that exist means employees are overwhelmed with messages being fired at them from all sides.

We use phrases like 'cutting through the noise' as internal communicators, which really means 'how can we make sure the right information is reaching the right people at the right time, and how can we make sure they can join a conversation about it?' That's hardly short and snappy, but it's something to think through. The mindset we need is one of coordination, where forward planning and predictable internal communication becomes the norm.

> TIP FROM RACHEL
>
> Ask yourself what constitutes *noise* in your organization. What stops communication from happening?
>
> It could be volume of content, timing, who is sharing the information, it's clashing with something else, topic isn't interesting, length, managers blocking it, lack of translation or localized content.
>
> Knowing what stops internal communication from 'cutting through the noise' will help you determine actions to take and what to prioritize in your IC strategy.

The logistics part of an internal communication strategy needs to be anchored by the insights you've gathered, which I examined in Chapter 3.

Determining logistics via a channels matrix

Companies 'face the choice between self-regulation and confusing clutter' (Quirke, 2008). To reduce information overload, Quirke encourages organizations to 'adopt a more sophisticated approach to managing information and interaction'. He says 'communication has to be orchestrated carefully via an "air traffic control" which has an overview of communication activities. This prevents mid-air collisions caused by would-be communicators taking to the air as and when they like.'

The proliferation of internal communication channels, both those owned and managed by the IC team, and those created by employees, means the airspace is a busy one. To expand on Quirke's metaphor, the rise of user-generated content and peer-to-peer communication means there are now many private jets and people taking to the sky. They can appear on internal communicators' radars without warning, which makes our roles as *curators*, not just *creators*, a critical one.

Defining the purpose

Do you know the purpose of each internal communication channel? How are you setting yourself, the IC team and employees up for success through channels?

When I am auditing or analysing internal communication inside an organization, the purpose of each channel is crucial. I want to determine how each channel earns its place, There should not be multiple channels with an identical purpose. If there is, it tells me one or more can probably be retired.

Employees need to know *what to use when*. Channels without a clear purpose make it hard for them to find what they need.

Using a channels matrix

A channels matrix is a useful tool to determine how internal communication happens inside an organization. I often produce two versions – one for the IC team to use and one for the business. I've included some examples in Tables 4.2 and 4.3.

TIP FROM RACHEL

A successful internal communication team isn't one that has rows and rows of channels on a channels matrix. Think *quality, not quantity*. Having scores of IC channels in place is not necessarily a mark of success. If you have unwieldy methods of internal communication, with no clear purpose and a team that is overwhelmed trying to keep them populated or working well, something needs to change.

Be ruthless in the way you prioritize sources of truth, and be respectful of the time employees invest in communication, to maximize everyone's efforts.

As a minimum, I include the following columns on a channels matrix:

- Channel
- Purpose
- Who it's for (audience)
- Direction
- Frequency
- Measurement

Tip: Consider all the methods, including those not owned by the IC team. Try to identify a named person or accountable department for those channels.

TABLE 4.2 Channels matrix: company version

CHANNEL	PURPOSE	WHO IT'S FOR	DIRECTION	FREQUENCY	OWNER	MEASUREMENT
Intranet	Source of truth Timely news and views	People with access via devices	Two-way via comments and reactions	Daily updates and interactions	IC team own core content and homepage IT team own the technology	Recall Actions taken Sentiment Reactions
Newsletter (email)	Go-to place for *need-to-know* info, plus people news	Factory workers	Mainly one-way, but includes calls to action	Published every Friday	IC team	Open rate Actions taken Questions asked Recall Responses

A version for an IC team needs to help them make informed decisions about the channels. Additional columns in their version could include:

- Budget holder
- Comms lead – named person in the IC team
- Risks
- How inclusive and accessible the channel is
- What makes a great story
- How long it takes to produce
- Owner
- Key dates
- When it was established
- Publication date

I've included some of these additional columns in Table 4.3 and shared example content, using an intranet as the example.

You can include your approach to channels management in your internal communication strategy.

I recommend including how your channels will:

- Align content with the business priorities.
- Enable effective planning and make sure you have a smooth editorial process.
- Reflect your organization and the needs of employees, particularly through accessible and inclusive content.
- Ensure colleagues are mindful of your brand, tone of voice, commercial sensitivities and internal sentiment.
- Set standards, for example using toolkits, templates and processes.
- Provide effective signposting between channels (helping employees know what to use when and how the channels work individually and together).
- Earn their place due to having a clearly defined purpose.
- Be continuously monitored and measured.
- Have a review in place – share their trajectory and any key milestones or dates.

TABLE 4.3 Additional channels matrix columns: IC team version

BUDGET HOLDER	COMMS LEAD	RISKS	HOW INCLUSIVE AND ACCESSIBLE IS THE CHANNEL?	WHAT MAKES A GREAT STORY?	HOW LONG DOES IT TAKE TO PRODUCE?	BUSINESS OWNER	KEY DATES
IT budget covers development and licences IC team holds content budget	Digital comms manager	Not all employees have devices, so can't access the intranet Avoid making it sole place for sign-ups	Ask IT for advice re: ALT text and screen readers Provide captions and transcripts Check for equal share of voice and representative content and images	Peer-to-peer Leaders being informal and unscripted	Digital comms manager spends five days a week overseeing the site from a comms perspective	IC team own core content IT team own the tech Comms director owns at exec level	Agency contract due for renewal Q4

Tip: You need to be thinking at least 12 months ahead, or even 24 months ahead. If you have a five-year vision or strategy in your organization, you could write a one, three or five-year aspiration for your channels and include this in your IC strategy.

Show your thinking in your IC strategy and what your expectations are. Make it clear what you are prioritizing and why. This will not be set in stone; you'll need to keep checking back in to see if any revisions are needed.

Creating the foundations

Successful internal communication relies on having solid foundations in place. An organization that I think does this well is Hilton. The company is over 100 years old and has over 7,000 hotels across 122 countries and territories. Hilton's portfolio spans 19 world-class brands and includes more than 400,000 Team Members (employees) globally, at the time of writing.

EXPERT VIEW
Rochelle Raven

Rochelle Raven leads Global Internal Communications at Hilton. With around 100 communicators based across the world, the team's purpose is described as 'the storytellers for the people, places and experiences that enable one of the most important drivers of human connection around the world – travel'.

Raven says they've introduced various methods to enable and drive a robust editorial strategy for internal communications. These include the 10 Internal Content Commandments, which serve as a reminder to their team when developing great internal content across channels.

Hilton's 10 Internal Content Commandments

1 Can Communications or our channels solve the problem?

2 Is it Team Member (employee) centric? Why should they care?

3 Watch tone of voice – informal, relatable, and acronym-free is key!

4 Assume a zero knowledge base

5 Remember that a picture says a thousand words, especially when communicating globally

6 Try to always include a hyperlinked Call to Action

7 Ensure you have double-checked property names/titles and name spellings

8 KISS (keep it simple, stupid!), content and language

9 Be globally relevant

10 Always come with an idea/solution for the team to build on

SOURCE Rochelle Raven, 2023

Editorial strategy

I love the fact Hilton's intranet is called *the Lobby* – what a fantastic choice! As part of its internal editorial strategy, Hilton has introduced an editor-in-chief across internal communications to help gauge the newsworthiness of a story and determine the best communications approach. The team set themselves up as an internal newsroom and run weekly and quarterly editorial meetings to brainstorm, share ideas and provide the opportunity to cross-pollinate great stories across multiple channels. The role also helps unite the brand from the inside out by providing a bird's eye view of storytelling across the business.

Raven says 'we have three parts to our editorial strategy: 1) Less is more; 2) Data driven and nimble; and 3) Team Member first. We are determined to have fewer, bigger, more impactful communications and use numbers and data to underpin our strategy.'

Less is more is not just about the length of stories, but volume too. Hilton reduced its yearly content across its internal channels by 80 per cent, which drove up engagement.

Data driven and nimble

Hilton produces a quarterly Global Internal Communications metrics report to look at performance of its channels and content on a quarterly basis and uses it to help tweak and optimize its internal strategy. It also uses technology to provide a 'bird's eye view' of content, so it can see conflicts and busy times and help ensure it is providing the right content, to the right Team Members, at the right cadence.

As a result of knowing its numbers, it has made changes and continually learns from how internal communication happens. For example, rather than quarterly hour-long all global Team Member town halls, it has developed a bite-sized 20-minute internal Hilton TV show to keep Team Members informed of the latest and greatest news from across the business in a way that resonates. This is a pre-recorded asset that Team Members can watch at a time that suits them.

Team Member first

As part of its channel ecosystem, it is able to target Team Members by brand and by region: 'It's important for us that Team Members can identify with the stories they are reading. We also ask questions before producing content such as why now? Why should Team Members be interested? We always come at things with a Team Member first approach. This is critical for us because we want to ensure every piece of content is impactful and it's clear to Team Members why it's being communicated.'

It has also seen a rise in user-generated content across its channels with Team Members increasingly using its platforms as a place to share best practice and recognition. Around 75 per cent of all content is being generated by Team Members.

Supporting documentation

What do you have in place to create firm foundations for an IC function? Gallagher's State of the Sector survey (2023) reveals common foundational documents among internal communicators include:

- Internal communication plan for a specific campaign or initiative (60 per cent)
- Crisis communication plan or process (48 per cent)
- Internal communication 'master' plan covering multiple campaigns over the course of a year (33 per cent)
- Channel-specific editorial calendar(s) (33 per cent)
- Channel framework (31 per cent)

Consider what you need to have in place and signpost towards via an internal communication strategy. What sets the function up for success? You need to have a consistent approach, and documentation such as these can aid this process.

Brilliant Basics

I have a *Brilliant Basics* checklist I use with internal communication teams. I developed it because I found I was looking for the same evidence every time I was reviewing an IC team or my team and I were auditing an organization.

The importance of Brilliant Basics is to create a strong foundation on which to build a successful and thriving IC team. We will examine establishing an IC team in Chapter 5.

BRILLIANT BASICS CHECKLIST FOR AN IC TEAM

- Overview of business objectives
- Internal communication strategy
- Internal communication plan template
- Editorial calendar for the business
- Editorial calendar for the comms team
- Tone of voice guide, including a glossary
- Sight of wider strategy, such as HR, external comms or public affairs
- Channels matrix
- Stakeholder map
- Overview of company values
- Mission, purpose and vision statements – for the business and team
- Comms principles or positioning statements for the team
- Monthly measurement report for comms team
- Communication guidance for leaders and people managers
- What makes a great story (one page guide)
- Channel templates, including email headers and footers
- Internal documents template (could include presentations and signage)
- Internal branding guide
- Online hub with resources to help others communicate

I also have an extended checklist of additional building blocks I look for when reviewing an IC team. These are some of the indicators I use to chart transformational internal communication. I look for evidence of how the team is thinking beyond what I would expect them to be doing, and how they are working alongside the business to think strategically about what is needed.

These additional building blocks include:

- Change communication plan template

- Briefing guide for IC agencies

- Cultural playbook

- Employer branding guidance or employee value proposition

- Standardized wording for job adverts

- Standardized wording for career-related letters

- IT road map

- Employee personas

- Benchmarked job descriptions for IC team

I also look at topics like people manager communication, environmental, social and governance (ESG), employee engagement, employee experience and employer brand. I like to see clearly outlined roles and responsibilities, typically alongside HR colleagues. Why? Because these are the topics that often fall through the cracks as there's a sense *someone is responsible*, but it's not clear who.

Testing maturity

How mature is your internal communication function? How mature is the organization's understanding of what internal communication is – and isn't?

EXPERT VIEW
James Robertson

James Robertson is Founder and Managing Director at Step Two. He specializes in digital employee experience, digital workplaces and intranets, and is headquartered in Sydney, Australia. He is the author of the best-selling books *Essential Intranets* (2013) and *Designing Intranets* (2010).

Reshaping communication

Robertson warns the internal digital landscape within organizations has become 'hugely more complex'. New platforms have been rolled out for collaboration and social, and multiple tools often run side by side, which 'make it harder, not easier to deliver internal communications'.

As IC teams grapple with the new tools in their toolkits, he says it's important to revisit internal communication strategies and start to reshape the way professional communicators and leaders communicate, to better match the digital age.

He has developed a digital maturity model for internal communication, to help teams understand their current state, and determine what changes to make. The days of having just two digital channels for internal communications – email and the intranet – have long gone. Driven by IT road maps and business expectations, there has been a proliferation of new tools and platforms in many organizations.

Digital channels for internal communication

Typical channels include:

- **Email**, which has grown in usage rather than shrunk, and may be supported by new email campaign tools.
- **Intranets**, which are still seen as the primary channel for corporate messages but may be left behind in terms of technological capabilities.
- **Social tools**, such as Viva Engage or Workplace by Meta (Facebook).
- **Collaboration tools**, such as Microsoft Teams, Workplace, Slack and countless others.
- **Employee apps**, which are being rolled out as mobile-only solutions for front-line workers.
- **Video**, which has shot up in usage during the pandemic crisis.
- **Shadow IT**, consisting of the continued use of non-corporate tools, such as WhatsApp and Telegram.

SOURCE James Robertson, 2023

The number of channels inside organizations varies – it's unlikely you'll have everything listed. However, having more than one tool for a given purpose increases complexity.

Robertson warns 'old internal comms approaches, including *scattergun* delivery of messages simultaneously across multiple channels, just won't work.'

In response to this conundrum, he developed a digital maturity model to help internal comms teams plot a clear way forward (Table 4.4). It includes the wider scope of digital workplace. Robertson says this is intentional 'as communication practices need to reflect the tools and practices that are in place, and then make the

TABLE 4.4 Digital maturity model for communications and collaboration

	1. Formal internal communications	2. Collaboration	3. Social & cultural	4. Intranet	5. Modern work practices
Low maturity	• Heavy use of email • 'Scattergun' comms generating comms overload • Newsletter/newspaper style comms	• Low rollout of tools • Low or no adoption • Poor digital literacy • Use of 'shadow IT' by early adopters	• Ad hoc communication regarding social and culture • Social activities are all offline • Digital engagement is low	• Corporate intranet in place • Intranet not a primary channel for internal communications • Information often shared via emails, not intranet	• Limited flexible working, primarily office-based • Traditional team practices • Limited adoption of digital tools to support new work practices
Medium maturity	• Regular, timely communication • Modern style, engaging messages • Clarity between 'content' and 'comms'	• Primary collaboration platform in place • Varying adoption across the organization • Wide range of digital literacy • No formalized purpose	• Enterprise social tool in place • Widespread but shallow interactions • Channel for some leader engagement	• Primary channel for formal communications • Trusted information source • Governance and management fundamentals in place	• Widespread flexible working supported by digital tools • Traditional work practices mirrored in use of online tools • Wide range of digital literacy

(continued)

TABLE 4.4 (Continued)

	1. Formal internal communications	2. Collaboration	3. Social & cultural	4. Intranet	5. Modern work practices
High maturity	• Comms strategy in place • Targeted and personalized comms • Two-way communication • Real-time metrics	• Clear purpose and business drivers • Proactive activities to increase digital literacy • Governance and management models in place	• Rich social interactions, including across org structure • Strong sense of shared culture online • Online employee recognition	• Key role as 'enterprise front door' into digital workplace • Targeted and personalized communications • Comprehensive governance in place	• Consistently high digital literacy • New work practices shaped by modern digital tools • Effective collaboration within and between teams
Potential benefits	• Improved effectiveness of internal communication • Increased staff satisfaction and engagement • Improved service delivery	• Increased effectiveness of teams and business units • Improved service delivery • Greater knowledge sharing	• Increased staff engagement • Strengthened organizational culture • Greater staff retention	• Improved effectiveness of internal communication • Improved service delivery • Enhanced management of knowledge	• Increased effectiveness of individuals and teams • Improved coordination of activities across the org • Increased organizational flexibility and resilience

SOURCE Reproduced with permission from Step Two, 2023

most of them'. It can also enable IC teams to identify the role they want to play, beyond 'basic corporate messaging'.

There are five different streams for internal communications:

1 **Formal internal communication**, the traditional work of comms teams, sharing leader updates, business changes and new policies.

2 **Collaboration**, encompassing all the ways employees work together in groups to achieve outcomes.

3 **Social and cultural**, helping to engage employees with the organization, and with each other.

4 **Intranet**, the mainstay of internal communications and content publishing.

5 **Modern work practices**, reflecting the changing ways that digital tools can help to get real work done.

Tip: Use the bottom of the table to focus on the potential outcomes and benefits that can be achieved if maturity increases across the five streams.

Gathering the data

Robertson says the way to use the model is to assess your current state against each of the streams, which you can use to make informed decisions about the future. There are a number of methods to use to research and gather insights, including an IC survey, employee research and broader assessment from external experts.

These activities will allow you to create a benchmark for your 'current' state and gauge your current maturity across the streams. You can then identify what you are aiming towards, or the 'target state' for each stream.

Bring together stakeholders to discuss and explore:

• **Business drivers and priorities**, which should shape the overall approach to communication and collaboration.

• **Internal comms strategy**, to provide an overall framework for improving internal messaging.

• **Best practices and leading examples** from other organizations, to ensure that the target state is sufficiently ambitious.

This information determines the target state for each stream.

Once you have captured your current and target states, you can then take action. Robertson says: 'Not all the streams need to be driven by IC teams, you need to work in conjunction with the business and your IT colleagues. All the information you have gathered allows you to determine the digital maturity of the organization and you can use this data to create targeted projects, have conversations to shape leader behaviour and build on the digital literacy of employees.'

Timeliness

In this chapter, we have examined how internal communication happens, techniques to use and what to prioritize. One key area to consider for an IC strategy is timeliness, particularly due to the rise of synchronous (occurring at the same time) communication channels. I describe this as your workflow and comms flow.

Questions to answer

There are two questions it's worth knowing the answers to:

1 From a timings perspective, how does work happen in your organization?

2 From a timings perspective, how does communication happen in your organization?

Knowing the rhythm, or cadence, of internal comms channels is commonplace for internal communicators. However, does the cadence align with how employees communicate daily? See Table 4.5 to compare asynchronous and synchronous communication methods.

We don't use this terminology much in the world of internal communication. However, it's worth thinking through, as any disconnect between how people work and the ways they communicate impacts an organization's internal communication. If you are striving to transform the way the organization communicates, you need to know what this looks like for the company. For example, if there are ambitions to have real-time collaboration and employees *working out loud* (Miller, 2016; Williams, 2010), but employees rely on email and receiving responses later, it can slow productivity.

'It's clear we need to rethink our traditional office-based methods and embrace the power of asynchronous collaboration and prioritize socialization' (Tsipursky, 2023).

TABLE 4.5 Comms flow

Asynchronous communication	Synchronous communication
Receive response later	Happens in real time
Emails	Social networks
Messages	Meetings and discussions
Pre-recorded video	Video and audio calls
Document mentions	Feedback
What is the workflow and what is the comms flow?	

EXPERT VIEW

Sonya Poonian

'Employees now expect a consumer-grade digital experience from their workplace, which has risen in importance from working in a hybrid or remote setting, and often asynchronously' says Sonya Poonian. She leads the digital workplace consulting division at Simply, where she works with global organizations to transform the employee experience through digital internal communications.

She's worked with multiple leading FTSE 100 organizations in a variety of senior leadership roles across marketing and transformation and is now using this experience to accelerate the digital transformation for employees with a focus on driving engagement, collaboration and advocacy.

Deeper understanding

Poonian says 'as the status of IC has elevated since the pandemic, it's increasingly becoming recognized as a point of differentiation in defining the employee experience. As a result, IC leaders and their teams require a deeper understanding of the technology and capabilities to target and reach employees. How to work alongside IT colleagues to utilize and adopt digital transformation across their channels has become a core part of their role.'

What sets internal communicators up for success? Poonian urges IC pros to focus on strong stakeholder engagement. 'It is a core component to digital transformation. IC leaders that spend their time cultivating these relationships horizontally across the organization are those that differentiate themselves from their peers. Regular cadence and clarity of roles and responsibilities are equally critical – with IT teams focused on integration of new technology and IC teams embedding standards and best practice for colleagues. Engaging through regular check ins or creating a steering board with the core stakeholder groups builds a collaborative relationship that helps to achieve the organizational goals, as well as individual objectives whilst reducing risks and setting expectations.'

I asked Poonian for any top tips she can share with internal communicators, based on her years of experience in this field. She recommends ' communicating with detail, objectives, and understand those of other core groups, such as IT. They are ultimately an enabler of the business and business strategy and aspire to support you with using the right technology to achieve your strategy.'

EXPERT VIEW
Deborah Copeland

The British Broadcasting Corporation (BBC) is the world's leading public service broadcaster. Its mission is to 'act in the public interest, serving all audiences through the provision of impartial, high-quality and distinctive output and services which inform, educate and entertain'.

Deborah Copeland is Director of Internal Communications and Engagement at the BBC. She says they categorize digital internal communication into three areas: Company comms, Divisional comms and Opt-in comms.

- Company comms is news that is relevant to all.
- Divisional comms is targeted for the audience.
- Opt-in comms is 'content you don't need to know to do your job, but might have an interest in'.

Copeland says they are endeavouring to transform the organization, and at the heart of this ambition is employee-first comms. 'We're focused on how we build understanding and belief in our strategy, how we engage our leaders and how we support a creative and engaging culture across the BBC. When trying to transform an organization, it's vital that two-way communication and engagement sits at the heart of that. That means developing deep understanding of our different audiences, being efficient and effective with our comms and increasing personalisation where we can.'

What resonates

Stories about the BBC, such as pay and benefits and licensing discussions, resonate with employees. However, Copeland says 'they have also been engaging with our business strategy and wanting to get involved'.

The BBC's Internal Communications and Engagement team hosted a series of strategy roadshows to help line managers understand what the BBC's Value for All strategy means to them. Copeland says 'there was a disconnect between what people were hearing at a senior level and what they were experiencing on the ground. Our roadshows are helping managers develop their own plans to operationalize the strategy and the appetite to want to learn more has been incredible.'

Building on legacy

One of the organization's flagship internal communication channels is *Ariel*, which launched in 1936. It was originally a printed publication and was the first internal communication channel I ever saw.

My cousin Jonquil Panting is a producer for BBC Radio Drama. When I was a teenager in the mid-1990s, she invited me to watch a radio play being recorded and I visited her at the BBC's old offices in London. As we went to get a cup of tea inside the building, I remember seeing a distribution bin full of printed copies of *Ariel*. My cousin encouraged me to pick it up to understand more about the BBC and how it works. I was fascinated that there was an internal magazine for a company, as I'd not seen one before.

The print edition of *Ariel* was replaced by an online version in 2011. Today it has been reimagined as an app. Copeland says 'it's the go-to place for employees to get involved in conversations about the BBC and we encourage everyone to register. One year since launch, 67 per cent of the BBC had registered and used it regularly, increasing to 90 per cent of all managers. It played a big role in our centenary celebrations, including employee award nominations, messages from BBC talent and was even used to curate a Top 100 songs playlist during the BBC's 100th birthday celebrations.'

This has been a shift for the organization, with Copeland recognizing 'a lot of our communication was broadcast, and we've worked hard to turn this into two-way. *Ariel* today allows us to create exclusive content for our employees, and gather feedback and sentiment on announcements and company news.'

Championing employee voice

Copeland says it has focused on how it delivers communication in line with the organization they are today. 'Overheard at the BBC' was a feature in *Ariel* and Copeland says that's the 'next big drive' for the platform. 'Two-way conversations reflect how we work, so our internal communication channels need to encourage this to happen. We're actively trying to create the conditions where people have choice, so we've been targeted in the way we position the platform. When people are registering to access *Ariel*, it curates the content for them and puts the control in their hands.'

Setting internal communication standards

What operating model is in place in your organization? How is internal communication structured? Your internal communication strategy should state whether you are working as a central team, or a hub and spoke model (Figure 4.5) with comms champions across the business.

An internal communication team sets the communication standards for the rest of the organization. They are the subject matter experts and determine what excellent internal communication looks like.

Varying degrees of communication accountability may sit with others, for example people managers may have job descriptions that state they need to meet with their teams and have conversations.

FIGURE 4.5 Hub and spoke model

The IC team should be viewed as the people who are role modelling outstanding internal communication and giving advice and guidance to the others. This could even be a team of one person.

The model depicts people who may have responsibility for communicating inside the business. Let's look at who a central IC team may be connected to, or rely upon:

- **Employee networks:** groups of employees, including employee resource groups.
- **Location-based champions:** people who can help the flow of communication across the business.
- **Editorial board:** a cross-functional group of employees who are asked their views on planned and previous internal communication.
- **Comms as part of their role:** people who have a percentage of their time dedicated to internal communication. This could include executive assistants.
- **Internal influencers:** employees who are well connected inside the organization.
- **Leaders:** at all levels, they need to know their communication responsibilities.
- **Comms champions:** elected volunteers who provide feedback, ideas and insights, and help the organization communicate.

The IC team needs to develop strong relationships with all these groups – the arrows illustrate the requirement for two-way communication. Listening to these respective groups of people will help shape the relevancy and accuracy of internal communication inside the organization. You may also have union representatives to add into the mix.

Creating robust advice and guidance for the organization, which they could use in a self-service capacity, could include producing one-page guides to writing stories, sharing tone of voice guides or tasking those groups to be roving reporters and storytellers. Be clear whether the IC team will be *crafting and drafting* content, or whether you're operating more in a *consultant and coach* capacity (Quirke, 2008).

Standards in action

Kimberley-Marie Sklinar is Group Internal Engagement Manager at AutoProtect Group. She joined the company as a communications manager who was brought in to build a strategy and create an IC function. When she arrived, she 'discovered an email inbox, a newsletter that went out whenever someone had time to do it, and the occasional content from marketing'.

Sklinar reflects: 'Due to the nature of their work, my more challenging audiences are vehicle technicians and salespeople. I talked to them to ask what they wanted to see from comms. Our mission as a business is to create remarkable journeys, so my role is to enable people to do that, make sure they know what's going on and how they can innovate, and provide a good employee experience. If you build a strategy only around the leadership team, it's not going to work.'

A function to be trusted

Sklinar communicated with employees to inform them there was an IC strategy in place, which she describes as 'a message to everyone that IC is a function to be trusted. Comms has a focus now, it's much higher on the agenda and regularly discussed at exec level. Before, there was no culture of self-service behaviour. But now managers say the strategy helps them have more time to do things, as they can point colleagues to the intranet. The CEO also asked me to speak at the town hall, which is unprecedented in internal comms.'

CASE STUDY
Setting comms standards in the Fire Service

A professional standard for communications and engagement for England's Fire and Rescue Services has been published. This standard is part of a move to professionalize communications in this high-profile area of the public sector. It clarifies the importance of effective communication and engagement in all aspects of a fire and rescue service.

The Fire Standards Board, which is responsible for the development of Fire Standards, approved the standard in 2023. The board is composed of major stakeholders in the fire and rescue sector, including the Home Office, the Local Government Association, the National Fire Chiefs Council (NFCC) and the Association of Police and Crime Commissioners, as well as being led by an independent chair and vice-chair. The board has responsibility for creating fire standards that cover all the activity that fire and rescue services do in England.

The standard was drafted with expert input from FirePro, the membership body for communication professionals working in fire and rescue, the National Fire Chiefs Council's Communications team, and communications and collaboration specialists from a wide range of fire and rescue services. The standard also covers engagement.

To achieve the standard a fire and rescue service must take a strategic approach to communications and engagement, including consultation. However, the Fire Standards Board understood that a one size fits all approach does not work recognizing how the differently located fire and rescue services vary, for example, by geography and demographics. Therefore, services are each left to decide how best to go about meeting the standard's stated requirements to achieve the outcome required.

'This Fire Standard will give an even bigger focus on where strategic communications and engagement can benefit services, encouraging consistency across the sector, reaffirming that good communications and engagement is everyone's responsibility' (Fire Standards Board, 2023).

Suzanne McCarthy, the Chair of the Fire Standards Board said: 'The Communications and Engagement Fire Standard has as its aim to drive improvement and enhance professionalism, helping to identify what good looks like for the benefit of both fire and rescue service personnel and the communities they serve.'

Approved standard for Communications and Engagement – Outcome Statement

A fire and rescue service whose leaders understand and champion its inclusive approach to communications and engagement, contributing to its positive culture and working environment. Through good leadership, everyone knows both when to use effective communication to support the safety and well-being of their communities and people, and when to engage to gain insight, encourage involvement and build trust.

A service where everyone recognizes and understands their important role in communicating and engaging, they communicate openly and effectively internally and externally and particularly through times of change. They actively listen and welcome feedback, especially through consultation to keep people engaged, informed and reassured. Its people develop and maintain positive relationships, within and outside of the service, building trust, creating advocates and resulting in successful collaborations and partnerships.

It ensures its vision, strategic objectives, and any information it needs to share are delivered in a way that is understandable and accessible to all because it tailors its communications and engagement approaches to suit its multiple audiences.

Based on its community risk management planning and driven by insight and engagement, the service knows who are the most vulnerable and in need in its community. It contributes to community resilience using effective techniques to connect with its communities. It draws upon established behavioural science methods to inform how it educates and encourages communities to adopt safer practices.

When carrying out its civil contingencies' role and in times of emergency and crises, the service communicates clearly to warn, inform, protect and reassure the public, coordinating with others when appropriate. It evaluates the effectiveness of its communications and engagement activities using learning to improve.

SOURCE Fire Standards Board, 2023

As a desired outcome, there is a lot of excellent information in there to help communicators know how to anchor their communications in the right way. There are many facets to that outcome statement. Could something like this be useful for your organization? What's the desired outcome of your internal communication?

Cohesive communication

How cohesive, or united, is the way your organization communicates and works?

Are your work, people, culture and organizational structure in sync – or congruent? (Nadler and Tushman, 1997).

'Organisations that communicate effectively with internal stakeholders are more productive, sustainable and successful. Effective communication improves team cohesion, engagement, productivity, innovation, reputation, talent attraction and retention, and leads to more satisfied and fulfilled employees' (IoIC, 2023b).

Accessibility

A barrier to cohesive communication is a lack of accessibility. One in eight people globally have some form of disability and struggle daily to access content and communications from brands and organizations of all kinds (PRCA, 2021).

The Public Relations and Communications Association (PRCA) published accessible communications guidelines to advise professional communicators. It categorized disabilities in the following ways: visual, hearing, mobility, cognitive, speech and neural.

ACCESSIBLE COMMUNICATION

Types of permanent disabilities:

- Visual: colour blind, low vision, blind

- Hearing: hard of hearing, deaf

- Mobility: arthritis, quadriplegia, spinal cord injury

- Cognitive: learning disabilities, autism, seizure

- Speech: speech impediment, unable to speak

- Neural: bipolar, anxiety, PTSD, OCD, depression

SOURCE PRCA, 2021

Research shows 'far too many global organizations remain in the dark when it comes to understanding what proportion of their workforce is comprised of people with disabilities' (Alexiou, 2023).

In a survey of 28,000 employees across 16 countries, 25 per cent of respondents stated they have a disability or health condition that limits a major life activity (Wool et al, 2023). This is significantly higher than stats reported by most large-scale enterprises, which place the proportion at 4–7 per cent (Alexiou, 2023).

This data reveals that employees with disabilities significantly under disclose to their employers; employers are missing a large-scale opportunity to enable a quarter of their workforce to bring their full selves to work; and employers are relying on inaccurate information (Wool et al, 2023).

As someone who is hard of hearing and who wears a hearing aid, I'm acutely aware of the impact of inaccessible content. Videos without subtitles, poor audio, and cameras not being aimed at mouths so I can lip-read make communication inaccessible for me.

TIP FROM RACHEL

Think about the impact of inaccessibility for your internal communication. This is going beyond the mindset of accessibility *via devices*, to accessibility in all forms.

What needs to be included in your IC strategy to reflect your commitment to making communication accessible for all?

EXPERT VIEW
Jill Spurr

How can you make your internal communication accessible? What do you need to bear in mind and how can you turn good intentions into action?

Jill Spurr is Head of Communications and Marketing at Affinity Trust. The organization supports over 900 people with learning disabilities across England and Scotland, enabling them to live as independently as possible. The charity has a track record of supporting people with more complex needs, including autism, mental health needs, and profound and multiple learning disabilities.

She says 'inclusion is never one-dimensional. We all have characteristics that afford more privilege and ones that give us less; lived experiences that present challenges and ones that bring benefits. We are the sum of our parts.

'The saying goes "If we can see it, we can be it", but 70–80 per cent of disabilities are invisible. I don't believe anyone should have to "out" their protected characteristics to be valid, that's not inclusive. Nor is assuming that if it isn't obvious and someone doesn't tell you otherwise, they don't represent a minority. I don't think there's an easy answer, but it's something that I always keep in mind in our communications. Challenge what you think disability looks like.'

Developing an accessible brand

Towards the end of 2022, Affinity Trust's Executive team wanted to align and refresh the charity's brand to reflect its new ambitious five-year strategy and refreshed organizational values.

Spurr says 'we wanted our brand to show what modern support looks like for people with learning disabilities and autism, by representing people in their best light living an active life. Being authentic to who we are means being people-centred and accessible to all our audiences.'

She describes the adult social care sector as having a 'bruising few years', due to the pandemic and cost-of-living crisis. Affinity Trust was also going through digital transformation, moving from a heavily paper-based organization to digital systems, so it also needed to bring people together and remind them that they are a vital part of an organization that makes a difference.

Gathering experts

A group of experts from across the charity were appointed to work with the partner agency, Alive with Ideas. This group, which included Trustees, brought diverse perspectives to the project about how the brand would work in their area of responsibility, as well as valuable insight into the relationship between the brand and the people they support. They also acted as a critical friend, challenging every iteration, and carrying out wider testing of the brand before the final sign-off.

Spurr encourages others to adopt a similar approach, as 'co-production is a powerful thing. Taking a diverse group on an inclusive journey produces outcomes that represent the best of everyone and can far exceed what you aimed to achieve in the beginning. That group also has a sense of ownership over the brand – they were part of creating it – so they have a stake in its success. They are proud of the project, and said they couldn't wait to start using the brand, which is a measure of its success.'

The rebrand gave the charity an interesting platform to engage people in accessibility internally and make them more aware of what that looks like. 'It's an important part of a wider programme embedding new ways of working into the organization. The way that the brand has been delivered has enabled us to balance what's familiar (we have many people who have worked with us for a long time) with something that feels new, exciting, and forward-focused, ready to deliver a very ambitious and challenging strategy.'

Understanding accessibility

Reflecting on accessibility, Spurr says 'most people understand accessibility in practical terms, like using our colour palette contrasts which are AAA-compliant. But our internal expertise meant we were able to bring in a great level of detail. Gems like not always having photos of people looking to camera because some people we support struggle with eye contact.'

A new brand narrative was created to engage existing staff and attract new employees. 'It was written in Plain English, as a key goal of the rebrand was to reduce the gap between what we *say* and what we *say to people with learning disabilities* – because that's inclusion! We employ people with learning difficulties, people who are neurodivergent, and people with a whole range of protected characteristics – our brand is for all.'

Storytelling in action

Encouraging people to share their stories is also central to the charity's approach. 'People are predisposed to connect through storytelling, so it helps engage staff and share best practice. We are changing opinions and attitudes about how people with learning disabilities and autism live a life of meaning and connection through telling their stories. We have even hardcoded respect into our brand and always use a people-first approach, internally or externally.

'Our imagery shows people in their best light. Our tone is human and rejects jargon like "non-verbal" or "access the community" – people go out, right? All of these details build a brand that supports an environment where everyone feels empowered to be their authentic self, whether that is someone we support or someone who supports.'

Making adjustments

I was curious to know what Spurr recommends IC pros learn from the work she's been doing. She says 'when we run inclusive sessions with the people we support, the adjustments we make may not seem obvious. Things like just using a first name and not a label like your job role or separating staff from people we support, because labels predispose behaviour and attitude.

'Our approach is incredibly empowering. And don't think that fidget toys are just for people with learning disabilities, they can be really beneficial for all kinds of people in group environments. Make sure you vary shape and feel to offer a variety of sensory experiences that help people engage more deeply. But I think our biggest message is that you do not need to compromise on style and creativity to be inclusive. Inclusion is beautiful and accessibility is creative. If accessibility starts with your brand, engagement is built right into its fabric.'

Reflecting accessibility in an internal communication strategy

Affinity Trust's internal communication strategy includes the phase *together, we make it possible!* 'That one phrase really embodies where we are with internal communications' reflects Spurr, 'that everyone is valued and valuable, and we all have a role to play in delivering excellent support.'

The charity's brand launch culminated with the relaunch of its staff recognition programme, the Star Awards. It has had internal awards for several years, but has reimagined them to reward the people who best live the organization's values and to share best practice, which Spurr says will 'ultimately drive continuous improvement of our support. And that's really the internal comms strategy: to help people keep delivery of quality support front and centre of all they do because that's why we are here and that's what makes a difference.'

You do not need to compromise on style and creativity to be inclusive. Inclusion is beautiful and accessibility is creative.

Jill Spurr, Head of Communications and Marketing at Affinity Trust

We've covered a lot in this chapter, as we've examined the logistics that shape the way an organization communicates.

STRATEGY CREATION CHECKLIST

Make notes and decisions on the following points, before moving on to the next chapter. This will help you write your strategy as you read through this book. As a result of working your way through this chapter, you should now have:

- Outlined what you are prioritizing in your internal communication strategy.
- Mapped how communication happens in your organization, using the relevancy model.
- Determined how mature your channels are.
- Completed a channels matrix, including channels not owned by the IC team.
- Spotted any channel gaps to include in your IC strategy, or identified key channel owners you need to communicate with.
- Determined a 12-month road map for your channels and aligned aspirations with your organization's strategy.
- Read the content commandments. Could something like this work for your organization? What would they be?
- Thought through what stops internal communication from happening.
- Analysed your organization's standards for internal communication, or written your own.
- Contemplated the IC team as a centre of excellence – what does your set up look like? Is it a hub and spoke? Add names to it.
- Considered how accessible your channels are and identified any potential changes that need to be prioritized.

Review the choices you've made while reading through this chapter. Make sure you've captured what has resonated and what feels appropriate for your organization. You may make notes on all of these points, but only include some in your IC strategy.

References and further reading

Alexiou, G (2023) Companies grossly underestimating how many disabled employees they have, study shows, *Forbes*, 28 May www.forbes.com/sites/gusalexiou/2023/05/28/companies-grossly-underestimating-how-many-disabled-employees-they-have-study-shows/amp/ (archived at https://perma.cc/Z7J8-6556)

Canva (2023) The Visual Economy Report, canvavisualeconomy.com (archived at https://perma.cc/DR5Q-Q6VB)

Chaker, A M (2023) So many ways to communicate at work, so many ways to misfire, *Wall Street Journal*, 26 April, www.wsj.com/articles/so-many-ways-to-communicate-at-work-so-many-ways-to-misfire-ec7d9f07 (archived at https://perma.cc/NR7P-E823)

Chick, J (2023), The Evolution of Employee Voice: Celebrating the 110th Anniversary of the CIPD! An Instutional History of Internal Communication in the UK, www.historyofinternalcomms.org/employee-voice-cipd-110/ (archived at https://perma.cc/X9E5-K4N2)

Cole, A S (1923) *Welfare Work*, May, Chartered Institute of Personnel Development, 85

Field, E, Hancock, B and Schaninger, B (2023) Middle managers are the heart of your company, *McKinsey Quarterly*, 17 July, www.mckinsey.com/capabilities/people-and-organizational-performance/our-insights/middle-managers-are-the-heart-of-your-company (archived at https://perma.cc/9X5B-8FMR)

Fire Standards Board (2023) Communication and Engagement Standard, 31 March, www.firestandards.org/standards/approved/communication-and-engagement/ (archived at https://perma.cc/443F-S3TR)

Gallagher (2023) State of the Sector 2022/3, www.ajg.com/employeeexperience/state-of-the-sector-2023/ (archived at https://perma.cc/4SUH-B8TV)

Grammarly Business and The Harris Poll (2023) The State of Business Communication 2023: The path to productivity, performance, and profit, go.grammarly.com/business-communication-report (archived at https://perma.cc/PR2U-NEB3)

Heller, M and Rowlinson, M (2020) Imagined corporate communities: Historical sources and discourses, *British Journal of Management*, 31 (4), 752–68.

Jones, R (2022) What's your next move? *Voice Magazine*, October, www.ioic.org.uk/resource/voice-october-2022-lr-pdf.html (archived at https://perma.cc/VH24-BHWX) (members only)

IoIC (2023a) IC Index 2023, Institute of Internal Communication, www.ioic.org.uk/resource/ic-index-report-2023.html (archived at https://perma.cc/N5JB-JGGJ)

IoIC (2023b) Our Mission, Institute of Internal Communication, https://www.ioic. org.uk/about-us/our-principles.html (archived at https://perma.cc/YB5V-LJUF)

Kahn, W (1990) Psychological conditions of personal engagement and disengagement at work, *Academy of Management Journal*, 33 (4), 692–724

Macaulay, K (2014) *From Cascade to Conversation: Unlocking the collective wisdom of your workforce*, AB Publishing, London

Marston, W M (1928) *Emotions of Normal People*, Kegan Paul, Trench, Trübner & Co Ltd, London

Miller, R (2016) How to work out loud, All Things IC Blog, 7 April, www.allthingsic.com/wol/ (archived at https://perma.cc/WX8J-KJSQ)

Nadler, D and Tushman, M (1997) *Competing by Design: The power of organizational architecture*, Oxford University Press, Oxford

PRCA (2021) Accessible Communications Guidelines, Public Relations and Communications Association, www.accessible-communications.com/wp-content/uploads/2021/06/PRCA-Accessible-Communications-Guidelines-1.pdf (archived at https://perma.cc/BCS9-RY8Q)

Quirke, B (2008) *Making the Connections: Using internal communication to turn strategy into action*, 2nd edn, Gower, Aldershot

Raven, R (2023) Interview/correspondence with the author

Robertson, J (2010) *Designing Intranets: Creating sites that work*, Step Two Designs, Sydney

Robertson, J (2013) *Essential Intranets: Inspiring sites that deliver business value*, Step Two Designs, Sydney

Robertson, J (2023) Interview/correspondence with the author

Shannon, C (1948) The mathematical theory of communication, *The Bell System Technical Journal*, 27, 379–423, 623–56, July, October, https://people.math. harvard.edu/~ctm/home/text/others/shannon/entropy/entropy.pdf (archived at https://perma.cc/H6NV-4UKR)

Tsipursky, G (2023) You can't use office-based leadership in hybrid work, *Forbes*, 27 July, www.forbes.com/sites/glebtsipursky/2023/07/27/you-cant-use-office-based-leadership-in-hybrid-work/amp/ (archived at https://perma.cc/RX8E-ME4Q)

Williams, B (2010) When will we work out loud? Soon!, TheBrycesWrite, 29 November, www.thebryceswrite.com/2010/11/29/when-will-we-work-out-loud-soon/ (archived at https://perma.cc/VV8A-SVMT)

Wool, H et al (2023) Your Workforce Includes People with Disabilities. Does Your People Strategy? Boston Consulting Group, 10 May, www.bcg.com/publications/2023/devising-people-strategy-for-employees-with-disabilities-in-the-workplace# (archived at https://perma.cc/2EY6-QHEQ)

PART TWO

Implementing an internal communication strategy

5

Leading organizational communication

WHAT THIS CHAPTER WILL COVER

This chapter is all about leadership, as we start to move towards implementing an internal communication strategy. The previous chapters examined the mindset, insights and logistics you need. The leadership stage of The MILLER Framework for strategy creation focuses on how to deliver a strategy and the role leaders and managers play. We'll also examine employee engagement and how to create a successful IC team. You'll discover how internal communicators work with a business to lead the way by transforming organizational communication. You'll find a checklist at the end of this and every chapter to help you keep on track.

The MILLER Framework: Leadership

Imagine you have your IC strategy on a large screen. You are presenting it to your CEO and senior leadership team.

Is it finished? Or are you giving them an early view and inviting them to contribute their ideas? What's the outcome you're looking for from that conversation? How confident do you feel presenting what's on the screen in front of your leadership team?

An internal communication strategy sets the standard for internal communication and the way it should happen inside an organization. As I said at the very start of this book, internal communication *is too important to be left to one team, department, or person. It is everyone's responsibility.* Through this chapter, we will analyse how to involve people at the right time and what internal communicators need to do, to turn ideas into reality.

FACTS ALONE DON'T COMMUNICATE

Journalist Sydney J Harris said 'communication is the beginning of a dialogue; information is a monologue. Information tells *what*; communication explains *why*.'

For organizations to move from the information end of the spectrum to communication, Harris (1972) said you need to:

> sacrifice false pride and act like persons who are fallible, uncertain, sometimes wrong and willing to learn from mistakes. When we inform we lead from strength, when we communicate, we lead from weakness – and it is precisely this confession of mortality that engages the ears, heads and hearts of those we want to enlist as allies in a common cause.

When you are creating an internal communication strategy, actively seek out the *ears*, *heads and hearts* of employees. Study the intentions framework from Chapter 2 and focus on the emotional connection you intend to make through your work.

An internal communication strategy should answer the following questions:

- Why is this approach the right one?
- Why are you encouraging certain things to happen?
- Why are you recommending certain decisions be made?

Learning from mistakes

As internal communicators we need to constantly review what we do and learn from mistakes and failures. Operating in such a visible role means everyone in an organization can see the errors we make – from the typo on a CEO's presentation, to not gauging the sentiment correctly when communicating change. Everything feels like it's up for scrutiny, and it often is.

There will always be the tricky people; the ones who point out errors in a gleeful fashion and make seemingly unhelpful comments or criticisms. This can be a source of frustration and overwhelm for internal communicators, but I've learnt to embrace that scrutiny in my career.

Reframe it to be *interest*. Stakeholders, employees and leaders are sharing views because they are *interested* in the way communication happens. What does that do to the way you respond?

Leading the way

An internal communicator needs to operate in a leadership capacity as the subject matter expert, regardless of position or experience. This gets easier in time and with practice.

You are advising on the way communication happens, setting standards, inspiring others and raising the bar. You're not simply *managing* internal communication, but *leading* internal communication. There is a difference, and the distinction between the two matters.

To boldly go

We need to show our thinking in an IC strategy, and be courageous and bold in the recommendations we're making. A lack of conviction or 'safe' targets and aspirations will not transform the way an organization communicates.

Internal communicators need to be aware of *how* they work, *who* they work with and the relationships they cultivate and their personal motivations (their *why*), in line with their personal values.

'The more genuine your character, the higher your level of proactivity' wrote Covey (1989). 'It goes beyond transactional leadership into transformational leadership, transforming the individuals involved as well as the relationship.' He highlighted the need to invest in an 'Emotional Bank Account' with people, particularly when seeking their support.

Beware the 'can you just?' request

As internal communicators we often say yes to someone because we know we can use our expertise to enhance their work. We know we can apply the rigour we practise in internal communication to turn their ideas into interesting stories inside the organization to elicit a response and improve the way communication happens.

However, most of the 'can you just do XYZ?' requests are often last-minute, with zero planning on the part of the stakeholder. Their to do list seeps into ours and their lack of planning does little to help our own.

Internal communicators need to plan and prioritize so they can make progress. Part of this is knowing how to implement your internal communication strategy in a way that allows you as an individual or team to work strategically. This means working proactively, rather than reactively, while leaving room for the inevitable last-minute requests and crisis situations.

Managing the volume of requests

How do you manage the volume of requests for help the IC team receives? Techniques in place inside organizations include:

- A work intake form – a one-page briefing document that needs to be completed before the comms team assigns time to a project.

- A shared mailbox, to which requests need to be emailed.

- Editorial calendar for the business, which has prioritized initiatives outlined. What doesn't get captured doesn't get prioritized.

- A categorization structure (Tier 1, Tier 2, Tier 3, or gold, silver, bronze response). This is often based on how strongly the request is linked to organizational priorities or size of potential audience.

- Clear guidance regarding what the IC team *does* and *doesn't* do.

Do you have any of this in place in your organization? If you are creating an IC strategy and focusing on how to implement successful internal communication, take time to think through how you manage the volume.

Employee engagement

Let's address employee engagement, I have referenced it at various times in this book but want to examine it further.

Within the world of internal communication, the terms internal communication and employee engagement are often used interchangeably (CIPR Inside, 2017), but they shouldn't be as there's a distinct difference between them.

It's not uncommon for IC roles to include an element of employee engagement. For example, the *strategically advising* level (level three) of the Institute of Internal Communication Profession Map mentions engagement under the strategy, planning and business acumen professional area. It says internal communicators 'need to have a depth of understanding of relevant theory to underpin strategy development, which includes engagement and employee voice, plus distinctions between transactional and transformational engagement/change' (IoIC, 2023b).

William Kahn (1990) talked about personal engagement and disengagement, rather than employee engagement, which is widely regarded to be the first mention.

The MacLeod and Clarke (2009) definition of employee engagement is 'a workplace approach designed to ensure that employees are committed to their organization's goals and values, motivated to contribute to organizational success and are able at the same time to enhance their own sense of well-being'.

Employee engagement in action

Engage For Success is a movement that was created following the publication of the 'Engaging for Success: Enhancing performance through employee engagement' report by MacLeod and Clarke in 2009.

I remember when the report was published, I was working in-house as a Senior IC Manager in the railway in London and studying for a Postgraduate Diploma in Internal Communication Management via Kingston University and the Institute of Internal Communication.

I pored over the report, attending various launch events and trying to absorb what it meant. The end word in that definition is well-being. I had to search what it meant. I had never encountered the term well-being in my professional practice, and I had been working in-house for six years at that point in time.

It is unthinkable today to contemplate internal communication without considering well-being. I remember writing about the 'Engaging for Success' report on my internal comms blog back in 2009, which I had just launched. I was analysing the definition, thinking through what well-being was and considering how I could use the enablers in the organization I was working for.

I then went on to accompany David MacLeod to Rome in 2013 on the invitation of Toni Muzi Falconi, Senior Counsel and co-founder of Methodos SpA and adjunct professor at New York University School of Continuing and Professional Studies, NYC, as well as The Libera Università Maria SS. Assunta (LUMSA), in the Vatican, Rome. Toni is also one of the founders and inaugural chair of the Global Alliance. He had read about Engage for Success via my blog.

David and I shared our expertise to advise PR professionals in Italy who had seen what was happening in the UK and wanted to determine what engagement meant from their perspective (Miller, 2013). The global community of internal communicators is something incredibly special. What unites most of us is our desire to make a tangible difference to the organizations we work for, helping to transform them from the inside out by unlocking the power of effective communication.

Over the years, the word engagement has increasingly been used in place of communication and it's fair to say it has caused confusion and division in the comms community.

What engagement isn't

For all the definitions of what engagement is, it's important to note what it isn't. According to Engage For Success, 'Employee engagement cannot be achieved by a mechanistic approach which tries to extract discretionary effort by manipulating employees' commitment and emotions. Employees see through such attempts very quickly and can become cynical and disillusioned' (Engage for Success, nd).

The word engage is also used in internal communication in place of *interact*. It's become shorthand to mean provoke a response or reaction. This isn't helpful! For example, when I hear internal communicators telling me they want employees to engage with stories on their intranet (internal website), what they often mean is they want employees to notice the information, click on a link, respond to a call to action and remember the information they've read. When describing internal communication in an IC strategy, be mindful of using broad terms, clarify what you mean by terms like engage or engagement.

Examining engagement

Gallup defines employee engagement as 'the involvement and enthusiasm of employees in both their work and workplace'. Its 'State of the Global Workforce' report estimates low engagement costs the global economy $8.8 trillion. 'That's 9% of global GDP – enough to make the difference between success and failure for humanity' (Gallup, 2023b).

Gallup categorised employees into three groups, and found 77 per cent are disengaged – or 'filling a seat and watching the clock':

1 Thriving at work (engaged) 23 per cent

2 Quiet quitting (not engaged) 59 per cent

3 Loud quitting (actively disengaged) 18 per cent

Leadership and management directly influence workplace engagement, and there is much that organizations can do to help their employees thrive at work. Employee engagement does not mean happiness, if you're only measuring contentment, you're missing engagement. True engagement means your people are psychologically present to do their work. They understand what they have to do; they have what they need; and they have a supportive manager and a supportive team. They know why their work matters. They are *work ready*.

SOURCE Gallup, 2023b

What does employee engagement look like in your organization? How does it impact internal communication and what do you need to consider for your IC strategy?

Tip: Define what both internal communication and employee engagement are in your IC strategy, if you use this terminology.

Deciphering engagement and internal communication

The UK's Government Communication Service (GCS) says engaged employees mean a productive workforce. 'It proves that internal communications is not just about "Sending out stuff". By influencing staff engagement levels, we can have a positive impact on the things that really matter' (GCS, 2023).

It states engagement matters because internal communication departments play a key role in developing the flow of messages across the organization and all employees play a role in ensuring effective communications. 'An engaged workforce has a direct impact on key organizational outcomes: profits, customer satisfaction, productivity, innovation, absence and turnover' (GCS, 2023).

Joe Salmon is Director of Communication Business Partnerships, Global Functions, Iron Mountain. He says driving employee engagement is 'essential, but it's just the first step on the ladder to building pride and driving advocacy'. Salmon says employees need to feel and believe they are part of a culture where they can thrive while being themselves. 'It's much more than just connecting employees with the business, purpose and values. Internal Communicators need to connect people with people. That team spirit and sense of belonging is when advocacy happens' (IoIC, 2023).

Busting the jargon

The Local Government Association describes internal communication as an action – a function that uses information and dialogue to inform, motivate and inspire. It says employee engagement is a reaction – the outcome you get as a result of investing time, money and strategy into communication with your people and making your organization a great place to work.

I've observed employee engagement being added to internal communication job titles and descriptions. Organizations need to be focusing on creating the conditions for 'employees to be committed to the organization's goals and values, motivated to contribute to organizational success and enhancing their own sense of well-being' (MacLeod and Clarke, 2009).

Who's responsible?

If you have a solo internal communicator inside your organization, it's unrealistic to expect them to be solely responsible for delivering everything in that description. If employee engagement is a reaction, then the action has to be a coordinated effort. An internal communicator can certainly be involved in that work; I view it as a peer to internal communication, not a parent and not a child.

The Local Government Association acknowledge there are 'other issues beyond communication that contribute to employees' general satisfaction and engagement with their work'. These include training and development opportunities, cultural and environmental factors, pay and benefits, recruitment and retention matters and management structures. 'These things can't be addressed by internal communication alone. It is for this reason that some councils and other organisations make broad employee engagement work part of HR, while internal communications sits as part of a wider communication directorate' (Local Government Association, nd).

EXPERT VIEW
Emma Bridger

Employee engagement and experience in action

Although the importance of employee engagement is acknowledged by organizations, only 42 per cent of practitioners have an employee engagement strategy in place (People Lab, 2017).

If you are thinking about creating an employee engagement strategy to sit alongside your IC strategy, I recommend looking up Emma Bridger's work. She is Managing Director at People Lab and Co-Founder at The EX Space.

Her books include *Employee Engagement: A practical introduction* (Kogan Page, 2018). The strategy road map is a useful mechanism to develop a succinct 'strategy on a page' that will enable you to communicate your strategy and plan clearly to stakeholders.

Bridger says: 'You need to define what employee engagement means for your organization and it's vital key stakeholders in your business understand and support your definition. It's an important building block of your engagement strategy, underpinning the subsequent plan and activity.'

TABLE 5.1 Your employee engagement strategy road map

Employee engagement definition	
Future vision	
Goals	Outcomes
Action plan – drivers	
Measurement	

SOURCE Reproduced with permission of Emma Bridger, 2023

Employee experience

Is your organization focusing on employee experience (EX)? I first discovered the term in 2016 and highlighted Jacob Morgan's model on my blog, which describes the 'employee experience equation' as a combination of culture + technology + physical space = employee experience (Morgan, 2016).

Bridger acknowledges there is no universally agreed definition of either employee experience or engagement. However, she describes a great experience as 'subjective – a brilliant experience for one person, team or organization might not be perceived as brilliant elsewhere'.

Whereas the market has a lot of employee engagement indexes and benchmarks, the industry has not yet been saturated with EX indexes and benchmarks, which Bridger says is a good thing. She advises using a range of different data points if you want to benchmark, to understand how your organization compares, and to give you richer insights. She urges 'don't just rely on the benchmarks of the survey company you happen to use.'

Looking through the lens

Over the past decade, Bridger has gained insight into the workings and experiences of thousands of employees across diverse, global organizations via hundreds of 'Best Experience' workshops. She says this has enabled the design of great experiences, which result in engagement. The workshops allow individual perspectives on what truly matters at work to be unearthed and understood.

Bridger says 'the information gathered has highlighted and reinforced universal themes for an exceptional employee experience that delivers engagement. This led me to develop The EX-Lens as a diagnostic tool, to give a full picture and help professionals understand what a Best EX means to your people.'

There are two equally important aspects to the model:

1 Universal Themes – common themes that featured across all Best EX stories and were evident in the data analysed.

2 Individual differences – while Bridger's individual research uncovered universal themes of what makes an experience great, there are also individual differences.

While you can use the universal themes as a blueprint for designing experiences, it's only half the story. Bridger says it's important not to forget about individual differences. 'We all have individual needs, motivations and preferences, which are on the inner ring of the lens in the figure [Figure 5.1]. It's critical to ensure these are not ignored if you want to genuinely understand how to improve employee experience and facilitate engagement.'

Employee experience: Universal themes

The following nine universal themes of a positive employee experience are common across the thousands of 'Best EX' stories collected and analysed. They are grouped into three broad categories: the organization, the work and the people.

FIGURE 5.1 The EX-Lens

SOURCE Reproduced with kind permission of Emma Bridger, People Lab, 2023

1 Trust

2 Growth

3 Meaning

4 Impact

5 Challenge

6 Autonomy

7 Connection

8 Belonging

9 Appreciation

Bridger says 'trust, growth and meaning are all driven by the organization and its culture. Impact, challenge and autonomy come primarily from the nature of the work itself. Connection, belonging and appreciation are about people and the way they interact.'

The organization: Trust, growth, meaning.

Trust: trust is a two-way thing and without trust there can be no employee experience. An individual (or institution) has to earn it – by being trustworthy – and another has to grant it.

Growth: as humans we have an innate need for personal growth. The 'best experience' stories always involve some element of growth. It's also linked to challenge; we often find ourselves experiencing personal growth when we have a challenge to overcome. Growth is also predicated by our mindset – highlighting the role of employee mindset in EX.

Meaning: we're hard-wired to search for meaning and it's subjective to our own individual experience. It sits under the organization category as it's linked to wider mission and purpose.

The work: Impact, challenge, autonomy

Impact: when we have a positive impact and make a difference, it stimulates a rush of positive emotions, our serotonin and dopamine levels rise and we feel good about that experience. Having an impact also teaches our brains that our actions matter.

Challenge: overcoming a challenge elicits positive emotions, but developing purposefully hard experiences is not the answer. Challenges provide us with intrinsic motivation. Building experiences into workplace practice with an element of challenge engages the essence of employee well-being in organizational culture.

Appreciation: when we experience appreciation it results in a release of positive emotions and all the benefits this brings.

The people: Connection, belonging, appreciation

Connection: experiences involving positive social connections – with your manager, company leaders, team-mates, colleagues or even people outside the organization – feature consistently. As social creatures, feeling connected is rudimentary to our well-being.

Belonging: a feeling of belonging at work is a place where we can be ourselves. It is associated with alignment between personal and organizational values. Belonging is the sum of everyday experiences that enable people not only to feel safe, but able to bring their full selves to work.

Autonomy: direction and control of our own lives is important and a key feature of intrinsic motivation. In work, autonomy brings flexibility, a feeling of respect, sets employees free from limiting micromanagement and demands good communication in the organization.

What do these nine universal themes mean in your organization? Consider any elements that you need to be mindful of for your internal communication strategy. You may find the lack of something, such as appreciation or autonomy, creates a barrier to effective internal communication inside your company.

Establishing a successful IC team

When you're creating an internal communication strategy, consider including information about the internal communication team. This could take various forms; it could be a list of names and photographs or an organizational chart showing the structure. The purpose is to show the person or people behind the strategy. If you have business partnering in place, you could show who is supporting which area.

Dewhurst and FitzPatrick (2022) say there are four 'value spaces' an internal communication function occupies in organizations and they all overlap: getting the basics right, driving outcomes, supporting others and building intangible assets.

What if a team isn't in place?

I built teams when I was in-house and now advise internal communicators who are introducing or restructuring teams. It's tempting for IC pros to focus on people who may already be in the team, or people they've worked with before.

However, creating a successful team can only be achieved by analysing the business and being clear why the organization exists (purpose), what the organization needs to do, how people work, what the priorities are and what the business strategy is. Only *then* can you determine the communication roles that need to be in place to support those ambitions and ways of working. Once the job descriptions are in place, then you turn to the people and see who can fill those roles or where the gaps are.

If you are creating an ambitious internal communication strategy, do you have the right roles in place and people who could share that vision and turn it into reality? A strategy can also provide a glimpse into the future, demonstrating what could be achieved with additional investment.

EXPERT VIEW
Pinaki Kathiari

Pinaki Kathiari is CEO and Owner of Local Wisdom, based in New Jersey. The firm's mission is to make communication teams into a 'strategic force' within their organizations. He is an entrepreneur, a leader in digital communications and an international speaker.

He has developed a framework for growth, to help internal communicators and digital content teams assess their maturity.

The Five Layers

Kathiari says there are five core elements that make up a team's maturity:

1 **Workday:** High-level summary of how the team manages tactical communication and what the typical 'day in the life' feels like for each level.

2 **Achievements:** Seven milestones to reach an effective and efficient communications function.

3 **Team:** Ten roles that are key to the team's ongoing production needs. The positions and full-time equivalent (FTE) are combined to help gauge the minimum time commitments.

4 **Work volume:** The volume of people-hours needed to accomplish the achievements for a particular level to progress to the next.

5 **Business outcomes:** The net positive results a comms team can bring to their organization and the overall business impact they can make.

SOURCE Local Wisdom, 2023

In this book, I have examined the need for internal communicators to plan their work to allow time to focus *on*, not just *in* our roles. We've looked at the requirements for strategic internal communication and the need for planned, proactive, rather than reactive, work.

Kathiari says internal communicators can find themselves in a zone where 'important but not urgent work is continuously superseded by more traditional and

FIGURE 5.2 Internal Communication & Digital Content Team Maturity Model (2023)

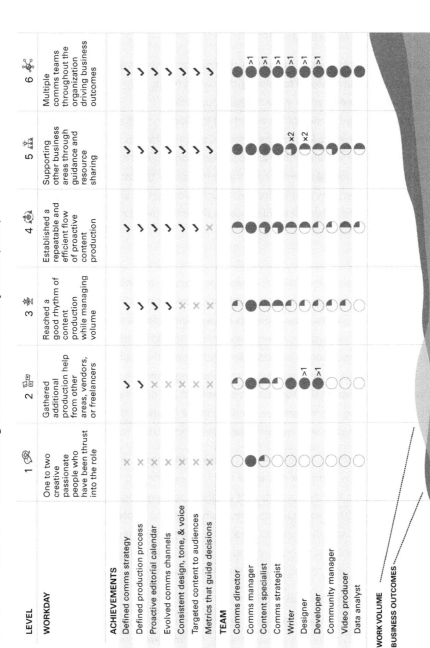

SOURCE Reproduced with permission from Local Wisdom

critical communications'. He says this gap often leaves room for only the day-to-day demands of the business, rather than the work that is necessary to help the organization grow.

How to use the Maturity Model

Kathiari has spent 20 years supporting communication teams and says Local Wisdom created the Maturity Model to help digital content teams keep up with the pace of organizational needs, while evolving their capabilities.

This is the third version of the model and Kathiari says it is a road map that can help anyone looking to level up their internal communications. 'Communicators can use the model to see where they are today, envision where they want to go, and plan a course there. Internal communicators are often under tighter budget constraints than their counterparts in other functions such as marketing and external comms. This model can help them determine how to maximize their time and strive for success.'

The levels

There are six levels in the Maturity Model. For example, organizations without a defined comms strategy and only a couple of communicators in place are typically at level one. Every level from two upwards has a defined comms strategy.

Kathiari says: 'A good communication strategy should be quick to come up with, convey realistic milestones, and consider what actions the team will not do (or defer until later). Without a destination, you're wandering without purpose or direction. I've seen strategies go sideways too many times. If you don't set yourself up with a plan, you're going to constantly be swept up in the "crisis" of the moment and not be able to approach your workload with the desired destination in mind.'

The sixth level includes more than one comms team across a larger organization. This is meant for larger companies, or those that have experienced massive growth or major expansion, like the acquisition of another company, opening a new location, or going global. 'How you stand up a new comms team is dependent on many different factors' says Kathiari, 'but a good starting point for most organizations is creating a role that first supports an area of the business that needs additional comms support, and then building up the team from there.'

Keeping organizational needs in mind

How can you match expectations with reality? Kathiari says as you use the Maturity Model to inform your team's growth strategy, he 'implores you to keep the needs of your organization top of mind. We've partnered with enough internal communicators to know just how high expectations can get, so please be realistic about what's achievable for your team and pace yourself accordingly. We cannot stress this enough: not every organization will need a level six comms team. Work toward the level that will best serve your organization, and you'll be on the right track'.

If you'd like a customized assessment of your comms team's level of maturity, you can take a five-minute quiz at maturity.localwisdom.com.

Designing teams

The Government Communication Service (GCS) in the UK uses a Modern Communications Operating Model (MCOM) to provide simplicity and clarity about the expectations of teams and leaders within the GCS.

It helps everyone working in government communications know the knowledge, skills and attributes they need, under the shared purpose of delivering outstanding government communication.

The model brings together all the policies and guidance needed to build and lead a team that delivers the GCS vision of exceptional communications that make a difference.

Designing and developing internal communication

What will be delivered is set out in the GCS Strategy 2022–25 'Performance with Purpose' and the annual Government Communication Plan. The policies and guidance in the Modern Communications Operating Model set out how to deliver exceptional communications, develop people and build great teams.

The MCOM 'house' has three pillars: People and Structure, Policies, and Guidance and Tools. The pillars sit underneath the overarching strategy framework for government communications.

The model is available via the GCS website and includes links to the policies and guidance outlined in the model. I like the language in use: what you must do, what you should do, and the guidance and tools you could use.

Team design principles

According to the team design principles, directors and heads of communication must clearly set out roles and accountabilities (e.g. in an organogram).

FIGURE 5.3 Modern Communications Operating Model 3.0

What you need to build and lead a successful communications team

GCS Strategic Approach		
GCS Strategy: Performance with Purpose and UK Government Communication Plan		
People and structure	**Policies**	**Guidance and tools**
Team design principles	Functional Standard: GovS011	OASIS campaign planning
Communication disciplines	Working with GCS (inc. governance)	Evaluation framework
Working across your organisation	Propriety and ethics	Crisis communications
		Mis- and disinformation
Equality, diversity and inclusion	Procurement and spend (inc AMC)	Behavioural science/COM-B
Building capability and talent	Data handling and protection	Models for disciplines
	Accessible communications	Media monitoring unit
	HMG brand guidelines	

SOURCE Reproduced with permission from Government Communication Service, 2023

Directors and Heads of Communication must take the following principles into account when designing their teams:

- Ensure, through tiered accountability, that it is clear who makes decisions and owns outcomes and processes.
- Work collaboratively in order to achieve clear, simple and consistent communication on behalf of government; manage duplication and minimize complexity.
- Keep processes simple, proportionate and user-focused.
- Define roles to suit the needs of the activity being undertaken.

The purpose and size of organizations will differ, but every communications team should apply the common, gold standard principle of using a multidisciplinary approach when structuring their teams.

Every communication team should have the core seven MCOM disciplines (GCS, 2023) represented to differing degrees depending on organizational need, size and focus. This does not mean needing seven separate siloed teams. In the spirit of a multidisciplinary approach, it means having those skills somewhere in the team and available to others. Design principles are also in place for digital content teams.

Four core functions of a modern digital communications team around which a digital team should be structured:

- Digital strategy and leadership
- Data insight analysis
- Technical content creation including these specialisms: graphic design and animation; videography; photography
- Copywriting, editing, channel management and strategic platform publishing, including all digital channels

Jo Pennington is head of standards and capability at GCS and coordinated the work bringing MCOM 3.0 together. Pennington says: 'MCOM is a living document and will be updated regularly to help everyone deliver world class communications.'

How to manage stakeholder expectations

Managing stakeholder expectations is a critical skill for internal communicators. According to research by Contact Monkey (2023), 75 per cent of internal communicators feel that 'leadership recognizes the value of internal communications'. Does that ring true for your organization?

Miscommunication is one of the biggest risks in an organization and a barrier to transformation and effective internal communication.

Leaders who assume that miscommunication is not a challenge in their organization will incur avoidable costs. Those who apply traditional systems to fill communication gaps will continue to funnel resources towards unscalable solutions. However, leaders who prioritize communication as a business imperative and act to strategically invest in communication solutions will unlock significant value across their organization (Grammarly Business and The Harris Poll, 2023).

Business leaders are feeling the downsides of poor communication, with 56 per cent saying they experience written miscommunications multiple times a week. Eighty per cent of business leaders (11 per cent more than knowledge workers) can think of concrete examples from the past year when unclear communication left them feeling anxious or stressed. However, business leaders (81 per cent) are still more likely than knowledge workers (66 per cent) to rate their organization's communications as effective (Grammarly and The Harris Poll, 2023).

I'm going to share an example with you of a team who have been working hard to refine their processes and manage expectations, to provide clarity for leaders and employees alike.

EXPERT VIEW
Cat Slatcher

Cat Slatcher is Senior Corporate and Internal Communications Manager at the Met Office, the national meteorological service for the UK. It provides critical weather services and world-leading climate science to help people make better decisions to stay safe and thrive.

It has around 2,000 employees based in 60 locations around the UK, including Heathrow Airport and a Marine Centre of Excellence in Aberdeen, plus global locations including Gibraltar, the Falkland Islands and even Antarctica.

Creating its IC strategy

The Met Office designed and developed its internal communication strategy using The MILLER Framework and has been implementing it inside the organization. Slatcher says: 'The MILLER Framework was so useful for our IC strategy as it's given us the structure and language we needed to create a comprehensive strategy. We didn't really know where to start and had various documents over the years. But now we're confident about our approach, we can show it to anyone who needs to see it internally and we're working in a consistent way.'

How the Corporate and Internal Comms team describe their role

At the Met Office, internal communication connects people to our vision and purpose, so we all feel involved, informed and inspired. We nurture a safe and inclusive environment where everyone can thrive.

We help the Met Office achieve its purpose by ensuring that our external and internal audiences understand who we are, what we do and what we stand for.

Ultimately, we promote positive engagement with the Met Office, encouraging people, both internally and externally, to act as advocates for the Met Office (Cat Slatcher, 2023).

The team developed a set of principles to help everyone communicate well with each other. They describe them as their mindset or ethos, and designed them as part of the Mindset section of The MILLER Framework, when creating their IC strategy.

Internal communication principles

At the Met Office we:

- communicate clearly, keeping things simple and understandable
- recognize and celebrate individuality
- make our communication accessible, inclusive and engaging
- are focused on who we want to communicate with
- choose the right channels and timing
- think with empathy and care about each other
- are open, honest and keep it real
- consider content, conversations and consequences
- are flexible and adaptable

Values

The Met Office's company values are a unique expression of the company's personality. They define their character and guide behaviours. They reflect who they are and the incredible work they do now – and in the future. The values underpin the internal communication principles:

- We live and breathe it.
- We keep evolving.
- We're experts by nature.
- We're a force for good.
- We're better together.

How the team supports the business

As part of their IC strategy creation, the team and I had conversations about how they advise and support the business.

To be able to implement and embed their internal communication strategy, they wanted to understand *where* work requests came from, *how* the team made decisions about *what* to support and then *how* they would support them.

This led to the creation of a service framework – *Internal Comms as a Service at the Met Office*. They defined three key areas: 1) Sources of demand, 2) Requirements gathering and baseline information and requirements, 3) Comms as a Service. We're going to look at each of these areas in turn.

Internal comms as a service at the Met Office

Sources of demand: Where does the IC comms requirement come from?

- Corporate and organizational comms, including central government comms
- Directorate comms affecting all staff
- Strategic action, projects or programmes supported by change management Tier 1-4
- Leadership comms support
- Incident management
- Staff networks

Tip: Consider this for your organization. Where do the internal communication requests come from?

Slatcher says: 'Change Management have a Triage Service in the Met Office, where they have four different levels and it determines what happens next. We realized the sources of demand felt like they came from a hundred different places. Unlike change management, you're not dealing with projects all the time, you're dealing with everything under the sun, from small to massive to crisis comms to incident management comms or senior leader comms. This makes it hard to plan and prioritize because everything happens daily.'

To help mitigate this situation, the team have become 'regimented' in getting people to complete an IC brief.

Completing an IC brief

An IC brief is a form that lives on their intranet, MetNet. It requires people to answer the *who, what, why, when, how* of their request for support and advice from the Communications and Engagement team. They aim to reply within two working days.

This forms the first formal interaction with the team. This is important because it helps them know the volume of requests and be able to plan effectively. It requires a change in behaviour from colleagues, who may be used to sending an informal note to an internal communicator, or stopping them in a corridor.

Implementing this process has become a fundamental way for the team to plan, prioritize and progress. The IC brief is part of the requirements gathering and baseline information, which is the second part of their *Internal Comms as a Service at the Met Office* framework.

Requirements gathering and baseline information

- An IC brief needs to be completed for any new IC work
- Access demand/workload assessed once a week
- Consult with change managers
- Determine capacity support for area of office
- Balance with other Met Office priorities

Before the team can assess the right level of support, they consider the following aspects, which they call *baseline requirements*:

- Clear comms driver
- Link to corporate strategy/strategic action
- Level of impact on the organization
- Level of interest/emotion/feeling/care
- Triage level of change management
- Change management support
- Part of existing comms plan
- Amount of comms collateral and required channel use
- Clear audience
- Time-bound – delivery schedule
- Lead time/advance warning
- Level of communication skills or experience resource
- Equality Impact Assessment completed or under way

Tip: Could an IC brief work for your organization?

Slatcher says: 'The baseline requirements are prerequisites. As a team we get together at least once a week to look at any work that has come in and we are asking the questions in the baseline requirements. We examine whether work has been triaged or given to us. Although we support different Directorates, sometimes there's one person who could be overloaded with a lot on, or someone in the team has prior knowledge to something. Having these discussions as team, with a consistent way of analysing the work, helps us plan.

'It took the team a while to get to this point, but they say the benefit of working in this way means they have clarity around the decisions they are making and ensuring they are prioritizing work which links to the business strategy.'

Comms as a Service

The final part of their *Internal Comms as a Service at the Met Office* framework is Comms as a Service. Depending on the criteria, the support and involvement they provide broadly falls into three categories: light touch, medium or high.

Using the IC brief and the three levels means they are working consistently as a small team and managing stakeholders' expectations. Slatcher adds: 'We tell people "this is the service you're getting from us, based on what you've told us the business requirements are". Sometimes something that seems small may become bigger, or something that seems larger may not turn out that way. But on the whole, the way we are approaching our work intake is proving successful.'

The categories denote the level of involvement from the IC team.

Light touch

- Provide high-level advice on messages, timings, audience, channels, comms plan.
- Signpost to resources toolkit, including templates and instructions, and encourage people to help themselves.
- Low time or resource commitment, or low priority.
- Reviewing and possible editing of communication content.
- Majority of work will be done by project lead, team members, subject matter expert or Change Manager.

Medium

- Initial support on messages, timings, audience, channels, comms plan.
- Signpost to resources toolkit, including templates, with guidance and collaboration – encourage people to help themselves.
- Medium time/resource commitment or priority.
- Reviewing or editing communications.
- Work will be collaborative and defined together with project lead, team members, subject matter expert or Change Manager.

High

- Provide detailed expert advice on, and often leading on, the delivery of messages, timings, audience, channels, comms plan.

- Signpost to resources toolkit, including templates, with guidance and collaboration.
- High time and resource commitment/priority – often embedded within project.
- Creating, editing and reviewing communications.
- Work will be collaborative and defined together with project lead, team members, subject matter expert or Change Manager.

Some organizations use a framework along these lines and choose gold, silver or bronze for the naming convention. The Met Office chose not to use these terms because Slatcher says they 'imply a hierarchy, which doesn't really help us. We did start out describing them in that way, but we discovered someone's bronze may seem better or worse than a gold. That's not the case, we're striving to be more "user-friendly" in how we're describing who we are as a team and what people can expect from our internal communication expertise. Sometimes things only need a light touch from us, so that's what they'll get, whereas others require more investment of our time and expertise, which means a higher level of service and intervention is required. Calling it gold, silver or bronze didn't help us in the way we hoped it would, but light-touch, medium and high are working well.'

The team worked diligently to develop criteria that would enable them to make informed decisions.

Creating a source of truth

The company uses SharePoint for its intranet, MetNet, and they have a Communications Team Site. This is the source of truth for how internal communication happens at the Met Office. It hosts resources and features information such as the IC principles and IC brief. Crucially, it also highlights 'what we offer' so colleagues can see immediately how to work with the team.

What we offer:

- Internal comms consultancy
- Stakeholder facilitation and analysis
- Project communications campaign planning
- Advise directorate level campaign planning
- Delivering of communication plans and activities
- Channel advice

- Translation and creation of key messages
- Creative advice and ideas
- Internal event organization
- Copywriting, editing and proofing
- Support with production of collateral and comms materials
- MetNet support – news items, briefs, announcements, events

SOURCE Cat Slatcher, 2023

They also link through to their service levels on the Communications Site. Slatcher says: 'The Communications Site has taken The MILLER Framework and made the sections visible for everyone to see. Creating the strategy was only one part, implementing it has saved us time and we're transforming how consistent we are as a team. We now have a rigorous approach to support the way we work strategically as comms professionals. It helps us hold ourselves and others to account and I've no doubt we will continue to build on it over time.'

Involving leaders in decision making

When is the best stage to involve leaders or an IC team when creating an IC strategy?

Are your organizational priorities clear and known? When you made a note of them earlier, you could have involved leaders, especially if you couldn't determine the priorities solo and needed input.

As you work your way through writing an internal communication strategy, consider involving leaders or key stakeholders as you prioritize your goals and objectives. This can help with buy-in and a sense of ownership.

You will be using these objectives to clearly outline what you will be focusing on (and therefore what you will be saying no to in future). It's worth thinking about involving leaders before you start writing, mid-way through and then at the end.

An internal communication team needs to demonstrate how their work is supporting the organization's business strategy and show the clear correlation between them.

EXPERT VIEW
Anthony Kluth

Anthony Kluth is Head of National Communications at the British Embassy in Washington, DC. His 20-year in-house internal communication career includes being Deputy Director, Group Head of IC at the Department for Environment, Food & Rural Affairs in the UK, Head of Strategic Communication at British Red Cross and Lead Communications Manager at Transport for London.

Kluth recommends involving the IC team first. 'We'll work together to identify the key areas within our organization's business plan where we feel IC can add the most value. We'll then pool our collective knowledge about what's happening in those areas, what we are already committed to and what sort of relationships we have or need. Once we have a useful framework we'll go out and engage leaders in a way that demonstrates we've done some of the thinking for them – but need their input to get the detail right. Once we have a credible working document, I'll present this to the top team. If all goes well, they will already have heard positive things about our work from their teams and are generally happy to see detail they recognize already reflected in the draft strategy. This can free up precious time with your most senior leaders to focus on which areas matter most to them.'

Seeking buy-in

Do you seek buy-in for an internal communication strategy in your organization? What does that look like? Kluth acknowledges this area can be 'surprisingly complex' and says it can depend on how IC is viewed. 'I've worked at organizations that understood and valued IC as a strategic function and others that prioritized delivery above all else, viewing too much strategizing as a distraction. In both cases it's important to ensure you have some form of strategy that identifies the areas where IC can add most value and captures the key pieces of work that underpin these. It can be important to get a few projects successfully delivered (to prove your value) before attempting to have a more strategic conversation with senior leaders – but having something you can reach for when you are in danger of being blown off course is vital.'

He recommends knowing what your organization is focused on. 'If your organisation focuses on delivery – pitch this as a succinct and clear delivery plan. If you feel a more strategic overview will be well received, work up a full strategy. Both routes are valid and it's fine to flex between the two if that's what will get you the buy in you need.'

> TIP FROM RACHEL
>
> If you are seeking additional budget to deliver what's in an IC strategy, involving key decision makers early can be useful.
>
> Some IC pros use their strategy document as part of a business case to ask for additional team members or to invest in certain channels. Think through who needs to be involved and kept updated about the proposals you are making.
>
> **Tip:** Demonstrating the impact of your recommendations can help ease the process. For example, if you are trying to build a team, can you have someone in a proposed role as a secondment or temporary opportunity? This can help you demonstrate the impact with real examples, rather than theoretical ones.

Why people managers need to be effective communicators

Think of the best manager you've ever had. What made them memorable?

I'm certain how they communicated forms part of your reason for choosing them. We remember people (or line) managers who listen well, encourage contribution, amplify their team's voices, and seek feedback. We remember their impact and that feeling remains, often years after parting ways.

'If communication is the sister of leadership, then motivation (to move) is its brother' (Adair, 1997). I love this quote and believe you cannot be a good leader without being a good communicator. Organizations need to motivate their leaders and help them be effective communicators.

Leaders who fail to make a connection with employees or are not visible during times of crisis or change are viewed negatively by a workforce. Some of the best leaders and people managers I've encountered in my career are those who are visible, motivational and personable.

Helping people managers to succeed

Throughout this book, I have highlighted the role of people managers, including the need for them to be actively participating in conversations, to increase relevancy and create a shared understanding and meaning for employees.

Managers form one of the four employee engagement enablers 'engaging managers who focus their people and give them scope, treat their people as individuals and coach and stretch their people' (MacLeod and Clarke, 2009).

It is not enough to merely acknowledge how critical people managers are to aiding communication inside an organization. We need to empower and equip them to communicate – and therefore lead – well. Organizations need to set their managers up for success, we need to train and counsel them to be the best communicators they can be.

At the start of this book, I outlined how internal communication is too important to be left to one team, department or person; it is *everyone's* responsibility. When it comes to people managers, organizations need to outline expectations clearly. They are not 'doing the role of the comms team' when communicating with their teams, but working towards 'creating the conditions in which employees offer more of the capability and potential' (MacLeod and Clarke, 2009).

My team and I often talk with clients about leaders being both a channel and a key stakeholder. It's useful to consider senior leaders and people managers through both lenses. They can be a channel as well as a group you rely on heavily to ensure internal communication is effective.

We live in an age of abundance of channels and choice. When I started working in this field in the early 2000s there was a much simpler channel landscape, but I still had to make a conscious decision to focus my efforts on leaders, to make sure they were equipped with what they needed to keep their teams informed and actively having conversations, in a timely way. I knew the monthly printed staff newsletter that was my primary channel back then was no use without a robust information flow in place.

Whenever I speak with an internal communicator who is launching a new channel, I urge them to consider the purpose – where will it fit in and what will the impact be on existing channels? Crucially, is there a clear mechanism in place for cascading?

How confident are you that information is flowing freely? This needs to underpin any approach to IC, see Chapter 4 to learn more about cascading.

What is expected?

The United States Office of Personnel Management (OPM) developed Executive Core Qualifications (ECQs) in 1997 to determine the attributes of successful executives in both the private and public sectors. They were updated in 2006 and 2012 and are: leading change, leading people, results driven, business acumen and building coalitions.

There are fundamental competencies within each ECQ, which are viewed as the 'foundation for success' in each one. The majority are rooted in communication: interpersonal skills, oral communication, integrity and honesty, written communication, continual learning and public service motivation (OPM, 2012).

Research among UK workers reveals 4 in 10 want their manager to 'better inform them about the team's priorities and goals, with another 3 in 10 wanting updates on their employer's performance' (IoIC, 2023a). That same research discovered one in three line managers 'don't feel equipped' to lead conversations with their teams about what is happening across the organization.

The language that is used often creates barriers for comprehension and action. If we're striving for managers to have conversations with their teams, the language and tone they use need to be conversational.

'The more formal the communication, the less likely it is to be repeated. Managers often feel uncomfortable "communicating" with their people because the language they're asked to use is so unnatural and artificial. The secret to effective leadership communication is to make it simple, memorable and repeatable' (Quirke, 2008).

Outlining expectations

When I was Head of Communications at London Overground, I inherited a monthly team briefing channel, which had been introduced by the HR team. At six sides of paper long, it was certainly not brief!

The length was certainly an issue as it had been designed to be read, rather than verbally briefed.

I sat in on team briefing sessions inside station mess rooms and depots across the railway network. I wanted to see and understand how it was being used. I could see it wasn't a great experience for the managers or team members, and I wanted to decipher why. Some sat in silence and read it, others read it verbatim and didn't add any additional information or relevant content for their station. It was formal and full of industry jargon, with a high level of assumed knowledge.

What I uncovered was a lack of clarity from the organization in terms of what was expected from the managers who were leading the team briefing sessions. Most leaders in the railway, not all, are appointed or promoted due to their technical expertise and knowledge. However, upon taking up the role, they were not told what the expectations were from a communication perspective.

This is what we expect

As a result of reviewing job descriptions with my HR peers, I introduced a competency framework into the organization. This was a document designed to outline expectations.

The wording I used was *'this is what we expect from you'* and *'this is what you can expect from us'*. It included a channels matrix and a commitment to help them communicate well. I launched it in-person with managers and trained them in-person on how to deliver a team brief.

Don't assume people managers know they need to talk with their teams, invite questions, localize content and provide feedback. That feels incredibly obvious to internal communicators; of course managers need to speak with their people. However, if the person who is newly appointed has not experienced it themselves, how are they to know?

When it comes to the cadence, or rhythm, people managers know their teams best, especially in an operational environment. I introduced 'flexibility within boundaries' in the railway. Give your leaders the information and tools they need to create sources of truth and certainty for their people, then trust them to know what's appropriate in terms of delivery. I made myself accountable to those briefers and invited them to have a constant dialogue with me, asking questions, checking for understanding and raising queries from their teams.

Considerations for an IC strategy

How are you setting line managers up for success? What needs to be reflected in your internal communication strategy? How well do line managers communicate in your organization? Are they equipped to lead their teams successfully? Is it clear what expectations are placed on them from an organizational communication perspective? Think these questions through for your organization and consider what needs to be included in your IC strategy.

Communication tasks for line managers

Research shows line managers are 'set up to fail' through a lack of communication preparedness (CIPR Inside, 2022). The Chartered Institute of Public Relations (CIPR) Inside's report 'Effective line manager communications' surveyed line managers, human resources professionals and internal communicators.

It revealed HR and IC professionals broadly agree on the communication tasks they expect line managers to carry out:

- Forward updates and cascades (94 per cent)
- Reinforce organizational values and behaviours (93 per cent)
- Initiate conversations in their teams (90 per cent)
- Listen to employees (90 per cent)

However, there is a gap between expectations placed on people leaders and the support they receive. Despite 73 per cent of respondents reporting that communication is valued as a leadership skill, just 15 per cent said training was mandatory for line managers, while 51 per cent said it was voluntary.

Dan Holden was Chair of CIPR Inside when the research was conducted. He says 'there are three key themes that were uncovered. They were organizations set the tone from the top, we expect a lot from line managers and need to start giving the priority and support that matches that expectation, plus the fact most organizations are communication heavy. The role of senior leadership in internal communication is vital. Management sets the tone, drive priorities and has the strongest influence across all levels of the organization.'

Operating as a strategic internal communicator

Working as a strategic internal communicator is evidenced through a variety of behaviours and experiences. It includes being brought into conversations early, so you're present when the thinking is being done, trusted with confidential information, and asked for your professional advice and recommendations.

In Chapter 1, we examined the levels in the Institute of Internal Communication's Profession Map. Level three is strategically advising and level four is leading. Level four states: 'working at a senior level to lead thinking on internal communication; ensuring communication strategies meet business needs and that effective communication is built into the fabric of the organization' (IoIC, 2023b).

An internal communication strategy is a demonstration of how a professional communicator is leading the thinking about how the organization communicates.

An internal communicator's personal brand

A personal brand sounds like something a celebrity has, and they certainly do. However, everyone has a personal brand, whether they realize it or not. I describe it as your *reputation and promise*, which includes your values and beliefs. It is *who you are and what you're known for.*

A brand is

> a perception or emotion, maintained by somebody other than you, that describes the total experience of having a relationship with you. It's definitely not trying to be something you're not. The difference between one personal brand and another is that the person with a *strong brand* utilizes their special qualities to make a difference in the lives of others (McNally and Speak, 2011).

Jeff Bezos, the founder of Amazon, says 'your brand is what people say about you when you're not in the room.'

What do your stakeholders say when you're not with them? Do they describe you as a trusted adviser and knowledgeable subject matter expert? Or do they describe you as someone who updates the intranet and organizes the all-employee meetings? More importantly, what are they thinking *when you are in the room*, or on a call together?

Why personal branding matters for IC pros

Your personal brand is critical as an internal communicator. When you are working inside an organization and striving to operate at a strategic level, having clarity around who you are and what you're known for can elevate your role.

It's essential if you are trying to influence at a senior level while creating an internal communication strategy. Throughout this book, we've examined the choices to make as you design and develop internal communication. As we move into implementation and transforming the way an organization communicates, knowing how you are perceived is an important self-reflection to make.

If the objectives you've set, the budget you require, or the channel recommendations you're making are bold, (which I encourage you to be!), are you able to take stakeholders *with* you? If not, what is holding you back? If it's the lack of relationship with them, or how you're viewed, this is something you can work on intentionally through analysing your personal brand.

> Your personal brand is your reputation and promise. It is who you are and
> what you are known for. I believe you own your personal brand and rent it to
> the organization you work for.

I started researching personal branding in 2017 and used my findings to
help me determine *what I was known for* and *what my internal communication business* was known for. Those explorations led me to have my personal
values analysed by values expert Dr Jackie Le Fèvre. I also developed a
personal branding checklist, which I now use with in-house internal communicators. There are 10 questions to answer to help you critically assess how
you are viewed.

PERSONAL BRANDING CHECKLIST

Ten questions to ask to gauge your personal brand as an internal
communicator:

1 What do stakeholders think of you?

2 How would you describe yourself in three words?

3 What three words would your boss or team use to describe you? What
about a friend or partner?

4 What image are you projecting inside your company? And at home?

5 What's the impact of the information above? Is it accurate?

6 What are you known for? What are your values?

7 Are you known for what you *want* to be known for?

8 How can you change perceptions? What do you need to do?

9 How can you celebrate your personal brand and build on the strengths?

10 When will you review what you've discovered?

Tip: Ask people whose opinion you trust, to answer these questions. Once you
know the answers, identify any gaps between what you're known for and what
you want to be known for, then create an action plan and put timings against it.

I believe you own your personal brand and rent it to the organization you work for. If your personal brand is your reputation and promise, that not only applies to us as individuals, but collectively as a communication function.

Being mindful of your reputation and promise is useful because if you want to be working strategically, you must break it down, to understand where your gaps are.

Who are you?

When I ask internal communicators how they are described by stakeholders, they give one of these four answers: comms police, trusted adviser, I don't know, people don't know me.

There isn't a perfect answer here. It is OK to be viewed as someone who safeguards your brand, comms police style. However, if that perception means people in the business are unaware of the insights you have about employees, and your skills, knowledge and experience to help create a shared understanding and meaning to align employees' efforts, you'll typically work tactically and reactively.

You may discover different stakeholders view you in different ways. What is the impact of the way they view you? Who do you need to work with to create your IC strategy? What are your relationships like with them?

TABLE 5.2 Personal branding answers

How IC pros say they are viewed	IC pros' reflections on what it means
Comms police	I'm known for correcting grammar, getting the red pen or tracked changes out and being the brand guardian
Trusted adviser	I'm known and trusted in the organization. I'm brought in early to conversations by stakeholders and my advice is usually listened to
I don't know	This isn't something I've considered. I've no idea how I'm viewed by people inside my organization, I couldn't say without asking them
People don't know me	I'm new to the company, or feel like people don't know who I am. They contact our shared mailbox and ask for a 'comms person' rather than by name

How to champion an IC strategy

Internal communicators need to be talking the language of the business when championing an IC strategy. We will examine sign-off and boardroom conversations in Chapter 7.

One of my favourite techniques for leading internal communication and championing an IC strategy is the creation of principles. I've used them constantly in my career and recommend them regularly to clients.

Internal communication principles

Having a set of IC principles as part of an internal communication strategy helps employees, stakeholders, leaders and the IC team know what is important and what's being prioritized.

IC principles are your promises – they are a check and balance for an IC team and educate the wider organization regarding the standards that are in place. I also use them as part of desk research when auditing or analysing the way a company communicates. If they don't have principles in place, I determine what I think they are, or could be.

Creating IC principles

There's a couple of ways to approach creating principles – the director of IC or head of IC could create them and present to their team for discussion, buy-in and revision. Or an IC team could start with a blank sheet and co-create them together.

Co-creation is powerful because the team will be the ones holding themselves and the organization to account, so there's a benefit to being consulted and involved.

IC principles in action

In Chapter 2, Debbie Chapman, Head of Communications at Battersea Dogs & Cats Home in the UK shared the thinking behind her internal communication strategy. Here are the IC principles in place inside her organization, which form part of her IC strategy.

Battersea has introduced the following IC principles:

- We are skilled and empowered, able to deliver engaging content.
- We have a clearly defined tone of voice.

- We have clearly defined ways of working – so we are clear about what is in our power to sign off or create and have ownership over our channels.
- Internal Comms are involved in projects from the start. We are trusted advisors to colleagues across the organization.
- We provide a clear connection in all our internal comms to our impacts for dogs and cats.
- We have insight into how our internal comms are received that helps us make evidence-based decisions.
- Our internal communications are timely, current and relevant (we cut down on noise).
- Our internal communications are inclusive, clear, concise. We have focus groups to test for understanding.
- We have an effective channel strategy in place, with clearly defined audiences and channels that deliver to them.
- Our intranet is a useful resource – not a dumping ground.
- Our channels are accessible. Staff are using Pawtal (intranet) on their mobiles.
- We empower colleagues to create their own content (to set guidelines).
- Internal Comms are curators of content and have more time to work on the biggest projects and priorities.

SOURCE Debbie Chapman, 2023

What do you think of this wording? I wonder if it resonates with you. What would your IC principles be? We have covered a lot in this chapter, including looking at leading internal communication and how to work with leaders.

STRATEGY CREATION CHECKLIST

Make notes and decisions on the following points, before moving on to the next chapter. This will help you write your strategy as you read through this book. As a result of working your way through this chapter, you should now have:

- Considered how you are leading, not just managing, internal communication in your organization.
- Thought about how to manage the volume of work requests.

- Analysed your personal brand and what the IC team is known for. Created an action plan if required.
- Thought about line manager communication and decided what to include in your IC strategy.
- Deliberated IC principles and determined if they could be useful for your organization.

Review the choices you've made while reading through this chapter. Make sure you've captured what has resonated and what feels appropriate for your organization.

References and further reading

Adair, J (1997) *Leadership Skills*, Cromwell Press, UK

Bridger, E (2018) *Employee Engagement: A practical introduction*, 2nd edn, Kogan Page, London

Chapman, D (2023) Interview/correspondence with the author

CIPR Inside (2017) Making it Count: The strategic value and effectiveness of internal communication, Chartered Institute of Public Relations, cipr.co.uk/CIPR/Network/Groups_/Inside_content/Resources_.aspx (archived at https://perma.cc/TJX7-HD6N)

CIPR Inside (2022) Effective line manager communications: A CIPR Inside study, Chartered Institute of Public Relations, September, newsroom.cipr.co.uk/line-managers-set-up-to-fail-through-lack-of-communications-preparedness/ (archived at https://perma.cc/2HBC-S47H)

Contact Monkey (2023) Report: Global State of Internal Communications 2023, https://www.contactmonkey.com/ebook/global-survey-2023 (archived at https://perma.cc/KYH4-78LA)

Covey, S R (1989) *The Seven Habits of Highly Effective People*, Simon and Schuster, New York

Dewhurst, S and FitzPatrick, L (2022) *Successful Employee Communications: A practitioner's guide to tools, models and best practice for internal communication*, 2nd edn, Kogan Page, London

Engage For Success (nd) What is employee engagement, engageforsuccess.org/what-is-employee-engagement/ (archived at https://perma.cc/M2LN-JQTZ)

Gallup (2023a) Employee Engagement Solutions, www.gallup.com/workplace/229424/employee-engagement.aspx (archived at https://perma.cc/U6T8-3BRC)

Gallup (2023b) State of the Global Workplace 2023 Report: The voice of the world's employees, www.gallup.com/workplace/349484/state-of-the-global-workplace.aspx (archived at https://perma.cc/3MJG-SZ7H)

GCS (2022) Performance with Purpose: Government Communication Service Strategy 2022–2025, strategy.gcs.civilservice.gov.uk/wp-content/uploads/2022/05/gcs-strategy-2022-25.pdf (archived at https://perma.cc/UP53-F7ZF)

GCS (2023) Modern Communications Operating Model 3.0, Government Communication Service, 27 June, gcs.civilservice.gov.uk/modern-communications-operating-model-3-0/#people-and-structure (archived at https://perma.cc/5GXK-KFGA)

Grammarly Business and The Harris Poll (2023) The State of Business Communication 2023: The path to productivity, performance, and profit, go.grammarly.com/business-communication-report (archived at https://perma.cc/KZ6R-NQ2H)

Harris, S J (1972) For the Time Being, Houghton Mifflin, Boston, MA

IoIC (2023a) IC Index 2023, Joe Salmon quote, Institute of Internal Communication, www.ioic.org.uk/resource/ic-index-report-2023.html (archived at https://perma.cc/GKY5-MPAG)

IoIC (2023b) The Profession Map: The core, Institute of Internal Communication, www.ioic.org.uk/learn-develop/the-profession-map/the-core.html (archived at https://perma.cc/E9NV-G2JY)

Kahn, W (1990) Psychological conditions of personal engagement and disengagement at work, Academy of Management Journal, 33 (4), 692–724

Local Government Association (nd) What is internal communications? www.local.gov.uk/our-support/guidance-and-resources/comms-hub-communications-support/internal-communications/what (archived at https://perma.cc/86U7-LD3J)

Local Wisdom (2023) Interview/correspondence with the author

MacLeod, D and Clarke, N (2009) Engaging for Success: Enhancing performance through employee engagement, Department of Business, Innovation and Skills, engageforsuccess.org/wp-content/uploads/2020/12/engaging-for-success.pdf (archived at https://perma.cc/46QG-8VXJ)

McNally, D and Speak, K (2011) Be Your Own Brand: Achieve more of what you want by being more of who you are, 2nd edn, Berrett-Koehler Publishers Inc, San Francisco, CA

Miller, R (2013) Engaging for success in Italy, All Things IC Blog, 3 June, www.allthingsic.com/italye4s/ (archived at https://perma.cc/295E-MX6F)

Morgan, J (2016) The Employee Experience Equation, 25 February, thefutureorganization.com/the-employee-experience-equation (archived at https://perma.cc/DW9E-9XPF)

OPM (2012) Guide to Senior Executive Service Qualifications, United States Office of Personnel Management, www.opm.gov/policy-data-oversight/senior-executive-service/reference-materials/guidetosesquals_2012.pdf (archived at https://perma.cc/45F6-6XBR)

People Lab (2017) Spotlight on the Employee Engagement Profession, https://peoplelab.co.uk/help-us-to-close-the-employee-engagement-gap-spotlighton-employee-engagement-2018/ (archived at https://perma.cc/YYE3-MBAJ)

Quirke, B (2008) *Making the Connections: Using internal communication to turn strategy into action*, 2nd edn, Gower, Aldershot

Slatcher, C (2023) Interview/correspondence with the author

6

Evaluation and measuring internal communication

WHAT THIS CHAPTER WILL COVER

We are at the penultimate stage of creating an internal communication strategy, which is evaluation. This chapter will examine why measurement is important, the role of data and why measuring impact matters. I've included expert views and frameworks to demonstrate measurement in action. You'll find a checklist at the end of this and every chapter to help you keep on track.

The MILLER Framework: Evaluation

Failing to measure or evaluate your work is like opening a brand-new board game, discarding the rules and trying to decipher what's in front of you. You'll be exerting effort with no idea what the purpose is, how to play or how to win.

Measurement creates a logical pattern for internal communicators, it determines the rules of the game and allows us to identify what we're aiming for. As a result of measuring we can review, adjust, and know whether our efforts are paying off. Measurement is defined by the Collins English Dictionary as 'a result, usually expressed in numbers, that you obtain by measuring something – the quality, value, or effect of something and the activity of deciding how great it is'. Evaluation is 'the act of appraising or diagnosing'.

What results are you aiming for and how are you appraising those results? Measurement isn't a nice-to-have skill for internal communicators, we need to have it. We need to know what is working in our organizations and what isn't.

Measuring for success

Lord Kelvin (1824–1907) is widely reported to have said 'if you cannot measure it, you cannot improve it'. The longer version of what he said is

> when you can measure what you are speaking about, and express it in numbers, you know something about it; but when you cannot measure it, when you cannot express it in numbers, your knowledge is of a meagre and unsatisfactory kind: it may be the beginning of knowledge, but you have scarcely, in your thoughts, advanced to the stage of *science*, whatever the matter may be' (Lord Kelvin, 1883).

In Chapter 3, we explored insights and how to use them to determine how an organization communicates. It's not enough to just collate reams of statistics, we need to gather the *right* data, make sense of it and use that data to inform our decision making.

Continuing to write articles, oversee channels, advise leaders and counsel the business without knowing whether what we're doing is *working* is unwise. A lack of data and measurement causes internal communication professionals to rely on *instinct* rather than *insight*. Communicators need to build evaluation into an internal communication strategy. I'll guide you through how to do that in this chapter.

Transforming organizational communication

People 'don't think in terms of information. They think in terms of narrative. But while people focus on the story itself, information comes along for the ride' (Berger, 2014). What's the narrative of your internal communication strategy? If it's transformational, what's the story you're telling? What information (measurement) do you need to have in place to reinforce the story?

What's your transformational story?

From *Beauty and the Beast* to *The Very Hungry Caterpillar*, transformational stories surround us. Transformation is tangible and requires a change from one state to another. Now is the time to evaluate your IC strategy. Appraise it to determine if you're playing it safe. Be honest. Is it an *evolution* or *revolution* of your organizational communication? Could you take it further?

'When it comes to transformation, there's a difference between disruption and destruction' says Tope Sadiku, former Global Head of Digital Employee Experience at The Kraft Heinz Company, one of the largest food and beverage companies in the world. She is now working as the Strategic Planning Lead, Transformation, Agile and Digital Revolution at Kraft Heinz, where her focus is to increase employee productivity and creativity using technology. 'There is some level of disruption and sometimes we can get very excited to the point of destruction. Knowing where that line is very, very important' (Firstup, 2023).

Transforming or improving an organization's communication takes time. Be ambitious when setting targets for what you are trying to achieve but remember to be time-bound too. What can you realistically achieve and what needs to change? Consider the fact 'All improvement requires change, but not all change will result in improvement' (Langley et al, 1996). What needs to be improved about the way your organization communicates?

TIP FROM RACHEL

Define transformation

If your communication objectives include transforming internal communication, you need to define what it means for your organization, so you have a chance of measuring it. What would it mean for your organization? How will you know transformation has happened?

Imagine it's 12 months from now, what's the journey you've been on? What are the milestones along the way and what are employees doing, saying, thinking and feeling?

The starting point

You need to know the 'as-is' state or starting point first, to determine progress and review the impact of your actions and recommendations. This is where knowing your transformation story comes in. What's the current situation? This will help you track progress and once you've made changes or improvements, you'll be able to reflect back.

> **Tip:** Screenshots of intranet homepages are worth capturing before you embark on a technology refresh or redesign as it's easy to forget what it previously looked like.
>
> Get specific
>
> Look at the objectives you've written for your internal communication strategy, to ensure they are specific enough to be measurable. If they're not, refine them until they are. Have you demonstrated how you will measure channels? What does success look like and how will you determine the value they've added?

Why should people care about the transformation story your internal communication strategy is telling? What business problems are you solving?

'Internal communication is continuing its steady rise in transforming organizational performance and working lives. Demonstrating value has to be part of that story' says Suzanne Peck, Institute of Internal Communication President. Peck says secrets to successful measurement involve 'having a clear purpose or objective that your leadership supports, benchmarking where you are before you begin, and measuring the difference at the end'.

Why measurement is important

If you are working as an internal communicator and struggle to know what and how to measure, you're not alone. Various industry reports acknowledge this situation. 'Tracking and measuring internal communications has been the main challenge facing internal communicators for years, with 63% of respondents citing it as their number one challenge' (Contact Monkey, 2023). 'Lack of analytics and measurement' is cited by 22 per cent of internal communicators as one of their top challenges (Gallagher, 2023).

According to the Institute of Internal Communication, the purpose and aim of internal communication is to affect a change in the knowledge, attitude and/or behaviour of people within an organization, in line with defined business outcomes (IoIC, 2019). When thinking about measurement, we need to demonstrate those outcomes.

The benefit of hindsight

How will you know if your internal communication strategy is successful? When it comes to strategies, 'the problem is that it is only with hindsight that you can see whether the right strategic choices were made and the right techniques were made to put them into practice' (Barthélemy, 2022). We don't have a crystal ball that allows us to see into the future, so we need to build evaluation into our strategies today. I encourage you to build hindsight into your internal communication strategy via the process of revision, which we will discuss in Chapter 7, as it's the final stage of The MILLER Framework.

Using insights for evaluation

I examined auditing internal communication in Chapter 3 and shared some hypotheses. Including a hypothesis can be a useful measure of success for an internal communication strategy. Creating a strategy because you know the business problem (or hypothesis) you're trying to address, gives you a clear mandate for measurement and evaluation. You're able to use the insights you collate through your work to demonstrate progress.

EXPERT VIEW
Caroline Cubbon-King

'Measurement comes in all shapes and sizes' says Caroline Cubbon-King, Communications Consultant at All Things IC. She's worked alongside the wider team and me to deliver internal communication audits and describes them as 'the most in-depth measurement and evaluation lens'.

'It can feel exposing to lay your approaches, channels, content and insights bare and for review' reflects Cubbon-King. 'My favourite part of an IC audit is the listening phase. The insights that come from meaningful listening are like gold dust.'

How to start an audit

- **Immerse yourself in information:** learn about the business strategy so you fully understand the context for the audit.
- **Analyse channels:** look at information flow inside the organization.

- **Assess the noise:** imagine you're an employee when reading content examples and experiencing digital comms channels. Assess the levels of noise in terms of volume and content.

'Internal communicators who are thinking of auditing usually know what's working well and what's not running so smoothly. They may even have measurement insights that back this up. This doesn't mean they are ready to act. Other teams desperately need investment in new channels or team members. Their measurement data might show loud and clear that there's an issue, but that doesn't mean they have the right evidence to make the case.'

Cubbon-King says 'well planned, thoughtful listening is where the magic happens. If you ask the right questions, your audience start to provide the evidence you need. They share experiences that back up your instincts. They can help you to focus your efforts too. We read lots of measurement reports that have so much detail, it's hard to know what to take on first. Let your people show you the way through the insights you gain via listening to them.'

Listening as a measurement approach

'Think about listening as a valid and hugely valuable part of your measurement approach' says Cubbon-King. 'Every week I speak to somebody who says they can't get accurate or meaningful analytics out of a system. That's sometimes used as a reason for not prioritizing measurement, which is not OK. You can always ask for feedback by talking with employees via focus groups or short surveys. Listen to see if messages are resonating and cutting through the noise, or test to see if leaders are briefing their teams well using the tools you have given them.'

Audit reports

'Audit reports are comprehensive, which reflects the detailed approach and care we apply. I recommend identifying prioritized findings and the actions that will have the most impact. Regardless of the complexity, we never identify more than five prioritized findings. Ensuring colleagues have a voice or embracing listening as part of your day-to-day approach is never far from my mind when forming audit recommendations and actions.'

Judging efforts

'Knowing how your stakeholders and audience will judge your efforts as a team is key when you're planning your approach to measurement and evaluation. I guarantee they won't be thinking about open rates. They will be judging you on how informed they are, whether they understand messages and receive them in a timely way and have a chance to ask questions or have their say. Leaders want to feel confident, equipped and able to communicate complicated messages or global messages in a way their local audience will relate to. There's nothing more satisfying than being able to say "you asked and we delivered". If you want to know the impact of your IC approach, the answers can be found through listening. I urge you to look for them.'

Making sense of data

'Communicators readily agree that communication is a means to an end. Yet all too often that end is either ill-defined or unmeasured' (Quirke, 2008). I read that quote when I was in-house and it resonated with me. I realized I had access to a lot of statistics, but hadn't determined what the end was.

What was I aiming for? How did the work I was doing align with the business strategy? How were the channels I oversaw contributing to the way employees felt about the business? How did I know if employees had the information they needed to do their jobs and understand how their roles aligned with the organization? It all felt incredibly overwhelming, until I understood measurement.

I made so many measurement mistakes in the early part of my internal communication career. It was tempting to measure something just because I *could*. I was surrounded by outputs, I took the numbers in front of me and dutifully reported them to whoever took an interest. However, I could not talk the language of outcomes, or the *so what?* as I call them. I had no idea what had happened as a result of all the stories I'd written, or advice I'd given to leaders, and I didn't ask.

How I measure

There are three things that have made a huge difference to the way I work and how I measure as an internal communicator:

1 Setting intentions
2 Defining the terms
3 Speaking with stakeholders

FIGURE 6.1 Intentions framework

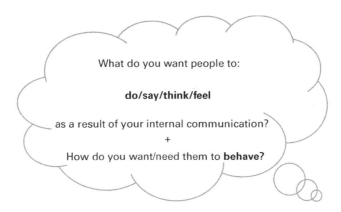

I revealed my intentions framework in Chapter 2 and how I ask myself these questions – what do you want people to do, say, think or feel as a result of your internal communication? How do you want (or need) them to behave?

If I don't know the answers to these questions, I cannot measure. Being clear what I am aiming for is critical, so I can capture those intentions and determine the route to achieve those aims.

Defining the terms and creating clarity

As internal communicators, we regularly collect numbers or outputs, but working strategically means focusing on outcomes.

These are some of the definitions I use for measuring internal communication. I have collated them throughout my career, so need to give acknowledgement to Melcrum, International Association for the Measurement and Evaluation of Communication (AMEC), Institute of Internal Communication and the Chartered Institute of Public Relations.

- **Evaluation:** the process of appraising to determine if you achieved what you set out to do.
- **Goal:** what you are aiming towards, the destination you're heading for.
- **Impact:** the effect caused by communication, typically the behavioural actions that are made.
- **Inputs:** 1) Defines the target audiences. 2) What you need in preparation for your communication, including your strategic plan, e.g. situational analysis, resources required and budgets.

- **Key performance indicator:** a quantifiable or measurable value that reflects a business goal or objective, and how successful the tactics are in helping you achieve it.

- **Measure/measurement:** a number that is derived or taken to determine the size or amount of something at a given point in time.

- **Metric:** a calculation between two measures, usually presented as a fraction or ratio to establish, monitor or compare impact or performance.

- **Objectives – organizational:** AMEC states all good measurement needs to start with organizational objectives. These can come in many different forms, whether they be awareness, advocacy, adoption or demand related.

- **Objectives – communication:** following on from organizational objectives are communication objectives. These should reflect and mirror the organizational objectives.

- **Objectives and key results (OKRs):** typically an objective, followed by action points.

- **Output:** something you do; it usually has a number attached and is quantifiable.

- **Outcome:** I call this the 'so what' – what's happened as a result of the work you've done? It's also what you want your audience to do, say, think or feel as a result of the internal communication. The outcome could be a change in behaviour.

- **Outtakes:** the result of the communication, what the audience is taking away as knowledge or behaviour.

- **Quantitative measurement:** all about the numbers or quantities. Usually gathered through employee surveys, polls, counting attendee numbers, website statistics and readership rates.

- **Qualitative measurement:** dives deeper and relates to qualities. It's what employees feel and is typically gathered via conversations such as focus groups, one-to-one interviews or free-text boxes in surveys.

Focusing on attention

Whose attention are you striving to attract through your organizational communication? Sustaining attention is

> less about making people feel good or bad, and more about opening up a curiosity gap that makes them want to learn more. Uncertain emotions, or

uncertain language more generally, keeps people engaged. If people already know who is going to win the game, there's no reason to watch the rest, but if the outcome is up in the air, they stay tuned to find out (Berger, 2023).

TIP FROM RACHEL

Determine how you – and the organization – talk about measurement. Create a glossary so you have a consistent approach and create certainty through language.

You could include some of these definitions in your internal communication strategy, to show what you are prioritizing.

Speaking with stakeholders

How often do you talk about measurement with stakeholders? It needs to be part of a briefing exercise, so when you are *planning*, not just *reviewing* internal communication. Don't wait until the end of a campaign or initiative to measure, as it will probably be too late to take action and improve or change something.

There is a trap many internal communicators fall into and it's measuring something just because you *can*. I shared a story with you in Chapter 5 of the monthly team brief I inherited at London Overground. When I joined the railway, I was given a spreadsheet containing pages of numbers. It was all the stations and how many people had been briefed each month.

It told me nothing. It was hundreds of rows of numbers, a whole list of outputs. But what was missing were the outcomes – or the so what? What happened as a result of employees participating in the team brief? What had they learnt? What did they have questions about? How did the brief make them feel? Was there anything missing?

Unless you are striving to mandate team briefings and want to ensure they're taking place, figures like that are meaningless. You need to outline expectations for people managers and trust them to conduct briefings.

The conversations leaders had with me about the team brief were to reassure me they'd taken place. They seemed surprised I wanted to *check-in*, not *check-up*, and move the conversation to be outcome-focused. There's a key difference in how people feel when they realize you're genuinely interested in helping them and their teams communicate, rather than chastising or chasing them to hold a team brief. Working strategically means communicating proactively; I made it my business to ensure employees saw that role modelling in action.

Focusing on employees

'There is often an overreliance on management-centric rather than employee-centric assessments' (Ruck and Welch, 2012). As a result of employee input from the questions I asked, I started including operational data such as how many miles trains travelled over the previous month, highest footfall in stations and updates on new fleet. Why? That information was what employees said they were interested in hearing about monthly, so I used those insights to evaluate and improve it.

After a few months, feedback revealed the perception of the channel and its overall usefulness had soared. Why? Because I had listened to what employees said and reflected their views in the content. After all, it wasn't *my* channel, it was overseen by me, but *for* them, to provide information to help people do their jobs and feel confident talking about the organization. Providing information to front-line colleagues equipped them to have better conversations externally with customers.

The role of data in an IC strategy

Use data and evidence to underpin aspirations and decisions in your internal communication strategy. Demonstrate why you are making recommendations, give context to the objectives and use insights to inform your work.

WHAT IC PROS ARE MEASURING

- **Reach:** email statistics, event and web call attendance, intranet and online analytics.
- **Understanding:** surveys, focus groups.
- **Behaviour change and business outcomes:** adoption rates, employee turnover.
- **Employees' satisfaction with IC:** audit, surveys, interviews.

Internal communicators turn insights into action, using data to:

- Provide evidence of value or show return on investment (ROI) to leaders.
- Refine channel frameworks.
- Adjust messaging.
- Tailor the types of content for different audiences, based on their interactions.
- Build business cases for additional investment.

SOURCE Gallagher, 2023

Include a section in an internal communication strategy called 'risks, barriers and mitigations'. Use it to highlight anything that will stop the strategy from being successful.

Clearly outline how you will measure impact and consider quantitative, qualitative and observational methods. This complements the SWOT analysis you'll read about in Chapter 7.

EXPERT VIEW
Liam FitzPatrick

Liam FitzPatrick is experienced in change management, PR and internal communications, in-house and for major consultancies. He lectures on developing teams, research and planning, and has served as an external examiner at UK universities. As well as contributing to several textbooks on PR and IC, he's co-authored a number of books including *Successful Employee Communications* with Sue Dewhurst (2019 and 2022) and *Internal Communications: A manual for practitioners* with Klavs Valskov (2014).

He says planning can be a 'real challenge' for communicators. One of the main reasons for this he says is because 'we're often at the mercy of events, providing responses to crises or external changes that our colleagues need to understand. Or, our perfect To Do list can be derailed by that "urgent" request which was brewing months ago but didn't bother to let us in on the secret!' FitzPatrick says getting 'out of the daily tumble dryer is every communicator's dream; the problem is that few of us stay out for long'.

Good intentions

Software company ICPlan discovered that fewer than 40 per cent of us are happy with our planning. We have good intentions, but often lack the time or the space to sit back and think about where we're headed and how we're going to get there.

Yet there is a clear link between teams that are strong planners and the respect and licence they receive in their organizations. That influence seems to stem from planning on three levels and is underpinned by the communicator's superpower – audience insight.

These are FitzPatrick's three levels of planning:

1 Strong project planning

2 The medium term

3 The big picture

FitzPatrick has addressed them all in turn, to reveal more detail.

Strong project planning

When we get the call to support a project, it is important to get a clear brief. However, many of us naturally jump straight into solutions mode. Our customer wants a poster, and we ask about design or where it will appear, neglecting to really understand what the customer wants to happen or why a poster is the right answer.

Just by asking the right questions, informed by how we know the wider team will respond, we can change the way the customer understands their own needs. Smart communicators have a standard battery of questions that they refer to and it is worth discussing with comms teammates what should be on the list. This will include the obvious things like timing and resources, but asking about *outcomes* and *outtakes* before looking at *outputs* makes a massive difference.

DEFINING THE TERMS

- **Input** – are we using our resources effectively?
- **Output** – did we do what we actually planned to do and, if not, do we know why?
- **Satisfaction** – did our audiences like what we gave them? Did they turn up in droves on our SharePoint page or did they talk about it on Viva Engage?
- **Outtakes** – did our audiences hear our core messages and did they make sense? Were they engaged by what they heard?
- **Outcomes** – are people doing what the organization needs them to do?

SOURCE Liam FitzPatrick, 2023

The medium term

Many of us, especially those responsible for channel management, find it useful to have a pipeline that covers at least three months in some detail but stretches to a year or more. Knowing that learning and development want to launch their new portal right in the middle of health & safety month is vital to stopping mid-air collisions.

Building the pipeline from the perspective of the employee is vital as well. How much can people really digest, and will they understand messaging about cost cutting just after we announced record profits? And, letting it be known that there is a calendar, endorsed by the leadership team, is useful for managing those last-minute 'oh, has anyone asked comms for help?' moments.

The big picture

Perhaps the most successful employee communications leaders can be spotted by the clarity of their longer-term plan.

Great comms starts with a link to overall organizational objectives and a statement of where we add value. Are we there to help retain and motivate committed people? Perhaps the biggest challenge in our world is collaboration or innovation. Or could our world depend on staff understanding operational messages or how to be safe or nice to service users? Are we on the payroll to grow ambassadors or is there some major transformation in the works?

A focus on what really matters and our ability to draw a line between that and our communication actions helps decide where resources are spent and explain, nicely, why a hitherto unknown project may have to wait a little bit longer for its moment in the sun.

The importance of audience insight

FitzPatrick says all planning draws on one of our superpowers – audience insight. Understanding our audiences better than anyone else gives us the wisdom to shape campaigns and the inner strength to resist the urge to pursue pop-up demands. It prompts us to ask questions that project teams may not have considered before and we can stop swamping people with messages they can neither understand nor digest.

Great communication begins with planning. And great planning begins, not with a spreadsheet, but time spent out and about really getting to know co-workers.

EXPERT VIEW
James Harkness

James Harkness is co-founder and partner at change and internal communication consultancy firm HarknessKennett. He has over 30 years' strategic communication expertise including working as MD of WPP's Banner McBride and Burson-Marsteller. He is also the former Head of Global Internal Communications at The Body Shop International Limited.

He says measurement is key for IC pros and 'the only way to demonstrate whether you (and your team) are effective. It needs to be central to everything you do.'

Reasons why internal communicators need to measure

- Effective measurement provides audience insight that will give you a voice and reason to meet with the C-suite and other key stakeholders.
- Measurement enables you to challenge based on data and facts.
- You need measurement to ensure IC is regarded as strategic, and not just focused on getting messages out, or managing channels. You have feedback that others will be keen to hear.

SOURCE James Harkness, 2023

Reflecting on the changes in the internal communication profession, Harkness says measurement has progressed 'so much' in recent years. He adds: 'when I first started in comms it was often the add on. It was something we did but didn't think about it until a campaign or programme was in full swing. Now measurement is one of the first things we think about. We always talk with clients before starting anything, to discuss the proof points and how we will measure them.'

Measurement mistakes

Harkness says some of the measurement mistakes he observes IC pros making include creating a measurement plan 'after the communication has happened. I think sometimes comms pros assume there needs to be a huge piece of research, which can raise expectations there will be a huge change. Lengthy surveys encompassing the whole organization for example, when often employees are experiencing survey fatigue. Sometimes a poll with a vertical slice of the organization will suffice.'

He encourages IC pros to continue listening to employees, recommending establishing a group of respondents internally who are asked every month or quarter how messages have been received and understood, or to feed back on specific activities.

'You should always share the results when you measure' he reflects. 'If you don't or people haven't heard how it's been used, they are less likely to participate in future. Commit to sharing the results and the actions emerging from the measurement.'

Involving others in strategy creation

Through the design, development and implementation of an internal communication strategy, Harkness recommends 'doing it *with* people, not *for* them and getting senior stakeholder input and involvement'. He also encourages senior stakeholder interviews to understand their views on business outcomes and messages at the start.

Harkness says in most organizations, human resources and marketing 'should have an input, but there may well be others, depending on your organization. Involve them at the start and share with them how they can contribute, so they don't feel like the strategy is something that's done *to* them. When you share with your top team, you want these key stakeholders' support and for them to feel they've helped to shape it.'

Measuring an IC strategy

Harkness's technique for writing an internal communication strategy includes putting measurement at the heart of it. 'The most important part about measurement is using it to contribute to the formation of your IC strategy and keep it alive.'

His key elements to writing an IC strategy include asking questions and focusing on:

- What is the business trying to achieve?
- What are the outcomes?
- Think three, four or five years hence – what does this look like?
- Include what you want people to think, feel and do.
- What do the audience insights tell you? Where are employees now and how do they feel?
- How far is the journey they need to make? He says the gap between what the business wants to achieve and where the audience are at is 'at the foundations of your IC plans and strategy'.
- How will we measure if we're successful?
- Look at existing measures and determine what else is required. This should be a mix of qualitative and quantitative measures, plus regular polling.

- He recommends developing a measurement framework for your strategy.

- Only then is messaging addressed – how do you create compelling content?

- What are the communication roles for leaders and managers at all levels?

- Finally, attention turns to channels. What existing and new channels will you use?

Harkness says 'looking at these elements in this order enables IC pros to be effective and remain strategic. Stakeholders, particularly senior ones, love to start conversations with channels – *I need an app* or *I think we need a video*. I'd rather start by asking what are you hoping to achieve? IC pros should be determining and recommending the message and channel, not the stakeholder!'

Harkness says there is merit in determining if leaders are aligned in how they articulate company messages. 'Spend time with line managers. What support do they need to "translate" these messages and make them relevant for their team? In what format? Would they benefit from training?'

Final steps

Once an internal communication strategy is created 'it can feel like a huge job done' says Harkness. However, 'that's only the start! Plan how you will review implementation of the strategy, how often you will update it and how you will share progress. The measurement plans you've created should enable you to report back on the strategy's success, ensuring IC remains central to your organization's success and your overall employee experience.'

Look again at the elements he shared and consider this for your own organization. How will you measure if you're successful? What do you have at your disposal?

Why measuring impact matters

Impact is defined as 'the effect caused by your communication. This should be behavioural rather than activity-based (what did employees do as a result, not how many people saw or read the communication) (CIPR Inside and IoIC, 2019).

'In the past, we've considered measuring IC to be too hard, too time consuming or beyond our budgets. Successful companies measure their communications' impact, a clear behaviour that differentiates them from less successful organizations' (Peck, 2019).

'Measuring internal communication means gathering data to demonstrate the reach, relevance and/or impact of your communication efforts. To measure internal communication effectively means to gather the right data, interpret it objectively and take or recommend appropriate action as a consequence of that data analysis' (IoIC, 2019).

EXPERT VIEW
Victoria Mellor

'Ever since the early 90s, when I started working in communications, measurement and evaluation have been our profession's Achilles heel. Despite the passage of time and advancements in technology, it seems we have only made modest progress. It's high time we break this cycle and usher in a new era of data-driven communication' says Victoria Mellor, a thought leader in strategic communication.

Mellor founded Melcrum in 1996 with the mission to elevate the communication profession as a critical driver of superior performance in business. In 2019 she co-founded Kademy with a focus on building high-performing communication teams. Mellor is also a board advisor to several entrepreneurial businesses helping them develop scale-up strategies and is married to her fellow Melcrum founder Robin Crumby.

I've long been an admirer of her work, and regularly met with Victoria and Robin at their offices in London during their Melcrum days, to discuss all things internal communication related.

How to shift good intention into daily habits

Data from Kademy's Communications Skills & Competency Assessment 2022–3, which had 1,200 respondents from global communication teams, revealed measurement continues to be the lowest-scoring skill for communicators.

The key to successful measurement is to make it a habit. Mellor describes it like a New Year's resolution.

We begin with great intention, but all too often, this falls by the wayside unless it becomes an ingrained habit. Behavioural science tells us that when a good intention becomes a habit, it becomes second nature. It gets done because it is part of our daily routine. A habit is *a learned sequence of acts* (Verplanken and Aarts, 1999).

Today's workplace is data and insight rich, as we discussed in Chapter 3. Mellor says 'we have numerous tools to help us measure, including AI. Data should become the currency that drives our interactions with stakeholders. It is the key to adopting a "business first" approach, allowing us to set objectives and formulate plans in an agile manner. The more we embrace data, the easier it becomes to navigate the complex landscape of our businesses. Insights derived from data hold the potential to unlock the connection between great communication and tangible business performance.'

Measuring your IC strategy

The three most important rules to get right when measuring your internal communication strategy:

1 **Measure only what you need to and measure your objectives directly**
   Setting the right measurable objectives for internal communication strategies requires engaging in meaningful conversations with the business and agreeing measurable objectives together. This collaborative approach ensures transparency, clarity, and fosters a shared understanding of the desired outcomes. Beware of having too many measures, it gives the impression of a lack of focus.

2 **Use data and insights to iterate**
   In an era of rapid change and evolving communication channels, being agile is paramount. Embracing data and insights allows us to iterate and refine our strategies continuously. By leveraging data-driven decision making, we gain valuable insights into our audiences, messages and priorities. This knowledge empowers us to adapt our approaches, tailoring them to the ever-changing needs and preferences of our stakeholders.

3 **Choose the method that matches the communication objective**
   Not all objectives are created equal, and similarly, not all measurement methods are suitable for every situation. It is crucial to select the appropriate measurement approach that aligns with the specific objectives at hand. By following this principle, we ensure that our efforts are focused, efficient, and yield meaningful results.

SOURCE Kademy, 2023

Mellor says now is the time to transform good intentions into daily habits. She concludes 'by integrating data, insights, and measurement into our interactions with the business, we will unlock a new level of effectiveness and impact.'

What is the best way of measuring your internal communication and how can you build measurement into your internal communication strategy?

EXPERT VIEW
Sia Papageorgiou

Sia Papageorgiou is managing partner at the Centre for Strategic Communication Excellence (CSCE) and co-founder of The Alignment People and Gifted Professionals & Communicators Community, based in Melbourne, Australia.

She says if internal communicators want to *be* strategic, they need to *act* like it, and measurement plays a big part. 'Your measurement plan is never a "set and forget" exercise. It should include initial, progress and final measures as you must monitor it along the communication lifecycle.'

Lines of responsibility

Papageorgiou encourages internal communicators to know the difference between *business outcomes* (what the business is responsible for) and *communication outcomes* (what communication is responsible for).

How to measure

The Centre for Strategic Communication Excellence says there are three ways to measure your internal communication:

1 **Quantitatively:** such as counting numbers
2 **Qualitatively:** such as exploring through a focus group
3 **Observationally:** such as observing what you have asked people to do as a result of your communication

Creating SMART objectives

Papageorgiou urges communicators to include measurement in their IC strategy and says setting SMART outcome-based objectives is a 'critical first step'. Here is an example of a SMART communication objective as it relates to a business objective:

Business need (the reason we are communicating)

• Reduce the number of safety incidents across the organization's manufacturing plants.

FIGURE 6.2 CSCE Internal Communication Measurement Matrix™

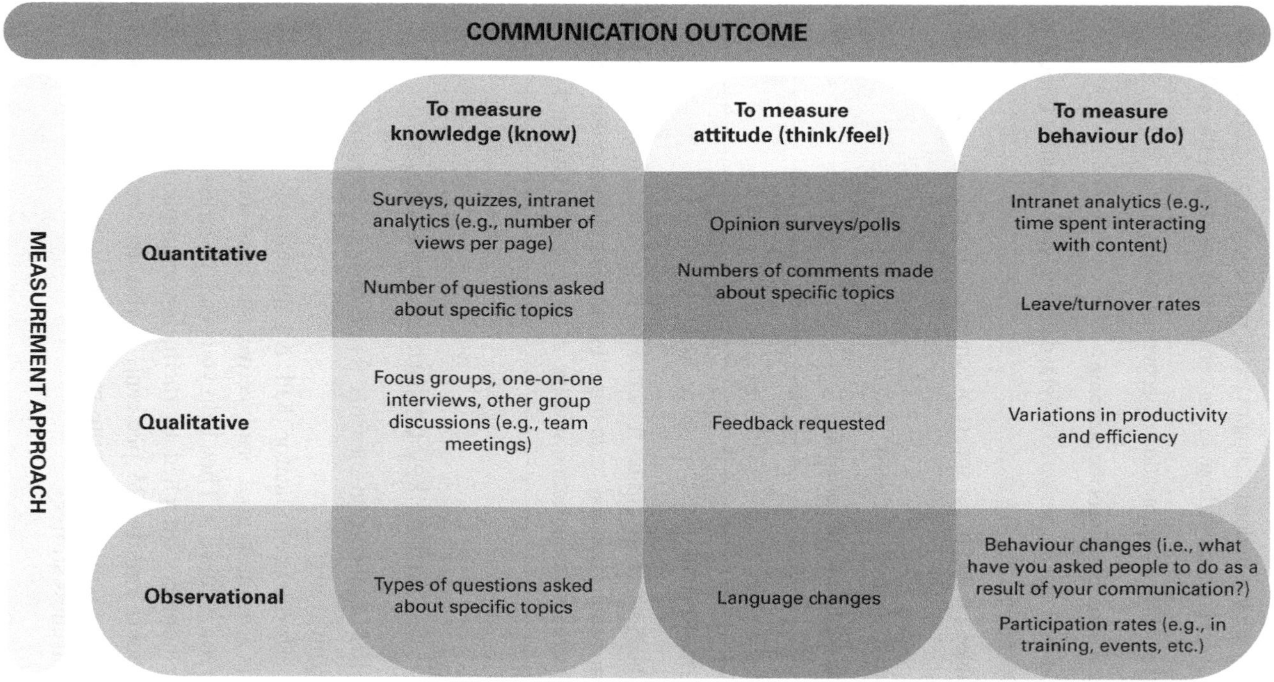

COMMUNICATION OUTCOME

MEASUREMENT APPROACH	To measure knowledge (know)	To measure attitude (think/feel)	To measure behaviour (do)
Quantitative	Surveys, quizzes, intranet analytics (e.g., number of views per page) Number of questions asked about specific topics	Opinion surveys/polls Numbers of comments made about specific topics	Intranet analytics (e.g., time spent interacting with content) Leave/turnover rates
Qualitative	Focus groups, one-on-one interviews, other group discussions (e.g., team meetings)	Feedback requested	Variations in productivity and efficiency
Observational	Types of questions asked about specific topics	Language changes	Behaviour changes (i.e., what have you asked people to do as a result of your communication?) Participation rates (e.g., in training, events, etc.)

SOURCE Reproduced with permission of Sia Papageorgiou, 2023

Business objective (what the business is responsible for achieving)

- Reduce work-related injuries across the organization's five manufacturing plants by 25 per cent by the end of Q4 2026.

Communication objective (what internal communication is responsible for achieving)

- Increase employee understanding of the organization's manufacturing safety protocols and procedures from 75 per cent to >90 per cent by the end of 2026.

As you can see, this communication objective is SMART:

- **Specific:** it describes a specific outcome
- **Measurable:** it can be measured several different ways including through a survey or poll
- **Achievable:** it is within our sphere of control and is based on current state of research
- **Relevant:** to the business need
- **Time-bound:** by the end of 2026

TIP FROM RACHEL

What is the *business* responsible for and what is the *IC team* responsible for in your organization? One way to do this is by outlining roles and responsibilities in your internal communication strategy, as we covered in Chapter 5.

Writing key performance indicators

How will the organization measure its performance against the objectives and goals you've set?

A key performance indicator (KPI) is a quantifiable or measurable value that reflects a business goal or objective, and how successful the tactics are in helping you achieve it. They help you track progress and make decisions. KPIs have numbers attached to them, for example increasing employee survey response rate by 25 per cent. If you are creating metrics around campaigns, these communications metrics are tactical, whereas KPIs align to the wider business strategy.

Deconstructing KPI

Darryl Sparey, Managing Director at Hard Numbers says 'you need to deconstruct the KPI acronym. What are the "key" metrics that focus the attention of senior leadership on the impact of communications? "Performance" tells you whether a campaign is working. "Indicator" highlights the sometimes uncomfortable truth that the numbers may show it's been a success, but they may not be the only factor behind a specific campaign outcome. You need to have a clear understanding of what the business needs the communication function to achieve and use the most relevant metrics that fit with your measurement work.'

He says 'if you're looking for key performance indicators for success, look for leading indicators of success, rather than lagging indicators of success. When thinking about internal communications, lagging indicators are employee churn – measuring current performance – rather than leading indicators which might be employee satisfaction or employee engagement. Then, think about how you can demonstrate your part in the increase of a particular metric. Does an increase in employee satisfaction correlate with higher engagement with content on the company intranet or specific company initiatives to drive employee satisfaction? And, in the future, does employee churn decrease, so you can show the impact on this indicator too?'

Return on investment

Some organizations use return on investment (ROI) for their internal communication. This is a profitability measure, to evaluate performance of a business by dividing net profit by net worth. The ROI formula is net profit / cost of investment × 100.

> We find that increasingly ROI is included as a question to determine whether internal communication activities will impact the financial part of the business, or help to achieve business goals. It is usually a question asked when IC is proposed as the solution for the organization. It is however, a business term and speaks to our need as a profession to understand business more (CIPR Inside and IoIC, 2019).

> To calculate ROI you need to be able to connect communication inputs with the outcome of a changed behaviors, because only behaviors have a positive or negative financial value… There is no financial value of increased knowledge or more favorable opinions until they lead to a person changing what they do with their hands, feet or mouth (Sinickas, 2018).

EXPERT VIEW
Caroline Kealey

Caroline Kealey is a communications strategist, change facilitator, trainer and author with over 25 years of experience in her field. She helps organizations focus on levels of performance and impact in internal communication and is based in Canada. She is a pioneer in working at the intersection between strategic communications and change, serving as Director and Lead Instructor of the Professional Development Institute's Strategic Communications & Change Cohort Program at the University of Ottawa.

Through her Results Map®, System she has codified communications, to help set internal communication teams up for success. The methodology has a suite of products, tools and templates for internal communicators to use inside their organizations.

Her Assessment Framework: Communications Function model helps IC teams assess their performance. It requires professional communicators to reflect on how their team is performing and determine whether they are working in a reactive, unmeasured approach, or a planned and measured approach.

Kealey says: 'This framework is used as part of our diagnostic process and can be valuable in zooming in on targeted areas for raising impact and value. One of the key areas for IC teams to focus on is integration. It requires communications professionals to analyse their current practice because if you have a fragmented structure and tactical delivery, you cannot work strategically. Being a strategic internal communicator requires you to integrate your work alongside the business priorities.'

She recognizes most communications teams are working without the crucial foundation of a relevant, practical, evidence-informed plan. Kealey cites various reasons for this including culture, time pressures, skills gaps and an 'increasing perception that planning doesn't make sense in a world that keeps changing'.

The Top 10 Questions in Strategic Communication remains one of Kealey's most-used and best-known Results Map tool.

They are:

1 What does success look like?

2 Why this, why now?

3 What are the project or corporate objectives?

4 What are the communications objectives?

FIGURE 6.3 Assessment Framework: Communications Function

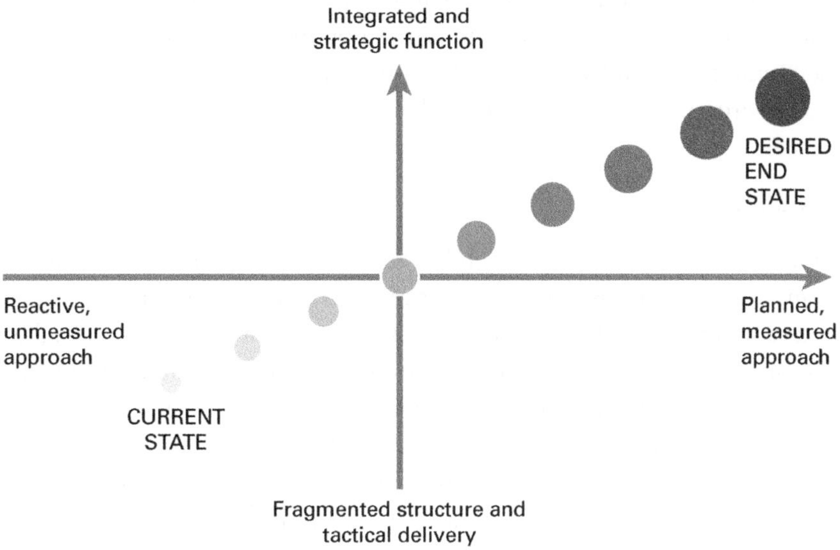

SOURCE Results Map®, 2023

5 How can effective communications help advance the project or corporate objectives?

6 What are the main risks and opportunities?

7 Thinking back about past communication activities, what worked and what didn't? Why?

8 Who are the key audiences and why are they important?

9 What are the project management parameters (time, budget and human resources)?

10 If we could change just one thing, what should it be?

Determining a cadence for evaluation

A critical aspect of internal communication measurement is the cadence, or rhythm. *When* you measure is as crucial as *what*, *why* and *how* you measure.

Internal communicators need to be listening and adapting in real time, determining what to change and what to keep. If you measure too late in a change comms campaign, you miss the opportunity to clarify or refine messaging to aid understanding. If you measure too early in a behavioural change situation, it's too soon to track results and see the impact.

Monthly reporting

I recommend implementing monthly measurement reports for a comms team. A monthly measurement report requires weekly, or even daily, input. You cannot wait until the end of a month to scramble for relevant insights, outputs and outcomes, because it makes the task an impossible one and it's easy to forget something. Internal communicators need to be in the habit of measuring your work and collating relevant data as you go.

Editorial content should be tracked weekly, themes should be reviewed monthly and strategic priorities analysed constantly. In Chapter 4 we examined logistics and how to create clarity around what you are prioritizing and why. Measurement aligns with this thinking; you need to demonstrate what you are prioritizing and show the results.

TIP FROM RACHEL

What does your organization measure? Research the metrics that are discussed at board level.

Working strategically means being proactive and horizon scanning, which you can demonstrate via measurement through spotting and mitigating risks.

Create a compelling measurement story and help senior leaders comprehend the incremental or transformational changes that are happening.

Remember to always keep the comms objectives and the business objectives in mind when communicating measurement.

A technique you could consider for your internal communication strategy is introducing measurement principles. I've recommended these to several clients over the years and I'm delighted to introduce you to Craig Scott.

EXPERT VIEW
Craig Scott

Craig is Head of Internal Communications at the National Trust, Europe's largest conservation charity. The charity looks after nature, beauty and history for everyone to enjoy and I've had the pleasure of advising them for several years.

The National Trust was founded in 1895 by Octavia Hill, Robert Hunter and Hardwicke Rawnsley, who pledged to preserve historic and natural places. Their aim was not only to save important sites, but to open them up for everyone to enjoy. Their mission remains at the heart of everything the charity does today. It has 10,000 permanent and seasonal staff, plus 50,000 volunteers. They have 5.3 million members, 250,000 hectares of land, 400 factories and mines, 76 nature reserves and 500 historic houses, ancient monuments and gardens and parks.

The internal communications team at National Trust has developed a set of measurement principles, to help them track and evaluate their work.

The National Trust's measurement principles

Effective measurement starts with strong objective-setting. We need to be clear with our partners on what it is they're trying to achieve. Measuring outcomes will need their commitment to monitoring the behaviour change they're looking for.

We'll measure for everyone. Not just laptop users. Using qualitative measurement will help us give voice to colleagues.

Our measurement approach will be aligned with our organization and directorate objectives, as well as our IC goals. We're a cause organization and it's important to track colleagues' confidence in supporting our public engagement messaging.

Our measurement will be continuous. We'll have a regular rhythm and dashboard of measurement to track trends as well as measurement of specific project outcomes.

We'll draw insight, learn and change from what we measure. We won't just understand what's worked, but why it's worked. We'll be willing to do things differently, and our measurement will give us intelligence we can use to influence what's asked of us by stakeholders.

Our measurement approach is about integrity. Being thorough and committed to quality in what we do. Honest with ourselves and our colleagues about what works and changing what doesn't. Demonstrating the value we add for our charity.

Scott says 'as a cause organization, the end goal of internal communications for us is advocacy: inspiring and equipping our staff and volunteers to be the most powerful exponents of our cause. The challenges we face are around reach and the sheer breadth of what our charity does, with the wide range of roles and places our colleagues work or volunteer in.'

Reflecting on what good looks like for the charity, he says 'we're looking for communications that give colleagues clarity on the connection from their own role to the purpose of the Trust, help them feel ownership and agency for it, and promote their own voices and stories. It's also particularly important for us to equip our people managers as communicators.'

Aligning measurement to purpose

Could measurement principles work for your organization? Scott says 'starting our measurement approach from principles made it much easier for us make sure we measure outcomes, not activity. It ensures we align our measurement to what we're seeking to achieve rather than just ticking a box; that we draw real insight and challenge both ourselves and our stakeholders to be purposeful and targeted in our communications; and most importantly that our measurement approach reflects our cause and values of being an organization that's for everyone.'

STRATEGY CREATION CHECKLIST

Make notes and decisions on the following points, before moving on to the next chapter. This will help you write your strategy as you read through this book. As a result of working your way through this chapter, you should now have:

- Defined what transformation means.
- Identified whether you need a measurement glossary.
- Reviewed your objectives to ensure they are specific enough.
- Considered the cadence, or rhythm, of your internal communication measurement.
- Determined whether measurement principles would enhance your IC strategy.

Review the choices you've made while reading through this chapter. Make sure you've captured what has resonated and what feels appropriate for your organization.

References

Barthélemy, J (2022) *Myths of Strategy: Dispel the misconceptions and deliver a winning strategy*, Kogan Page, London

Berger, J (2014) *Contagious: How to build word of mouth in the digital age*, Simon & Schuster, London

Berger, J (2023) *Magic Words: What to say to get your way*, Harper Business, New York

CIPR Inside and IoIC (2019) Research Report 2019: Measurement and ROI for internal communication, Chartered Institute of Public Relations in partnership with Institute of Internal Communication, cipr.co.uk/CIPR/Network/Groups_/Inside_content/Blogs_/Research_Report_2019.aspx (archived at https://perma.cc/G5AM-UDEP)

Contact Monkey (2023) Report: Global State of Internal Communications 2023, https://www.contactmonkey.com/ebook/global-survey-2023 (archived at https://perma.cc/MS7J-JAA3)

Firstup (2023) Boosting productivity with a digital toolkit, Cruising Altitude Podcast, 31 May, firstup.io/podcast/cruising-altitude/boosting-employee-productivity-with-a-digital-toolkit/ (archived at https://perma.cc/4AV5-DG3L)

FitzPatrick, L (2023) Interview/correspondence with the author

Gallagher (2023) State of the Sector 2022/3, www.ajg.com/employeeexperience/state-of-the-sector-2023/ (archived at https://perma.cc/6JT9-T28K)

Harkness, J (2023) Interview/correspondence with the author

IoIC (2019) Factsheet: Measuring internal communication – the basics, Institute of Internal Communication, 12 September, www.ioic.org.uk/resource/ioic-factsheets---measuring-internal-communication---the-basics-pdf.html (archived at https://perma.cc/FT9T-MWGY)

Kademy (2023) Communications Skills & Competency Assessment, kademygroup.com/how-we-work/skills-assessment/ (archived at https://perma.cc/9UUU-78G6)

Kelvin, Lord (William Thomson) (1883) Electrical Units of Measurement, in *Popular Lectures and Addresses*, vol 1 (1889), Macmillan & Co, London

Langley, G J, Moen, R D, Nolan, K M, Nolan, T W, Norman, C L and Provost, L P (1996) *The Improvement Guide: A practical approach to enhancing organizational performance*, Jossey-Bass, San Francisco, CA

Peck, S (2019) Research Report 2019: Measurement and ROI for internal communication, Chartered Institute of Public Relations in partnership with Institute of Internal Communication, cipr.co.uk/CIPR/Network/Groups_/Inside_content/Blogs_/Research_Report_2019.aspx (archived at https://perma.cc/G5AM-UDEP)

Quirke, B (2008) *Making the Connections: Using internal communication to turn strategy into action*, 2nd edn, Gower, Aldershot

Ruck, K and Welch, M (2012) Valuing internal communication; management and employee perspectives, Public Relations Review, 38 (2), 294–302

Sinickas, A (2018) quoted in Boysen, Y (2018) Calculate the ROI on Your Communications, *Nonprofit Communications Report*, 16 (3), PRSA, New York.

Verplanken, B and Aarts, H (1999) Habit, attitude, and planned behaviour: Is habit an empty construct or an interesting case of goal-directed automaticity? *European Review of Social Psychology*, 10 (1), 101–34

7

Why revision is essential for an IC strategy

WHAT THIS CHAPTER WILL COVER

This chapter focuses on revision, which is the final stage of creating an internal communication strategy. All the hard work you've done to date culminates in this chapter. We'll examine how to critically review it, what to do once it's written and how to get sign-off. This chapter also features a recruiters' view on the skills IC pros need. You'll find a checklist at the end of this chapter to help you keep on track.

The MILLER Framework: Revision

Writing an internal communication strategy is the first step. Implementing it into the way an organization communicates takes a lot of hard work. Completing the strategy puts you in a strong position because you have absolute clarity about the path ahead. However, without developing techniques to bring it to life and ensure it remains relevant, it can date incredibly quickly.

This chapter focuses on revision, which is the final stage of The MILLER Framework. Revision determines what happens next in the life cycle of an IC strategy and when it will be updated.

Let's turn the *thinking* into the *doing*. In other words, acting based on what you have read in this book to date. If you have worked your way through the chapters in sequential order, you should have nearly completed your internal communication strategy. Now is the time to critically review what you've written and make some decisions.

FIGURE 7.1 The MILLER Framework

Mindset	Business priorities, vision and why internal communication is important.
Insights	What we know about the organization and its people.
Logistics	How internal communication happens and what we're prioritizing.
Leadership	How we will deliver this strategy and the role leaders and managers play.
Evaluation	How we measure and evaluate internal communication.
Revision	What happens next in the life cycle of this IC strategy. Next steps and when it will be updated.

QUESTIONS TO ASK YOURSELF

- Am I happy with what I've created so far?
- Is the format right for my business?
- If I was going to present the strategy to stakeholders, does it contain everything it needs to? Do I know who I would present to?
- Does it need any tactical elements? If so, could this be an appendix?
- Who needs to see it next?
- What will I be asking of people who see it – to endorse, approve or own parts of it?

EXPERT VIEW
Naomi Jones

Naomi Jones is Corporate Affairs Director at Mars Wrigley UK and part of her role includes overseeing internal communication. The internal communications team, led by Rachel O'Brien, developed their internal communication strategy using The MILLER Framework.

A strong culture

'We have a wonderful culture at Mars driven by the fact that as a family-owned brand, we see things in generations rather than quarters' says Jones. 'We call our employees Associates, as we see ourselves as owning and being empowered to take the company forward. Our internal communications, however, were not always representative of this strong culture, based too much in the "tell and share" model.'

Using The MILLER Framework

'Our Associates fed back that they felt very engaged and empowered; however, they wanted our internal communications to be more engaging. The MILLER Framework was perfect in enabling us to see what we needed to do to provide best-in-class communications to excite and engage – bringing our unique culture to life by connecting Associates to our goals, strategy and purpose.

'It helped us to get the right mindset and set our goals based on what our Associates were telling us, achieve buy-in from our leadership team and then set a strategy which was measurable and could be evaluated.'

Creating the structure

Mars's internal communication strategy is built around the goal of 'providing best-in-class communications to excite and engage – bringing our unique culture to life by connecting Associates to our goals, strategy and purpose'. Under this sit five pillars – empowering our leaders; bringing our strategy and purpose to life through compelling storytelling; building confidence in our strategy; enabling and encouraging two-way conversations and championing and driving accessible and engaging communications channels. Evaluation has been built into the IC strategy by underpinning each of the five pillars with a 'how' and 'evaluation' section.

Invest time getting it right

Jones advises not rushing the beginning and end stages in The MILLER Framework. 'Too often we rush to the actionable elements and trying to get stakeholders on board. However, setting your goals based on your employees' feedback and doing the thorough evaluation are absolutely critical. And ensuring your strategy is measurable and achievable is fundamental. We spent a lot of time on a risk analysis to determine what our barriers to success might be and how we might overcome them.'

I asked her whether she found anything surprising about using the framework. 'No surprises, which is a good thing! As it makes sense and is grounded on solid principles. It has helped to guide and steer us and this is what we needed. Rachel and her team are known as the best in the business because she truly understands and values internal communications and sees where it should be within business – at the heart and forefront!'

Conducting a SWOT analysis

What will *stop* your IC strategy being a success and what will *help* make it a success? Be honest with yourself and determine the answers to these questions. I find one of the best ways to do this is via a SWOT analysis when you're at the final stage of creating your strategy.

SWOT stands for strengths, weaknesses, opportunities and threats. It's an ideal way to capture the answers to the questions. You may decide to swap some of the words and meanings around – that's your prerogative – the intention of conducting the analysis is to encourage you to objectively view the work you've done.

You can use a SWOT analysis to:

- Identify your key strengths
- Consider any issues that might threaten your strategy
- Help you make informed decisions

I've included some examples against each of the categories in Figure 7.2.

The example is completed from an internal communicator's perspective and not designed to be included in a strategy. It is designed to be a conversational tool with an IC team or boss.

However, you *could create* a SWOT analysis to be included in your strategy and complete it from the business's perspective. **Tip:** Be mindful who would read it, particularly if it includes commentary on stakeholders and leaders.

Determining the strategy life cycle

What is on the horizon that you're aware of? To future-proof your internal communication strategy, you need to be clear how you'll prioritize your professional recommendations and aspirations over the next 12–24 months. What will the business's priorities be and what will your key priorities be? (**Hint:** they should align.)

FIGURE 7.2 Example SWOT analysis

S	W	O	T
Strengths	**Weaknesses**	**Opportunities**	**Threats**
• Strategy feels ambitious and exciting • Clear objectives in place • IC team can now talk confidently as we have clarity on what we're striving for • We have two formats of the strategy document. Short-form for employees and long-form for stakeholders	• There are still some unknowns around budget, which could limit what we do • Need to recruit new IC manager, which impacts deliverables • Waiting for Exec to determine refreshed business priorities • Relationships with IT and HR need attention	• Can share IC strategy with external and HR colleagues, to minimize duplicated effort and missed opportunities • Strategy is an excellent onboarding tool for new hires and comms champions • We can demonstrate what we are prioritizing and why we say no	• Business has been expecting this strategy for two years. There are high expectations • Lack of resource in IC team to deliver what the business needs • Aware of budget cuts • Leaders not seeing IC as their responsibility as we now have IC strategy in place

Questions to answer:

1 It's 12 months from now and the actions I've prioritized are…

2 In 12 months' time, I will be pleased if I have achieved the following…

3 Within two years, it's critical I achieve…

Preparing the answers to these questions is useful so you can talk confidently with stakeholders and demonstrate the robustness of your thinking.

TIP FROM RACHEL

If you are in a fast-paced organization, which works in an agile way, creating certainty and determining priorities may be trickier. However, this is where having themes or internal communication principles works well to provide unequivocal certainty of excellent internal communication, regardless of what changes may happen.

EXPERT VIEW
Krishan Lathigra

Krishan Lathigra is a Deputy Head of Internal Communication at UK Home Office. His career includes positions at the Central Office of Information, Foreign and Commonwealth Office, Department for Exiting the European Union, Department for Digital, Culture, Media and Sport and HSBC. He leads on all internal communication and engagement relating to the Permanent Secretaries, Executive Team, Ministerial Team and key Home Office leaders.

He says it's important to revise an IC strategy because 'organizations need to react faster to changes in their external environment, such as technological advances, consumer expectations, and competition from new entrants to their sector. The internal comms strategy needs to adapt as the organization responds to external and internal shifts. Your strategy – ultimately – is there to support the delivery of business objectives. Internal comms needs to keep making sense of the broader context and the organizational priorities to help colleagues understand what is changing and what it means for them. Otherwise, the internal communication function loses its influence and its ability to deliver strategic advice.'

When to update an IC strategy

When updating or revising an internal communication strategy, Lathigra says 'there isn't a right or wrong answer about the frequency of updating or revising a strategy. It depends on the context in which the organization is operating; some environments are more stable than others. An annual review should be done at the very least but where the strategy has been co-created with internal stakeholders to align with other key initiatives – a quarterly or mid-year review could be useful.'

What to do once it's written

We discussed formatting an IC strategy in Chapter 2, and Lathigra describes his personal preference as PowerPoint. 'It's versatile – it gives a sense of pace with pithy bullet points and visuals. Brevity is an absolute must because you are competing for the time and attention of senior stakeholders. I'd aim for seven slides maximum with other supporting slides in an appendix. Remember that it's a strategy and not an implementation plan. Also strip out ambiguity and ponderous "corporate" language.'

Deep understanding of purpose

As someone who has produced and overseen countless IC strategies in his career, I asked what advice Lathigra has for someone creating an IC strategy for the first time. 'Ensure you have a deep understanding of your organization's purpose and strategy. This is the foundation around which you will build your internal communication strategy, giving you credibility and influence. By linking your internal communication strategy to the organizational strategy you are demonstrating your strategic value – much in the way that other professional functions do (for example, HR, finance, marketing, sales, audit and risk). You'll also need to understand: the external context for the organization; your audience and how they like to consume content; your key stakeholders and their requirements. And finally, root your strategy in insight and think about the outcomes you want to achieve from the start through developing an evaluation framework.'

Revisit the format

Once your internal communication strategy is written, determine whether you need an alternative version. Would having a visual summary in PowerPoint to accompany a Word-based document, or vice versa, be helpful? Decide the purpose of each document and be clear how you will use them.

Strategy sign-off

Chapter 5 explored who leads internal communication and seeking buy-in for an IC strategy. If internal communication is viewed and valued as a strategic function, approval is an easier conversation.

You are not asking whether your professional recommendations are the right ones; have confidence in your abilities as the subject matter expert. What you're seeking is endorsement of the approach, which should be informed by the conversations you've had with stakeholders throughout the strategy creation process.

WHAT TO THINK THROUGH

- Who do you need to present your IC strategy to?
- Refer to your stakeholder map to determine who needs to be involved.
- Who can help bring it to life?
- Who owns the strategy? You? Your boss? The organization?
- What is it called? Does it need to be referred to as anything else?
- You may want to give your IC strategy a title, particularly if it tells a story.

  Tip: It could be called 'how we need to communicate' or 'the future of internal communication at our company'.

- When will you review the strategy?
- When will you update the strategy?

Set a cadence, or rhythm, for revision that specifies how often you will update your internal communication strategy. When business plans and priorities change, your strategy will need to adapt to mirror and align to them, or it will be out of date.

TIP FROM RACHEL

Specify who owns the strategy and put a named person on the document. Add the version number, date and when it will next be reviewed.

Put a reminder in your diary every quarter to read your internal communication strategy, to check it's still relevant. You may find there's nothing to update. But if there is, it's important you update it and change the version number.

EXPERT VIEW
Dan Holden

Dan Holden is a Communication Consultant at All Things IC. He's a Chartered PR Practitioner, a Fellow of the Chartered Institute of Public Relations and a member of the Institute of Internal Communication (IoIC). He has focused his communication career on internal communication, working in various sectors, including aviation, defence, charity and manufacturing, all of which have seen him support remote-based colleagues.

Holden has worked in internal communication since 2014 and says 'when creating an IC strategy, I've seen everyone from the CEO and people and talent director to HGV drivers helping to create the final strategy document. When I worked in-house I'd spend time understanding the objectives of the departments within the business, not only to be an indicator of their priorities but to make sure the focus of internal comms was aligned with priorities across the business.'

Listening to colleagues

'A key part of my role as an internal communicator was to listen to colleague groups within organizations and understand my stakeholders' needs' says Holden. 'I would sit with senior stakeholders, such as department directors, to understand the support they needed from me and to build that into my strategy. I also tested some of the key priorities within my IC strategy with front-line colleagues, such as HGV drivers, to sense-check my thinking and identify gaps between what senior leaders think and their colleagues' experience.'

Signing off the strategy

Reflecting on internal processes, Holden says 'in every organization I've experienced different sign-off processes. In some, the IC strategy went to the head and then the director of communication who had the final say. In another, the objectives from the strategy had to be approved by a central business planning team to check alignment and ability to track progress against organizational key objectives. When the strategy needed to work in partnership to support employee engagement, I went to the head of human resources to secure their approval. This helped pre-empt later questions as I knew my senior stakeholders would ask whether the HR team had seen my strategy.'

Avoiding approval by committee

Holden also worked in a role reporting into the CEO, who signed off on the strategy. 'I then presented to their senior management team what I set out to achieve over the upcoming one to two years. This avoided "approval by committee" where too many people get caught up in the details and miss the bigger picture of what my IC strategy was setting out to achieve. My IC strategy updated as much as the business priorities and objectives changed. Sometimes this was annual, other times, it was every six months. Changes could be minor, perhaps adjusting the order of priorities or updating objectives to reflect recent business performance or engagement survey results. There's not a definite time frame of when to update a strategy, it should work as an overarching approach to your internal communication and continually reflect your organization's and colleagues' needs. I found having a delivery plan, showing the tactics, allowed me to respond quicker to organizational changes and not need to continually update my strategy.'

Co-ownership opportunities

'I'd view your IC strategy as a co-ownership opportunity with key stakeholders and colleagues' says Holden. 'As the subject matter expert, you are best placed to create it, but as everyone in an organization is responsible for internal communication, bring them into your strategy. Clearly outline the role of senior leadership teams, line managers and change project boards so they know what you need from them. This highlights a team effort is needed to succeed. It's also worth thinking outside your own department/division about who can help set you up for success, and this can surprise you. I recall a compliance director who turned out to be a big advocate of IC, recognizing the value that (if done well) IC could bring in helping to improve the safety culture. They championed my strategy alongside the comms and HR Directors and even provided budget to support campaigns! Help can come from those you least expect.'

Holden says 'your IC strategy should be a tool that acts as your guiding light. You might not use it every day, but have it available to sense-check your thinking. Know you can bring it out at key meetings to challenge stakeholders or explain why something should or shouldn't happen.'

Ownership and sponsorship

Communications leaders' priorities are focused on growth and their team. The top three priorities for comms leaders, determined by The CMO+CCO Meter from The Conference Board (2023), are: set the strategic direction for contribution to business growth, inspire and drive team performance and advocate for team's performance to leadership.

Do not go into a boardroom to talk purely about internal communication and seek approval for fresh ideas you've not shared with anyone on the board before. The hard work preparing your board or leaders for an IC strategy starts before you enter that room or join that call. Internal communicators need strong and established relationships across the organization, including at the highest levels.

An IC team is not a *nice to have*, it's a *need to have*. That's evident when internal communicators demonstrate the power of clear communication and how it saves an organization time, money and effort.

The language of the boardroom is not the same as the language on shop floors, hospital wards and in drivers' cabs. The role of the internal communicator is to mirror the reality of the workforce through their strategy, using the language of business. Internal communicators need to mitigate risk, spot opportunities to advise others and prioritize their work based on how it aligns with the business strategy. That's the mindset to bring into the boardroom.

EXPERT VIEW
Monique Zytnik

'Plans are perfect in the moment they are created' says Monique Zytnik, Global Employee Communication Expert, based in Germany. 'As we all know, circumstances change – new stakeholders enter the mix, the environment shifts, something might break, and new information comes to light. This is why communication strategies need to be regularly reviewed to make sure what you plan to do matches the reality of the moment. For me, this is on a weekly basis when in the midst of a regular campaign. During a crisis, it could be daily or hourly. Your understanding of the moment and your audiences' needs must be based on the constant organizational listening that you're doing. The constant pull of data from many sources, both qualitative and quantitative. Using your knowledge and judgement of what is needed. These changes need to be clearly negotiated and communicated with your stakeholders.'

Checking in and planning ahead

Zytnik recommends setting aside '10 minutes of your weekly check-in with stakeholders to go through any proposed changes, making sure you document decisions. A strategy that has been written lays dormant until it is implemented. This is when it is brought to life for all to experience. A strategy that is never implemented and evaluated is really just an ideas exercise. The impact of implementation and learning from the evaluation are never able to exist. Without implementation, you cannot reach your business goals, and this is ultimately the purpose of internal communication.'

Influencing and advising

Seeking approval or sign-off from a board should only happen *after* the internal communicator has had separate conversations with several people who sit on the board. You need to know who your allies are and involve them in the creation. This creates a sense of ownership and accountability.

It is unrealistic to make the overarching way a company communicates the *sole* responsibility of a director of internal communication. They can influence, advise and make recommendations, but those day-to-day conversations between a line manager and their team are not the responsibility of that director. Their responsibility is to equip, empower and inspire the line manager to increase their skills, knowledge and confidence on all things internal communication-related.

There needs to be a shared understanding and meaning at the highest levels regarding what internal communication is, why it is important, how communication helps the organization achieve its purpose, plus clear roles and responsibilities.

TIP FROM RACHEL

Have conversations with stakeholders before entering a boardroom for sign-off. Be clear what the intended outcome is from your conversation. If it's ownership and sponsorship, specify that's what you're seeking. Talk the language of the business, not just communication.

In Chapter 3, I stated internal communicators need to deeply understand what employees care about and what concerns them. The same is true for your senior leaders. You need active working relationships with the people behind *all* job titles.

EXPERT VIEW
Anthony Kluth

Anthony Kluth is Head of National Communications at the British Embassy in Washington, DC. His 20-year in-house internal communication career includes being Deputy Director, Group Head of IC at the Department for Environment, Food & Rural Affairs in the UK, Head of Strategic Communication at British Red Cross and Lead Communications Manager at Transport for London.

Operating at a senior level in internal communication roles, he is well versed in not only designing and developing internal communication strategies, but implementing them too.

Kluth says having an IC strategy is 'probably the most important factor in moving your team from being an organizational postal service to embracing its role as a strategic delivery partner'.

The benefits of having an internal communication strategy

Having an IC strategy achieves three things:

1 **It does the vital job of aligning your team's priorities with organizational goals**
   It's so important to have a written contract that sets out which organizational goals IC will support, why and how. Without this it is incredibly difficult to define the value your IC function adds, so your IC strategy can also act as your ticket to the top table and the basis for engaging senior leaders.

2 **It gives you a platform to engage and direct your IC team**
   The happiest and most successful teams I've been part of have successfully used their IC strategy as the core document that workload planning, objective setting and evaluation flows from. It helps people put structure and meaning around their work and provides them with something to reach for when receiving new asks and working with challenging clients.

3 **It provides a framework for you to track what you have achieved**
   By treating your strategy as a live document, you can use it to follow what you have achieved, when and why you had to change direction, how well you supported core themes and where you need to focus your efforts. It tells the story of your team and what you are achieving. Without it, it's too easy to bounce from project to project without pausing and taking stock.

SOURCE Anthony Kluth, 2023

Must-haves for an IC strategy

I was curious to know what Kluth always includes in his IC strategies. 'Whether I'm working on a light-touch strategy or a more detailed version I always include: the organization's priorities; themes for engagement; audience; outcome and evaluation.' An additional element is an explanation of what IC is and the value you add (don't assume senior leaders will always know this!), some audience insight – such as people survey results – something to demonstrate you know the mood and needs of your people and, if you can, a section that sets out your previous successes, and learning to demonstrate where you are and where you are trying to get to.

Implementing an IC strategy

Kluth says successfully delivering an IC strategy isn't about capturing and diligently working through a 12-month to do list. 'It's impossible to know with real certainty what your people will need 12 months out. So for me, IC strategy is about tracking themes for engagement that underpin business goals and focusing your work on these. Your strategy should be a live document that your team reviews regularly to ensure it's still providing you with a guide on what matters most. If there's a mismatch between what's in your strategy and what your team is being asked to deliver, it's time to pause and take stock with leaders.'

Bringing a strategy to life

An internal communication strategy is an excellent way to work in partnership with the business. 'Ideally you would position your IC strategy as a shared endeavour with senior sponsorship from your head of HR or (ideally) CEO' says Kluth.

'This helps raise the profile of your work but also tackles issues about how much more your IC function can achieve when it works in partnership with other business units – so that all the teams that hold a stake in people engagement are pulling in the same direction. Agreeing at the outset how you will work with other teams and what you will collectively prioritize enhances your impact and also helps make evaluation easier.'

Don't underestimate how useful your strategy is as a tool to engage your direct team. 'Everyone in your IC team can use it as a way to structure their work, to understand what to prioritize and what to gracefully move away from. It's also key to celebrating success and helping your team understand the difference they are making.'

Measuring an IC strategy

Kluth advises measuring an internal communication strategy carefully. 'As the saying goes, *measure what you treasure* – it's important to set a benchmark using annual people survey data (if available) or at least dip-testing engagement levels with your key audiences. Once you have this you can target your activity accordingly and focus evaluation on this small number of big-ticket projects to track understanding of your messages, sentiment and engagement levels.'

He says this should ideally be 'underpinned by some analytics to help you understand how successful you are at reaching your audiences through your mix of channels. Be really selective and only evaluate the projects and channels that matter most to you.'

His final piece of advice is to regularly review an IC strategy and to 'view them as live documents that the IC team reviews quarterly, involving key partners if possible, with a complete review at year end – as part of your annual planning process with senior leaders'.

TIP FROM RACHEL

When creating objectives for an IC team, mirror the wording of the IC strategy. If you've included principles, add them to the team's objectives. A strategy needs to be a living document, which means it needs life breathing into it via actions. Creation can only turn into implementation when you plan for it. You've captured the thinking, now you need to put as much effort into pulling the strategy through to conversations and ways of working. Role model the communication your organization needs to see.

Strategic skills

Throughout this book I've identified the mindset and skill set internal communicators need. Writing an internal communication strategy requires communicators to use everything at their disposal. Creating an IC strategy regularly features in job descriptions, so I wanted you to hear the perspective of a recruiter, to put it into context.

EXPERT VIEW
Andy Macleod

Andy Macleod is Director at Comma Partners. He has over 20 years' experience in internal communication, including 10 years as a senior in-house professional and 10 years specializing in communications recruitment.

His area of expertise is recruiting mid- to senior-level roles for organizations, across internal, change and corporate communications.

Macleod says companies are looking for internal communicators who have a 'strong set of skills, that will set them in good stead today and in the future'.

His recommended future skills for internal communicators include:

- **Understanding data** – not only knowing how to analyse it, but how to relate communication activity to it.
- **Being digitally adept** and keeping updated with trends in AI and social media. Knowing how to incorporate it as and when appropriate in internal communications.
- **Being alert to other opportunities** that communicators can influence, such as employee experience.
- **Knowing how to design and develop** an internal communication strategy and being able to implement it.
- **Recognizing internal influencers** and knowing how to connect with them and make the most of their influence.
- **Keeping updated with changing attitudes** and able to assert influence with those who need to respond to those changes internally.

These skills are in addition to the skills he says internal communicators need to be able to demonstrate today:

- **Being able to see the bigger picture** in an organization and know how it impacts internal communication.
- **The ability to recognize what internal politics are at play** and know how to navigate them.
- **To be able to put themselves in the shoes of each of their stakeholders** and see their perspectives.
- **Knowing how to manage stakeholders** and deciding when their input is (or isn't) needed.
- **Being alert to human behaviours and traits**, and to show empathy and understanding.

As someone who spends his working life advising internal communicators and the companies that are hiring them, I asked what advice he would give to IC leaders who are looking to build strong teams.

Macleod says the IC team 'needs to understand the business they are in and how they fit in; they need to spend time learning about their organization. This includes networking throughout the company, and building networks they can leverage or call upon as and when needed.'

He encourages IC leaders to set a common goal for the team to align their efforts with, which could form part of their internal communication strategy. Macleod says leaders need to ensure they have both breadth and depth in the team from a skill set perspective – 'not everyone has to be able to do everything, but make sure the team knows what each can do. Make expectations clear, but allow for initiative.'

He advises meeting face to face regularly as a team, but to allow for flexible working too, creating a culture where feedback and praise are readily given and expected. Encouraging creativity and innovation is important to build a strong team says Macleod, advising teams to 'think outside the box, to try new things and spark new ideas to try inside their organization'.

Career paths for IC pros

There are several new and existing career paths for internal communication professionals. Macleod says the most traditional path is for IC professionals to work their way up to become a head of IC or director of IC.

However, he acknowledges there is a wider career path too, to become a head or director of communications. This could include internal and external communication responsibilities and even marketing.

Other options include becoming an interim communication consultant or contractor; this can include specializing in one area, such as change communication. Change management creates career paths for many IC professionals, who take their existing change communications skills and expand into wider change manager roles.

There has been a rise in two roles as potential career paths for internal communicators – chief communications officer and chief people officer. These are both growing in popularity and prominence. Macleod says many IC teams are now reporting through a chief people officer role, and this route is emerging as a new option. Employee experience is emerging as a separate role for IC professionals. It had been coupled with IC; however, it is starting to be recruited for as a stand-alone role, which Macleod says is a 'superb option' for both IC and human resources professionals alike.

How to stand out

What sets the great apart from the good?

Here is what internal communication recruiters look for:

- Your CV tells a story, it's outcome-focused with clear achievements – it's not a copy and paste of the job spec.
- You talk about the IC landscape, the evolving working environment, recent IC-related books, as well as sharing insight from those you follow/network with – you don't limit yourself to 'what I did in my last role...'
- You think about what makes you unique – especially in times when the recruitment market is competitive and you're up against many peers.
- You keep an eye on the latest IC trends, research and influencers.

SOURCE Andy Macleod, 2023

STRATEGY CREATION CHECKLIST

Make notes and decisions on the following points, before moving on to the next chapter. This will help you write your strategy as you read through this book. You are now at the final stage and as a result of working your way through this chapter, you should now have:

- Worked through the questions I've posed in this chapter.
- Identified your IC strategy's strengths, weaknesses, opportunities and threats.
- Decided what you'll do once your strategy is completed.
- Determined who you need to speak with, and what the intended outcome/s from those conversations are.
- Thought about formatting and the need for a second version.
- Considered how the IC team will bring the strategy to life.
- Set the cadence for revision and put dates in the diary.

Review the choices you've made while reading through this chapter. Make sure you've captured what has resonated and what feels appropriate for your organization.

References and further reading

CMO + CCO Meter (2023) The Conference Board, March, www.conference-board. org/research/CMO-CCO-Meter/CMO-responsibilities-priorities-pressures-CMO-CCO-Meter (archived at https://perma.cc/JM6C-C2EH)

Kluth, A (2023) Interview/correspondence with the author

Macleod, A (2023) Interview/correspondence with the author

Zytnik, M (2024) *Strategic Internal Communication in an Age of Artificial Intelligence*, Business Expert Press, New York

8

What happens inside is reflected outside

WHAT THIS CHAPTER WILL COVER

This chapter recaps what I've covered in this book and looks ahead to the future. It includes artificial intelligence, working strategically and my aspirations for the internal communication profession.

Reflecting on topics covered in this book

As we come to the end of this book, I hope you are feeling equipped, empowered and inspired to be courageous with your internal communication. If you are faced with crumbling infrastructure, scarce resources and leaders who won't listen, there is hope.

It is *always* worth improving the way an organization communicates. If you're looking for permission to make the bold decisions, amplify employees' voices and bring conversations into the boardroom, this is it.

Strategic choices are those which are thoughtful and aligned with how a company operates. Work out loud, show your thinking and help organizations design, develop and transform the way they communicate. I've written at various times in this book how *it is our business to know our business* as professional communicators. You *can* and *will* make a difference.

Sometimes the results are immediate, and you can see the tangible difference effective communication is making on the way an organization works. Sometimes it takes months or even years to change behaviour, form new habits and positively enhance organizational communication. However long the timescale is, your efforts and energies matter because they are creating connections, improving employees' experience and helping leaders lead.

Working in this field is invigorating, fascinating and challenging, it's why I'm still in this profession after more than 20 years. If that description doesn't resonate with you, I challenge you to consider the role you are doing today. I've lost count how many of my Masterclass delegates have listened to other attendees and said 'I had no idea internal communication could be like this!'

This book has covered key topics including accessibility, people manager communication, measurement, neurodivergent employees, audits and hybrid working. You've discovered the building blocks to create your own IC strategy and read inspiring stories from your peers. I hope by working your way through this book you've increased your skills, knowledge and confidence about the wonderful world of internal communication and you know what to do next.

What happens inside is reflected outside

What happens inside is reflected outside is the ethos of my business, and I had this artwork created in 2018 to commemorate All Things IC's fifth birthday (Figure 8.1).

If you have a toxic culture inside an organization, it will seep out. If you have a positive culture, it will seep out. The notion of *controlling* internal communication is a fallacy. I started working in internal communication in 2003, and for the past 20 years, I've witnessed leaders and organizations try – and fail – to control communication. You cannot control what employees say; you can only control how you react and respond.

If you want an excellent employer brand, employee experience and high levels of morale and motivation, you need to work hard to earn, maintain and keep them. Employees will only speak positively if that's genuinely how they feel.

Recognizing the significance

If you're working for an organization that fails to recognize the significance of internal communication you have two choices: stay and try to improve it, or leave. Life is too short to put your efforts and energy into an organization – or its people – that doesn't set you up for success. Your mental health

FIGURE 8.1   What happens inside is reflected outside

Illustration by Lisa Kirkbride for All Things IC

and well-being is too valuable to sacrifice for a company that doesn't appreciate the incredible potential and commercial benefits of investing in internal communication. I came to that verdict during my in-house career. Leaving a particular role was one of the hardest, but most important, decisions I've ever made.

The MILLER Framework

I have guided you through The MILLER Framework, prompting you to make choices at each stage, to help you write an internal communication strategy for your organization.

You've read how three companies have successfully used the framework to develop their IC strategies. Do let me know how you get on creating yours.

THE MILLER FRAMEWORK

- **Mindset:** Business priorities, vision and why internal communication is important.
- **Insights:** What we know about the organization and its people.

- **Logistics:** How internal communication happens and what we're prioritizing.

- **Leadership:** How we will deliver this strategy and the role leaders and managers play.

- **Evaluation:** How we measure and evaluate internal communication.

- **Revision:** What happens next in the life cycle of this IC strategy. Next steps and when it will be updated.

Unlocking the power of corporate communication

Organizations that understand and harness the power of corporate communication can revolutionize from the inside out. This book has explored how communication is happening within companies around the globe. I've highlighted over 40 examples of how your peers are transforming organizational communication.

Internal communication needs to be treated as the strategic function it is and recognized for its ability to transform organizations. My vision for IC professionals is for them to be acknowledged as strategic partners whose expertise unlocks the power of corporate communication.

An internal communicator's role is critical to support senior leadership teams. We work as trusted counsel to help leaders think about the impact of their decisions and behaviours. Through our discipline we hold leaders to account and give constructive feedback and advice. We need to have outstanding relationships with peers in external communication, HR and across the company.

Organizations need to prioritize the way they communicate, motivate and inspire their employees. Internal communication must not be left to chance.

Listening is one of the most underrated skills inside organizations. Companies and leaders eradicate their relevancy when they fail to listen to employees. Knowing in real time how your people feel and what they're saying is vital. This means developing listening mechanisms for employees to contribute, not spying on them using software.

Companies and leaders eradicate their relevancy when they fail to listen to employees.

The rise of enterprise social networks and user-generated content in the 2010s rocked the industry. No longer were leaders the sole voices. We equipped employees to share their views, experiences and stories; now we need to listen. 'If employees don't have a positive Employee Experience (EX), they will leave, disengage or even sabotage organizations from the inside' (Whitter, 2023).

The rise of employee-generated content is fascinating, it's always been present, but previously invisible people and ideas have been made visible via technology. Horizontal networks have busted through hierarchical silos. We've moved beyond purely two-way communication, it's multidirectional, which creates dynamic environments inside organizations.

The key to transformational communication is giving flexibility within boundaries. Does your corporate language need to be so formal? Experiment and embrace the rawness of *human* communication, rather than *corporate* communication.

EXPERT VIEW
Shaun Randol

Shaun Randol is the founder of Mister Editorial, a newsletter about mixternal communications, with thousands of subscribers from around the world. He is also the Editor-in-Chief of Digital Publications for Lam Research, where he manages mixternal storytelling. Shaun has over 13 years of experience in internal + external communications (mixternal communications) for multibillion-dollar global corporations, including Bloomberg, BlackRock and Splunk. For more than 10 years Randol ran an online magazine and indie publisher dedicated to philosophy, arts and culture, international affairs and literature. He lives in a small town in Oregon, US.

He says 'humans born today will never know a world without artificial intelligence (AI). The students entering university now will graduate having used AI tools as fluently as Millennials use smartphones to communicate. Therefore, before we know it, every rookie in comms will be semi-expert in using artificial intelligence to get their work done. Unless retirement is on the horizon for you, comms pros need to learn how to use AI to enhance your workflow, operations and output. If you don't, someone who knows how to use these tools will outperform you and use less time to do so.'

Randol is an authority on mixternal communications and says it 'blurs the boundaries between internal and external communications. Internal + external = mixternal. Why mixternal? Because nothing about what the company says about itself (or what is said about the organization) remains external. Plus, everything that is said within an organization is shared externally'.

He adds 'external news and information circulating internally is easy enough to grasp. *Business as usual* communications, such as press releases, earnings calls and ESG reports will be shared with employees as a matter of doing business. Media coverage the comms team has helped create or support – through earned or paid means – will be shared internally through formal and informal employee networks. A story about the company, its personnel, or products and services that appears in the *Financial Times* or on the BBC will be shared internally whether positive or negative, and whether management likes it or not.'

Information finds a way out

Randol reflects that internal information 'always finds a way out. This goes beyond executive memos and internal research leaked to the media. The most seemingly mundane news and information—organizational changes, updates to benefits plans, promotions and demotions, employee profiles on the intranet—are shared by employees with their spouses over dinner, friends at the pub, and colleagues through LinkedIn messages.'

Since 'nothing ever stays within or outside a company's walls', Randol recommends embracing blending the traditionally divided comms functions into mixternal communications. What would that look like? 'It would mean combining the internal and external comms teams into a group with a singular understanding: that what we say will always be created for both employee and external audiences and whenever appropriate, published to forums easily accessed by and promoted to both audiences.'

What about a content strategy? 'Mixternal comms does not require a content strategy that is unique from internal or external editorial plans' says Randol. 'Content should always be created under the assumption that every employee will access the material and so will anyone outside the company. The difference in content strategies comes down to measurement, specifically how one gauges the effectiveness of content for distinct audiences. Product announcements should be aimed at specific audiences, such as salespeople internally and trade magazines externally. Understanding whether the messaging had an effect on salespeople (increase in signed contracts) or the media (increased web traffic to the product web page) requires different metrics, regardless of whether the content is the same. The blending of internal and external communications is teleological – a purposeful development of two functions that traditionally have worked well together, but separately. Forward-thinking comms teams would do right to combine their internal and external teams now to prepare for the inevitable mixternal communications future.'

Looking ahead to the future

Back in 2012 I wrote a chapter in *Share This: The social media handbook for PR professionals*, looking at the rise of social media and its potential impact on internal communication and employee engagement. When writing about the future, I stated: 'the focus will be on connections, collaboration and communication – who's doing what, where they are doing it, what they think of it and how others can get involved' (Miller, 2012).

I also predicted we'd see remote working becoming more popular 'as technology means people don't need to physically be in the same building to feel connected and engaged with their peers and managers across the globe' and described the role of internal communicators to 'ensure the right channels are in place to enable communication to happen'.

My predictions have been realized in ways I couldn't have anticipated, not least due to the Covid-19 pandemic. Internal communication has always been critical to help people and organizations thrive. At a global scale we experienced the importance of credible, accurate and reliable information to keep employees and their loved ones informed and safe. Communication unites workforces, nurtures a sense of belonging and creates opportunities for leaders to be visible and reassuring.

Companies are striving to make meaningful connections among employees. Internal communication is used as the medium, to aid the flow of information and knowledge sharing.

Looking ahead to the future, the fundamental principles of internal communication will remain unchanged. The purpose of internal communication is not telling people what to do. It is to create a shared understanding and meaning. Only when this happens can employees work together towards a company's goals. That irrefutable role will not change.

Every decade the methodologies we employ to create a shared understanding and meaning evolve, as we have better technology and techniques available.

Today's world: AI

Artificial intelligence (AI) refers to 'the simulation of human intelligence in machines that are designed to think and act like humans. It is achieved by developing algorithms and computer programs that can perform tasks that typically require human intelligence, such as visual perception, speech recognition, decision-making, and language translation' (CIPR, 2023).

I have written this book without using AI. The only exception is the play-list I've listened to via Apple Music every single time I've sat down to write. I associate the AI-generated sounds with my intention to write, and it's allowed me to hyperfocus.

EXPERT VIEW
Shaun Randol

Shaun Randol has been publishing a series online called Intellicomms, exploring the intersection of artificial intelligence and mixternal communications. It is a forum that offers practical examples and guides on how to use AI to enhance productivity, efficiency, innovation and creativity in a comms role.

He says 'for at least a decade AI has been used to write news headlines and articles, and human resources departments have used the technology to screen job applications. So if AI has infiltrated sister jobs like journalism, PR, HR and marketing, it's only reasonable to expect that internal comms is next. Already it's being used by enterprising IC pros and the results are convincing: AI is a game changer.'

Employee comms professionals can use AI to:

- create images to support content
- draft material for cyclical campaigns (culture moments, open enrolment, etc)
- enhance interviews with video components
- conduct research quicker
- boost social media efforts
- streamline workflows
- create multimedia (infographics, gifs, video, etc) using text
- use music to enhance the audience's experience with videos, audiocasts, and podcasts
- get a head start on comms activities you've never been asked to do before
- be creative and have fun
- and so much more

Let's look at this area in more detail, particularly as 92 per cent of comms pros think that AI use in PR is 'worth exploring' (PRophet and The Harris Poll, 2022).

EXPERT VIEW
Stuart Bruce

Stuart Bruce is internationally recognized as a PR futurist and pioneer in modernized public relations and corporate affairs. His primary areas of expertise are PR strategy, corporate communication, communication measurement and evaluation, public affairs, crisis communication, digital and social media, and digital transformation, including the selection and implementation of public relations technology. He is co-founder of communications team performance improvement consultancy Purposeful Relations, and founder of reputation and crisis communications consultancy Stuart Bruce Associates.

The rise of CommTech

The proliferation of communication technology, or CommTech, in recent years continues to grow. According to research conducted by Purposeful Relations and PRovoke Media, more than half (56 per cent) of PR and communications practitioners globally say they are 'extremely competent or competent' in their use of communication technology (Purposeful Relations, 2023).

The research revealed the gap between in-house and agency practitioners is widening in terms of competent use of communication technology. It stated many still use spreadsheets for business-critical processes including project management (41 per cent) and managing contacts (39 per cent).

Bruce says there is a reality gap between how good respondents think they are at using technology and how they are really using it. 'The results show that respondents often aren't using the right tools or even using a tool at all. One of the main costs for most PR and communications activity is staff time. Despite this, time is not being used effectively, often respondents aren't adopting and using even the most basic communication technology.'

He cautions this has a negative impact on the results that are delivered, querying how it's possible to deliver the best possible results without using the most effective tools.

Increasing levels of knowledge

With the increase of available tools comes a requirement for an increased level of knowledge and understanding. However, Bruce says this remains low, as typically the PR and communications sector is traditionally slow to modernize and innovate. He says even professions that are perceived to be traditional such as law and accountancy are often faster to innovate and modernize than PR.

Measurement and evaluation are the most important skills of the future of PR and communications. Bruce cautions 'there's too much chaotic data around, which is hard to make sense of. Some is missing or worse is wrong, or it's in a silo so other teams have it but corporate communications doesn't. There's also frequently a lack of understanding about what it means and it lacks any clarity or consistency. Above all, there is an inability to identify opportunities and act on the insights available.'

The biggest challenge

Revolutionary advances in technology, including artificial intelligence, provide opportunities for comms pros in areas such as data and analytics.

Bruce says excellent communication measurement and evaluation goes beyond reporting results, citing the real value as providing insight so you can plan and create better campaigns to consistently and incrementally improve the way you work. However, he warns despite the many uses of AI, including message and sentiment analysis, AI doesn't crack the biggest challenge of communication measurement and evaluation, including setting communication objectives that support business objectives to make a real impact on an organization's performance.

'We are closer than ever to cracking the conundrum of measuring and evaluating the success of communication campaigns, but that's not enough. The future of measurement and evaluation is to understand the complex interactions of the reputations and relationships that give companies their licence to operate.'

Rapidly emerging AI tools will make it easier for communications professionals to analyse and understand these complex interactions. A lot of the early AI focus has been on using generative AI based on external data sources from the internet. The ability to use AI technology to analyse a myriad of previously inaccessible internal data sources will unlock huge opportunities for corporate communications. It's essential in doing so that safeguards are in place to ensure the ethical use of AI.

TOP 10 ACTIONABLE INSIGHTS FOR PR AND COMMS PROS

1 Ensure you know how to use existing technology effectively before investing in technology. Often you will have tools in existing platforms that you aren't using effectively.

2 Public relations and communications is about reputation and relationships so do it more effectively using tools like contact relationship management (CRM) software.

3 Effective teamwork requires collaboration and coordination to be effective, so use professional technology tools to collaborate more successfully.

4 Professional project management tools save time and improve the effectiveness and performance of teams.

5 Ensure you stay on top of the latest developments in professional practice and communication technology.

6 Before investing in new technology, audit your existing technology stack, alongside team skills, professional practices and workflow.

7 Integrate and connect technology platforms to improve workflow, save time and make the team more effective.

8 Investing in technology is never enough. The most important aspect of digital transformation is always culture, training and new approaches to working.

9 Consider how technology can be used to improve every aspect of your work from public affairs and crisis communications to insight and planning and media relations.

10 Ensure you have a communication measurement framework in place that everyone knows how to use – and uses.

SOURCE Purposeful Relations, 2023

The potential of AI for internal communication is evolving and I'm excited to see what the future brings. It won't replace the job of an internal communicator, but someone who understands its role may.

Automating tasks should create capacity for humans to do what only we can. It will save you time, but you still need to apply emotional intelligence, company-specific terminology and tone. Check the facts and verify information generated by AI, be cautious and do not share confidential company information.

EXPERT VIEW
Stephen Waddington

How can you make artificial intelligence (AI) part of your learning and development as an internal communicator? 'Experiment with AI tools in day-to-day tasks and establish an innovation team within your organization to explore potential benefits' says business advisor and troubleshooter Stephen Waddington.

He's the Founder and Managing Partner of Wadds Inc and has a distinguished public relations (PR) career including roles at Metia Group, Ketchum and Speed. A former President of the Chartered Institute of Public Relations (CIPR), Waddington has authored and co-edited several books, including the fifth edition of *Exploring Public Relations and Management Communication*, with Ralph Tench (Pearson, 2021). He is a PhD research student at Leeds Business School where he is investigating the contribution of public relations to management.

The impact of AI on PR and comms

In 2023, Waddington produced a management paper for corporate communicators and public relations practitioners, highlighting the rapid development, application and impact of artificial intelligence. He says AI will 'significantly impact the public relations profession in the same way as the internet and social media before it' and urges professionals to give it 'urgent attention' for two reasons:

1 The potential impact on relationships and reputation that gives your organization and customers their licence or permission to operate.

2 AI will disrupt how you work, displacing functional and junior roles within PR practice.

There are various ways practitioners can use it today and there are many more platforms and uses on the horizon. Waddington says 'AI can assist in tasks such as text and image generation, editing and summarization, evaluation and modelling, and planning and decision-making.'

Ethical practice and AI

In Chapter 2 we examined how critical ethical practice is for internal communication. There are several risk areas, says Waddington, related to disruption and lack of oversight. 'Issues that should be on your risk register relate to bias, copyright and privacy. You should also be concerned about the ease with which tools hallucinate and generate misinformation.'

Waddington warns its potential misuse could lead to bias, misinformation and other ethical concerns, all of which were foreseen by the Ethics Guide to Artificial Intelligence in Public Relations, published by the CIPR AI Panel (CIPR, 2020).

The key areas and issues highlighted in that report by Professor Emeritus Anne Gregory and Jean Valin remain 'entirely valid' says Waddington. 'These are the use and application of AI; social change; the impact on the nature of work; privacy control and transparency issues.'

He concludes that the arrival of a new generation of generative AI and machine learning technologies available at scale and inexpensively only brings these into sharper focus for today's practitioners. 'These should be an area of research and investigation for any practitioner seeking to provide guidance to their management team.'

JARGON BUSTING

Generative artificial intelligence describes algorithms (such as ChatGPT) that can be used to create new content, including audio, code, images, text, simulations and videos.

SOURCE McKinsey & Company, 2023

EXPERT VIEW
Jennifer Sproul

Jen Sproul is Chief Executive Officer of the Institute of Internal Communication. I asked her how she views strategic internal communication in action. She says 'strategic leadership in the internal communication context involves a multifaceted approach. All internal communication must align with the organization's wider objectives. Rather than simply focusing on day-to-day tactical tasks, strategically minded internal communication professionals will adopt a forward-thinking mindset to anticipate future challenges and opportunities.'

How internal communicators can anticipate future challenges and opportunities

This demands the following mindsets and attributes:

- **Visionary and creative:** a strategic internal communicator must be able to leverage all media available to envision the organization's future and articulate a clear direction for all stakeholders across all media preferences.

- **Adaptive:** whilst organizational strategy sets a direction of travel, unforeseen events will inevitably arise. Maintaining curiosity and a learner's mindset will yield the necessary agility to successfully navigate challenges, maintain relevance and drive continued impact.

- **Data literacy:** strategically minded internal communicators are data driven. They blend quantitative data with qualitative insights to raise the profile of employee voice for enhanced organizational cohesion.

- **Collaborative:** meaningful progress only happens when all stakeholders commit to working collaboratively. Progressive internal communicators leverage their skillset to remove any communication blockages, for optimal alignment and execution.

SOURCE Jen Sproul, CEO, Institute of Internal Communication, 2023

'Internal communication plays a crucial role in steering organizations towards success' says Sproul. 'Commercial landscapes are fast-paced and ever-changing. In hyper-connected environments, unexpected and seemingly random events can converge quickly to create unanticipated fallout. Organizational leaders need to be able to think critically, get comfortable with complexity and foster world-class communication skills to maintain internal connection and community that yields resilience in the face of external market forces.'

However, she says market ambiguity is now so pronounced that strategic leadership can no longer be confined to the executive suite. 'To make sense of and successfully adapt to continuously shifting contexts, *all* contributors within an organization's ecosystem must clearly understand its vision, mission and values. All stakeholders must nimbly and adeptly make decisions that align with strategy and reduce vulnerability to the myriad unknowns that surround businesses. All organizational stakeholders must practise progressive and inclusive communication that fosters the collective intelligence of the many, rather than the few.'

The pivotal role of IC professionals

The role of the internal communication professional here is key. As the primary conduit between leadership and the wider workforce, Sproul describes the role of internal communication professionals as 'pivotal, to ensure the company's strategic direction is clearly understood throughout the organization, and that all subsequent activity is aligned'.

She says it is 'incumbent on internal communication professionals to role model the communication and relationship behaviours that foster cohesion, build engagement and embed collaboration as simply *"the way we do things around here"*.

These activities ultimately underpin the achievement of shared strategic goals, and while it's easy to rely on digital channels to distribute key messages, it's embodied, person-to-person communication that garners most goodwill.'

Sproul acknowledges workplaces are in the midst of profound transformation, driven by a range of interconnected meta-trends. 'Since Covid, these trends have accelerated, creating acute pressure for organizations to innovate and adapt. Sociocultural shifts in attitude mean organizations must work far harder to attract, inspire, motivate, and retain their staff. In a labour market that is gradually shrinking, this is no mean feat. Successful and meaningful innovation and transformation requires the active participation of everyone in the organization.'

Adapting to uncertainty

'Knowing where we're going and how we're going to get there, while remaining flexible enough to adapt to uncertainty are cornerstones of 21st-century business strategy' says Sproul. 'Success depends on clearly articulated and understood pathways forward, alongside the ability to remain receptive to market feedback and to course-correct as and when required. Collective action in pursuit of strategic objectives can only happen when internal communication plays a leading role.'

Forging strong relationships

'Internal communication leaders embrace employee advocacy, acting as community builder and connector so that everyone in the organization feels welcome, included and respected' says Sproul. 'Forging strong relationships with senior executives enhances the seamless and multidirectional flow of information and knowledge within the organization, fostering authenticity and transparency to yield positive workplace cultures. Leading strategically is a fundamental responsibility for internal communication professionals seeking to deliver value and drive organizational success.'

Navigating complexities

'By successfully role modelling world-class internal communication, both across agreed channels and in person, internal communicators play a key role in navigating the complexities of modern business environments' notes Sproul. 'Research data tells us the extent to which leaders and managers need support to develop their communication skills. As the pace of global change accelerates, organizations of all stripes must embrace agility and structural fluidity. The rapidly moving landscape of AI provides a good example of this. As emergent technology renders certain tasks obsolete, all organizations will need to prioritize informed and sensible debate about how best to adopt these new tools, platforms and software.

'With its cross-function knowledge and company-wide relationships, internal communication is uniquely equipped to convene inter-departmental focus groups and facilitate these conversations. As much as these new technologies create efficiency, they also demand the uniquely human skills of sensemaking and critical thinking, for optimal and contextual integration. While by no means straightforward, internal communication acts as the glue to maintain cohesion in increasingly fragmented work environments. Ultimately, internal communicators are instrumental in fostering engaged workforces, ensuring that the organization's vision becomes reality.'

The chief communication officer

Failing to prioritize and invest in communication impacts the way companies function. The commercial implications are evident with duplicated effort and wasted resources, while employees search for information to help them do their jobs.

As we come to the end of this book, my final thoughts are on the role of chief communication officers (CCO). Companies are increasingly appointing to this role and I welcome this move.

Internal communication needs to be discussed at all levels inside an organization; it's too important to be left to one team, department or person, it is everyone's responsibility. Internal communication is not a final agenda item, it should weave into every facet of the way an organization operates. Therefore, it needs to be discussed in the boardroom and, even better, be represented at a senior level.

Almost half of the boards and management teams in the FTSE 100 have no director of comms, director of corporate affairs or similar dedicated position at this level (CIPR, 2022).

> Like other members of the Exec team, the Chief Comms Officer will have the ear of the CEO, weighing in and counselling on executive decisions, and their potential ripple effects on the company's reputation, brand and strategic communications. The CCO role transitions any company's communications to be proactive, anticipatory, and intrinsic to brand and operational success (Simpson, 2023).

Prioritising the focus of the team and nurturing the talent are the two biggest challenges for CCOs and other C-suite executives. Proximity to the CEO is an indicator of the power of the function. The power of the CCO continues to grow and solidify (Pollard, 2023).

More teams than ever are now led by a Chief Communications Officer or head of comms who oversees both internal and external communicators. A communicator operates at their peril if they don't understand that what's conveyed internally will be shared externally. And external campaigns impact the organization internally, too – what's internal is external and vice versa. Mixternal communications recognize this truth, and communicators who craft mixternal strategies will see more airtight outcomes (Schwartz, 2023).

The role of the CCO is becoming more important to the CEO as one of strategic influence fostered by a balance of shaping long-term corporate narratives and executing immediate crisis response (Pollard, 2023).

The respective disciplines of internal and external communication should be recognized and funded, and in the words of Simpson (2023), it is time to bring the Chief Communications Officer into the C-suite.

References

CIPR (2020) Ethics Guide to Artificial Intelligence in PR, Chartered Institute of Public Relations, www.cipr.co.uk/CIPR/Our_work/Policy/AI_in_PR_/AI_in_PR_guides.aspx (archived at https://perma.cc/MQS6-HGGZ)

CIPR (2022) UK's largest companies face reputational risk as almost half of management teams lack comms expert, Chartered Institute of Public Relations, 10 October, newsroom.cipr.co.uk/cipr-research-finds-uks-largest-companies-face-reputational-risk-as-almost-half-of-management-teams-lack-comms-expert/ (archived at https://perma.cc/PG5V-LZD6)

CIPR (2023) Artificial Intelligence (AI) tools and the impact on public relations (PR) practice, Chartered Institute of Public Relations, www.cipr.co.uk/CIPR/Our_work/Policy/AI_in_PR_/AI_in_PR_guides.aspx (archived at https://perma.cc/MQS6-HGGZ)

McKinsey & Company (2023) What is generative AI? www.mckinsey.com/featured-insights/mckinsey-explainers/what-is-generative-ai (archived at https://perma.cc/MS9T-EZLZ)

Miller, R (2012) Employee engagement: How social media are changing internal communication, in *Share This: The social media handbook for PR professionals*, ed S Waddington, pp 195–204, Wiley, Chichester

Pollard, I (2023) CCO: Responsibilities, priorities and pressure, The Conference Board, www.conference-board.org/pdfdownload.cfm?masterProductID=46551 (archived at https://perma.cc/GY4M-2E6D)

PRophet and The Harris Poll (2022) PRophet AI Research, 13 September, www. prprophet.ai/wp-content/uploads/2022/09/PRophet-AI-Executive-Summary.pdf (archived at https://perma.cc/KD9R-UQVL)

Purposeful Relations (2023) Global CommTech Report 2023: How public relations professionals think about and use technology and artificial intelligence, www.purposefulrelations.com/global-commtech-report-2023/ (archived at https://perma.cc/5CSJ-QCAX)

Schwartz, D (2023). Focusing on a return to culture puts to rest the return-to-office debate, Ragan PR Daily, 22 August, www.prdaily.com/focusing-on-a-return-to-culture-puts-to-rest-the-return-to-office-debate/ (archived at https://perma.cc/T9W2-BYR8)

Simpson, K (2023) Introducing the CCO: Why it's time to bring communications into the C-suite, Hanson Search, 31 May, www.hansonsearch.com/our-insight/articles/introducing-the-cco-why-its-time-to-bring-communications-into-c-suite/ (archived at https://perma.cc/92TK-J8KF)

Sproul, J (2023) Interview/correspondence with the author

Waddington, S (2023) The Impact of AI on Public Relations, Wadds Inc, www.wadds.co.uk/the-impact-of-ai-on-public-relations-management-paper (archived at https://perma.cc/YD47-HH33)

Whitter, B (2023) *Employee Experience Strategy: Design an effective EX strategy to improve employee performance and drive better business results*, Kogan Page, London

INDEX

Looking for another book?

Explore our award-winning
books from global business
experts in Marketing and Sales

Scan the code to browse

www.koganpage.com/marketing

Also from Kogan Page

ISBN: 9781789666137

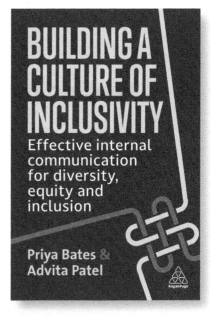

ISBN: 9781398610392

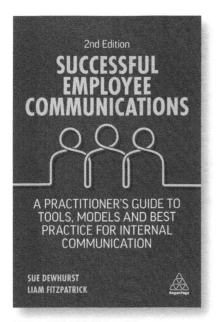

ISBN: 9781398604483

ISBN: 9781398606975

www.koganpage.com

Printed and bound by CPI Group (UK) Ltd, Croydon, CR0 4YY

10/04/2024

14481708-0005